797,885 Books
are available to read at

www.ForgottenBooks.com

Forgotten Books' App
Available for mobile, tablet & eReader

ISBN 978-1-332-70780-5
PIBN 10453523

This book is a reproduction of an important historical work. Forgotten Books uses state-of-the-art technology to digitally reconstruct the work, preserving the original format whilst repairing imperfections present in the aged copy. In rare cases, an imperfection in the original, such as a blemish or missing page, may be replicated in our edition. We do, however, repair the vast majority of imperfections successfully; any imperfections that remain are intentionally left to preserve the state of such historical works.

Forgotten Books is a registered trademark of FB &c Ltd.
Copyright © 2015 FB &c Ltd.
FB &c Ltd, Dalton House, 60 Windsor Avenue, London, SW19 2RR.
Company number 08720141. Registered in England and Wales.

For support please visit www.forgottenbooks.com

1 MONTH OF FREE READING

at

www.ForgottenBooks.com

By purchasing this book you are eligible for one month membership to ForgottenBooks.com, giving you unlimited access to our entire collection of over 700,000 titles via our web site and mobile apps.

To claim your free month visit: www.forgottenbooks.com/free453523

* Offer is valid for 45 days from date of purchase. Terms and conditions apply.

English
Français
Deutsche
Italiano
Español
Português

www.forgottenbooks.com

Mythology Photography **Fiction**
Fishing Christianity **Art** Cooking
Essays Buddhism Freemasonry
Medicine **Biology** Music **Ancient Egypt** Evolution Carpentry Physics
Dance Geology **Mathematics** Fitness
Shakespeare **Folklore** Yoga Marketing
Confidence Immortality Biographies
Poetry **Psychology** Witchcraft
Electronics Chemistry History **Law**
Accounting **Philosophy** Anthropology
Alchemy Drama Quantum Mechanics
Atheism Sexual Health **Ancient History**
Entrepreneurship Languages Sport
Paleontology Needlework Islam
Metaphysics Investment Archaeology
Parenting Statistics Criminology
Motivational

ANNALS

OF

STATEN ISLAND,

From its Discovery to the Present Time.

BY

J. J. CLUTE.

"If we look for a spot which forever is blest
By Nature with her perennial smile,
. . . .
We never need leave our own green isle."

ANON.

NEW YORK:
PRESS OF CHAS. VOGT, NO. 114 FULTON STREET.

1877.

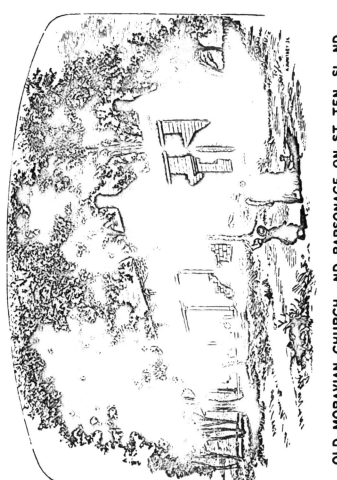

OLD MORAVIAN CHURCH ND PARSONAGE ON ST TEN SL ND.

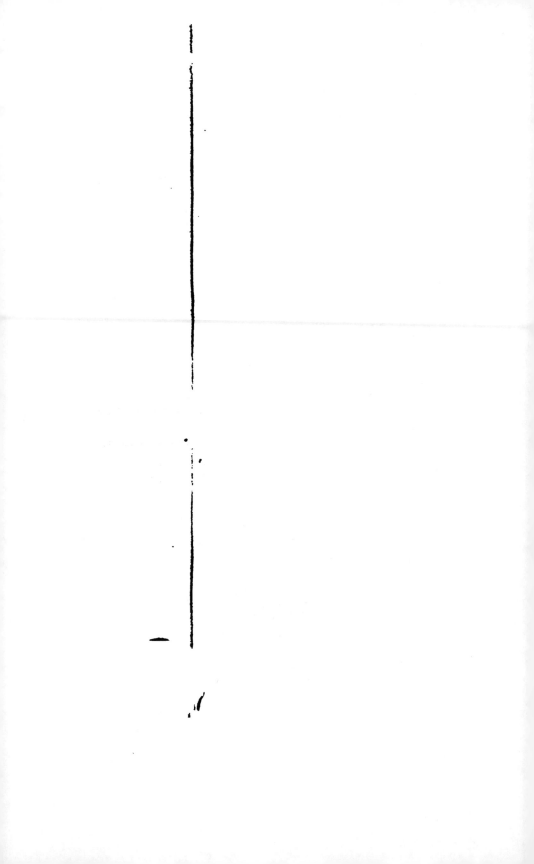

1883. Feb. 7,
Bright fund

Entered according to Act of Congress, in the year 1877, by
JNO. J. CLUTE,
In the office of the Librarian of Congress at Washington.

PREFACE.

This work was undertaken at the suggestion of several citizens of the county, who were aware that the writer, during a residence of between forty and fifty years, had accumulated a large amount of interesting materials relating to the history of Staten Island. These were collected from time to time, for the purpose of publishing them in our local journals in the form of historical sketches, and not with the ulterior view of giving them to the public in their present form. They have now, however, been arranged, so far as was practicable, in chronological order, and a large amount of new matter introduced. For the local anecdotes and personal incidents, which might be extended almost indefinitely, the writer is indebted to the memories of several old people who have now passed away, some of whom were almost centenarians when they died, but whose memories abounded in reminiscences, and with whom he was on terms of close intimacy. He has thus preserved the memory of many events of local interest, which otherwise would have passed into oblivion.

By far the most eventful period in the history of Staten Island was during the war of the Revolution, but the generation which was active then, has long ago disappeared, and many events in the local history of the community, made up of personal experiences, remain forever unwritten. It is undoubtedly true that at the commencement of the war, the greater part of the people of the Island were in sympathy with the enemies of the country; but the licentiousness and rapacity of the soldiery had inspired them with such enmity towards the British government, that at its close a revolution in the popular sentiment had taken place, and those who adhered to their loyalty, and followed the fortunes of their fellow loyalists, were probably not more than half a dozen in number, and these were they whose zeal for the royal cause had led them into the commission of acts, which, if they had remained on the Island, would have exposed them to public contempt, if not to public justice. Nevertheless, there were a few whose insignificance protected them, and who continued to "talk tory" as long as they lived, and grieved over the departure of the "times of the king when guineas were plenty." It has been the fortune of the writer to come in contact with two or three of these garrulous old mourners for royalty, the remnants of a class now totally extinct, whose reminiscences were not the less valuable, because they were tinctured with toryism.

We acknowledge with gratitude our obligations to the Rev. Dr. Brownlee, the late Rev. Dr. Goddard, and the Rev. W. L. Lennert, for access to such records and documents as their respective churches, the oldest on the Island, possessed. The clergymen of several other churches have cheerfully furnished brief, but comprehensive data for historical notices of their respective churches. To the Hon. B. P. Winant, of Rossville, we are indebted for the original record of the establishment of Methodism on the Island. We are also indebted to a gentleman well known in literary circles, for the historical part of the article on the Sailor's Snug Harbor.

Difficulties, in some instances insuperable, have been met in the effort to trace the genealogies of many of the oldest families on the Island. In very few can a correct or intelligible record of descent be found, and in some of these the records have been commenced at a date so recent as to be utterly useless for our purpose.

Were it not perplexing, it would be amusing to note the variety in orthography of many of the patronymics; for instance, the name of the Decker family is spelled as follows: Dekker, Deceer, Deeceer, Decker, etc.; the Depews, as follows: Depuy, Depew, Dupue, Depeue, etc.; the Disosways, as follows: Dussauchoy, Desuway, Dusachoy, Dussoway, Dissoway, etc.; the Bodines, as follows: Bodoin, Boudoin, Boudin, and Bodin, which is probably the original orthography.

Another difficulty, and one entirely insurmountable, is found in a custom which obtained among the early Dutch, in an entire and unrecognizable change in the family name; thus, for instance, Hans Jansen may be described as Hans Jansen, van den berg, or John Johnson, from the hill or mountain, or Hans Jansen van de zant—that is, John Johnson from the sands or sea-shore—and his descendants, or some of them, would adopt the name of Vandenburg or Vanzant, thus annihilating at once all trace of their descent from the Jansen family.

In the few instances in which the writer differs from the published histories of individuals and families, he will be found to be strictly correct, when the proofs which he has submitted are examined.

The limited area of Staten Island, about fifty square miles, its isolated position, and, in consequence, the isolated condition of its inhabitants, render it improbable that many important historical events have transpired upon it. Personal incidents and reminiscences might have been multiplied almost indefinitely, but sufficient have been given to enable the reader to form an opinion of the condition of society upon the Island, during the several periods of its history.

INDEX

CHAPTER I.

Discovery—Verazzani—The first death—Hudson River—Hostages—The first battle—Localities inhabited—Food—Animals.............................. 1

CHAPTER II.

Name—Dimensions—Surface—Climate—Geology—The fur trade—The first English claim—The Dutch take possession—The Brownists.................... 6

CHAPTER III.

The West India Company—English claims—Arrival of settlers—First settlement on Staten Island—At the Wallabout—Birth of the first child—Purchase of Manhattan Island—The Patroons—Communipaw—De Vrie's grant—Melyn's patent—Staten Island massacre and its consequences—Still, &c., upon Staten Island—Indian murders and murder of Indians........................... 14

CHAPTER IV.

Long Island Indians—Roger Williams—Expedition against the Staten Island Indians—Searches for the precious metals—Toad Hill Iron Mine—Misgovernment of the Directors—Bogardus and De Vries—Their Policy—Decline of the Fur Trade—Kieft recalled—His Death—The several Sales of Staten Island. 28

CHAPTER V.

Appointment, arrival and character of Stuyvesant—His silver leg—Disputes respecting boundaries—Disputes between Melyn and Kieft—Melyn's troubles with Stuyvesant—His sentence, and the reversal thereof—Stuyvesant summoned to Holland to answer—Sends his attorneys—Local troubles—Charges against Stuyvesant by the English—Early condition of the Island. 37

CHAPTER VI.

A hard winter—Melyn's character—His return to America—Sale of the ship and cargo—Van Dincklagen—War between England and Holland—Stuyvesant's perplexities—Ferry rates—John De Decker—Stuyvesant's proclamation against preachers—Indian war of 1655—Staten Island ravaged—Melyn forsakes the colony—Sells his title to the Island—Waldenses and Huguenots settle on the Island—Dom. Drisius—Defence of Melyn—Kieft's shipwreck and death.. 88

CHAPTER VII.

The province wrested from the Dutch by the English—A change of masters—De Decker banished—New grants on Staten Island—Elizabethtown settled—The establishment of courts—Berkley and Cartaret's patent—Nicoll surprised and indignant—Treaty of Breda—Nicoll's resignation, and appointment of Lovelace.. 42

CHAPTER VIII.

Tradition and legitimate history—Doubts as to the proprietorship of the Island Circumnavigated—Christopher Billop—The Bentley manor—The Billop family—Tomb-stone records—Errors of Dunlap corrected—Col. Billop's capture and imprisonment.. 47

CHAPTER IX.

Purchase of the Island in 1670—Indian reservations—De Decker restored to his rights—Death of Stuyvesant—Preparations for war—War between England, and France and Holland—Capture of the province by the Dutch—Restoration to the English—Manning's punishment—Duke of York's new patent—Staten Island separated from the Long Island courts—Excise—The dreadful comet-star—Dongan's administration—His patent to Palmer—Dongan's manor house—Historical errors corrected—Papist alarms—Dongan's mill—Leisler's administration—Officers of the county—Sloughter—Plowman's law suit.. 53

CHAPTER X.

Complaints against the sheriff—Census from 1698 to 1771—Slaveholders—Civil and military officers—Disappearance of old families—Cold winter of 1740-'1—Traveling in the olden time—A traveler's adventure in the woods—Cold winters of 1761 and 1768—Baron DeKalb—Domestic life of the olden time. 69

CHAPTER XI.

Gov. Hardy—The Delanceys—Expedition against Louisburg—Gen. Amherst—Conquest of Canada—Moncton's army on Staten Island—Amherst invested with the Order of the Garter on Staten Island—Extracts from old papers—Beginning of the Revolution—Tories on Staten Island 80

CHAPTER XII.

Military value of Staten Island—British take possession of Staten Island—Brutality and insolence of the British soldiers on Staten Island.......... 84

CHAPTER XIII.

The tories and whigs of Staten Island—Submission of Kings county—Interview between Howe and the American commissioners at the Billop house—Richmond—Great fire in New York—Howe's expedition into New Jersey, and attempt to reach Philadelphia by land—Knyphausen's expedition into New Jersey—Murder of Mrs. Caldwell—Invasion of the Island by the Americans—Stirling's invasion...................................... 89

CHAPTER XIV.

Lt. Col. Simcoe—His adventures in New Jersey—His capture—Negotiations for peace—Was Washington ever on Staten Island ?—His opinion of the people—Dwellings of the Hessians.. 99

CHAPTER XV.

Capt. Hyler's adventures—Nathaniel Robbins—The Prall families robbed—Futile attempt to rob John Bodine—Insolent conduct of two British officers—A soldier scalded with boiling soap—Soldiers stabbed with hay-forks—Attempt to kidnap a young lady frustrated—Instance of prompt decision—Soldiers shot by a boy—Attempt to rob a farmer of his horse—Burglars discovered by means of a button—Evacuation of the Island—An eye witness' account of it... 111

CHAPTER XVI.

The Quarantine—Murders.. 131

APPENDIX "A."—CIVIL LIST.

Members of the provincial Congress................................. 140
Representatives in Congress....................................... "
State Senators from Richmond County............................... "
Judges of the County Courts...................................... 141
Presidential electors from Richmond County......................... "
Members of the Colonial Assembly from Richmond County............. "
Members of Assembly from Richmond County......................... 142
Members of the State Constitutional Conventions from Richmond County... 144
School Superintendents of Richmond County......................... 145
Clerks of Richmond County .... "
Surrogates of Richmond County.................................... "

Sheriffs of Richmond County.. 145
District Attorneys of Richmond County...................................... 146
Regents of the University from Richmond County....................... "
Supervisors of Castleton and Northfield...................................... 147
    "   of Southfield, Westfield and Middletown......................... 148
    "   prior to 1766... 149
County taxes from the year 1766...

APPENDIX "B."—EXTRACTS FROM OLD RECORDS.   151

APPENDIX "C."—ANECDOTES, &c.   183

APPENDIX "D."—GOVERNMENT.   203

APPENDIX "E."—STATEN ISLAND 200 YEARS AGO.   210

APPENDIX "F."—VILLAGES.

New Brighton... 218
Port Richmond... 220
Edgewater.. 222

APPENDIX "G."—NOTED LOCALITIES.

Toad Hill... 226
Watchogue... 228
The Rose and Crown... 229
The Bull's Head... 230
The Clove—The Finger-board road... 232
Holland's Hook—Morning and Blazing Stars............................ 233
Kill Van Kull—Arthur Kull—The Old place............................. 234

APPENDIX "H."—HOSPITALS, &c.

The Sailors' Snug Harbor.. 238
The Retreat.. 247
Seamens' Children's Home.. 249
The S. R. Smith Infirmary—Y. M. C. A................................... 250

APPENDIX "I."—CHURCHES.

Reformed Church, Port Richmond.. 254
                    Richmond.. 259
                    Brighton Heights....................................... 260
    "   "   of the Huguenots....................................... 261
St. Andrew's Church.. 263

Calvary Presbyterian Church, W. N. Brighton	268
Presbyterian Church, Edgewater	270
Church of the Ascension, W. N. Brighton	271
St. John's Church, Clifton	272
St. Paul's Church, Middletown	273
St. Luke's Church, Rossville	274
Church of the Holy Comforter, Eltingville	"
Moravian Church	275
Baptist Church, Park	282
" " Mariner's Harbor	285
" " Graniteville	286
" " South	287
Methodist Church—Woodrow	288
" Bethel and St. Paul's	290
Asbury, Summerfield	291
St. Mark's—Trinity	292
" Grace—Cebra Avenue	293
St. John's—Lutheran	
Unitarian	294
Roman Catholic—St. Peter's	297
St. Mary's, Clifton	299
St. Joseph's, Rossville—St. Patrick's—St. Mary's	300

APPENDIX "J."—BIOGRAPHIES.

Individuals	303
Nicholas Garrison	304
Abraham Jones	306
David Mersereau	307
Nathan Barrett	310
Cornelius Vanderbilt	313
Daniel D. Tompkins	317
Samuel Russell Smith, M.D.	319

APPENDIX "K."—INDUSTRIES, &c.

New York Dyeing and Printing Establishment	322
Barrett, Nephews & Co's Fancy Dyeing Establishment	324
Fire-Brick and Gas Retort Manufactory	326
Linoleum Company	327
Whitelead and Linseed Oil Manufacturers	328
De Jonge's Paper Factory	329
The Oyster Trade	"
Staten Island Railroad	331
Breweries	333

APPENDIX "L."—Old Families.

Preliminary Notice... 336	Haughwout family... 388
Alston family... 338	Hillyer " ... 389
Androvette " ... 339	Holmes " ... 390
Barnes " ... 341	Housman " ... 391
Bedell " ... 342	Jacobson " ... 392
Blake ... 343	Johnson ... "
Bodine ... 344	Jones ... 395
Bogart ... 346	Journeay ... 396
Braisted ... 347	Laforge " ... 397
Britton ... 348	Lake ... 398
Burbank " ... 349	Larzelere ... 399
Burgher, &c. " ... 351	Latourette " ... 400
Bush " ... "	Lisk ... 401
Butler " ... 353	Lockman ... 403
Cannon " ... 354	Martling ... "
Christopher " ... "	Martino " ... 404
Cole " ... 356	Merrill ... 405
Colon " ... 357	Mersereau ... 408
Conner ... "	Metcalf " ... 412
Corsen ... 358	Morgan ... 413
Cortelyou ... 363	Perine ... 414
Cripe ... 364	Poillon ... 416
Crocheron ... '	Post ... 417
Cruser " ... 366	Prall ... 418
Cubberly " ... 368	Ryers " ... 419
Decker ... 369	Seguine ... 420
De Groot ... 371	Sharrott " ... 421
De Hart ... 373	Simonson ... 422
Depuy ... "	Stillwell " ... 424
Disosway ... 375	Sprague " ... 426
Dubois ... 376	Taylor " ... 427
Dustan ... 377	Totten ... "
Eddy " ... 378	Van Buskirk ... 428
Egbert ' " ... 379	Vanderbilt " ... 429
Enyard " ... 380	Van Name " ... 431
Fountain ... 381	Van Pelt " ... 432
Frost ... 383	Wandel ... 434
Garrison ... 384	Winant " ... 435
Guyon " ... 386	Woglom " ... 437
Hatfield ... 387	Wood ... "

APPENDIX "M."—MISCELLANEOUS. 439

APPENDIX "N."—NOTES. 451

ANNALS OF STATEN ISLAND.

CHAPTER I.

Discovery—Verazzano—The First Death—Hudson River—Hostages—The First Battle—Localities Inhabited—Food—Animals.

BRIGHT and calm, over the heights of Neversink, broke the dawn of the third day of September, 1609;* the early breeze rippled the surface of the slumbering ocean, and rustled through the leaves of the forest trees, awakening the songsters which nestled beneath them to pour forth their matin hymn to greet the king of day; the world seemed glad that light had once more dispelled the darkness. But all this beauty and harmony were lost upon the human denizens of the woods and mountains, who stood in groups upon the strand, gesticulating eagerly, and gazing intently, over the vast expanse of water which stretched out illimitably before them. Far off towards the Southeast, the unusual sight of a mere speck upon the surface of the ocean excited their wonder. Long and patiently they watched it as it slowly approached and grew larger and larger, until it had assumed proportions far exceeding that of any moving object which had ever before met their vision. What could it be? Was it some great bird which had flown over the great sea from some distant islands? Or, was it the Great Spirit who had descended to earth to visit and to bless his children? Slowly and majestically the object swept past, turned around the sandy

* Vide App. N. (1.)

point of land beyond them, and stopped. It was the Half-Moon, and bore Henry Hudson and his fellow voyagers. They supposed, erroneously, however, that they were the first white men who had ever looked upon the enchanted scene which surrounded them. Hudson was ignorant that, nearly a century before (1524), Giovanni Verazzano had entered the bay, and anchored near the same spot; that he lay there until the next morning, when a violent gale compelled him to put to sea again. Though not the first to behold, Hudson was the first to penetrate the mysteries of the land and water which extended to an unknown distance before him. In one boat he visited Coney Island, and sent another, containing five men, on an exploring expedition Northward. These men passed through the Narrows, coasted along Staten Island, and penetrated some distance into the Kills. On their return they suddenly encountered two large canoes, containing twenty-six Indians, who, in their alarm, discharged a shower of arrows at the strangers, and killed one man, an Englishman, named John Coleman, by shooting him in the neck. Both parties became frightened, and pulled away from each other with all their strength. Coleman's body was taken to Sandy Hook, and there interred, and the place was called "Coleman's Point."

The discovery of a northwest passage to the East Indies had, for a long time, been an object of great interest to the merchants of Europe, and in 1607 Hudson was sent to ascertain its practicability. He penetrated as far north as eighty-two degrees, discovered Spitzbergen and part of Greenland, and, encountering an impenetrable barrier of ice, he returned to England.

The next year, 1608, another expedition was fitted out by the same parties, and the command again entrusted to Hudson. This also proved a failure, as far as its principal object was concerned. The English company having declined to make another experiment, Hudson entered into the service of the Dutch East India Company, and was sent out in the Half Moon to renew the attempt. He sailed from Amsterdam on the fourth day of April, 1609, and once more directed his course for the northern seas. Again the ice presented an insuperable barrier, and he was obliged to abandon the object of his search. In the hope of discovering something to indemnify his employers for the expenses of the voyage, he sailed for the Continent of America, and arrived in the vicinity of Newfoundland in the month of July. Thence he followed the coast until he reached Virginia, which it appears he recognized as belonging to the English, and knowing that all south of that had been appropriated by Spain, he turned about and sailed northward again, until the third day of September, when he saw the highlands of Neversink, and, as we have already narrated, anchored within Sandy Hook.

Notwithstanding the mishap, as the death of Coleman was regarded, the natives proved to be friendly, and freely bartered with the strangers such articles as they had to dispose of, such as tobacco, maize, wild fruits, etc. Hudson remained at anchor until the eleventh, when he sailed through the Narrows, and anchored in the mouth of the great river which now bears his name. On the thirteenth he again weighed anchor, and proceeded to explore the beautiful stream upon whose bosom he was floating; he was eleven days in ascending as far as the site of Albany, and as many more in descending. Before starting, he had had considerable intercourse with the natives, but had always prudently kept himself and his men prepared for any emergency, and though the natives frequently came on board armed, they made no hostile demonstrations; Hudson, however, detained two of the Staten Island Indians as hostages, and took them with him on the voyage up the river, as far as the site of West Point, where they escaped by jumping overboard and swimming to the shore. On his way he encountered many of the Indians, who, though they manifested a friendly disposition, were nevertheless suspected of entertaining hostile intentions, and it was supposed that the dread with which they regarded the arms of their visitors alone restrained them.

On his return down the river, while lying at anchor off

Stoney Point, numerous canoes from both sides surrounded the ship, from one of which an Indian entered the cabin by climbing through a stern window, from which he stole several articles of clothing. As he left the ship with his plunder, the mate detected him and shot him, killing him instantly. This was the first blood shed by the whites. When the ship's boat was sent to recover the stolen articles, one Indian, who appeared to possess more courage than his fellows, while swimming, laid hold of the boat, apparently for the purpose of overturning it, but a sailor, with a single blow of his sword, cut off his hands, and he was drowned. It was supposed that the two Staten Island savages who had escaped at West Point, on their way down the river, had alarmed the several tribes, so that when the ship arrived at the upper end of Manhattan Island, it was met by a large fleet of canoes filled with armed savages, who discharged their arrows, but fortunately without doing any serious injury. A cannon was twice discharged at them, killing some of them, and tearing their canoes to pieces, the sailors meanwhile firing at them with small arms. The result of this engagement was that nine Indians were killed, and many more wounded, while the whites had sustained no injury whatever. Having escaped all the perils which surrounded him, Hudson put to sea on the fourth day of October, having spent a month in his explorations.

The chronicler of this voyage of Hudson, Robert Juet,[*] says:

"1609, Sept. 6. Our master sent John Coleman with four men to sound the river four leagues distant, which they did, but in their return to the ship they were set upon by Indians in two canoes, to the number of 26; in which affair John Coleman was killed by an arrow shot into his throat, and two others were wounded. The next day Coleman was buried on a point of land which to this day bears his name.

"Sept. 8. The people came on board us, and brought

---

[*] Vide App. N. (2.)

tobacco and Indian wheat to exchange for knives and beads, and offered us no violence. So we, fitting up our boat, did mark them to see if they would make any show of the death of our man, but they did not.

"Sept. 9. In the morning two great canoes came on board full of men; one with bows and arrows, and the other in show of buying knives, to betray us, but we perceived their intention. We took two of them, to have kept them, and put red coats on them, and would not suffer the others to come near us, and soon after the canoes leave them. Immediately two other natives came on board us; one we took and let the other go, but he soon escaped by jumping overboard.

"Sept. 11. The ship had now anchored a considerable distance up the river. The people of the country came on board, making show of love, and gave us tobacco and Indian wheat.

"Sept. 12. This morning there came eight and twenty canoes full of men, women and children to betray us, but we saw their intent and suffered none of them to come on board. They have great tobacco pipes of yellow copper and pots of earth to dress their meat in.

"Sept. 15. Sailed twenty leagues further up the river, passing by high mountains. This morning the two captive savages got out of a part of the ship and made their escape.

"Sept. 18. The master's mate went on shore with an old Indian, a sachem of the country, who took him to his house and treated him kindly.

"Oct. 1. The ship having fallen down the river seven miles below the mountains, comes to anchor. One man in a canoe kept hanging under the stern of the ship, and would not be driven off. He soon contrived to climb up by the rudder, and got into the cabin window, which had been left open, from which he stole a pillow, two shirts and two bandoleers. The mate shot him in the breast, and killed him. Many others were in canoes about the ship, who immediately fled, and some jumped overboard. A boat manned from the ship pursued them, and coming up with one in the water, he laid hold of the side of the boat and endeavored to overset it; at which one in the boat cut off his hands with a sword, and he was drowned.

"Oct. 2. Fell down seven leagues further, and anchored again. Then came one of the savages that swam away from us at our going up the river, with many others, thinking to betray us, but we suffered none of them to enter our ship. Whereupon two canoes of men with their bows and arrows shot at us after our stern; in a recompense whereof, we discharged six muskets and killed two or three of them. Then above an hundred of them came to a point of land to shoot at us. There I shot a falcon at them, and killed two of them; whereupon the rest fled into the woods. Yet they manned off another canoe with nine or ten men, which came to meet us; so I shot at it also a falcon, and shot it through and killed one of them. Then our men with their muskets killed three or four more of them."

The Indians dwelling upon Staten Island at the time of its discovery were the Raritans, a branch of the great nation of Delawares or Leni-Lenapes. From indications found in various localities, such as large collections of shells and bones, it is evident that they dwelt on or near the shores of the island, where fish, scale and shell, were easily procurable; this is also confirmed by the fact that their burial places have been found in the same vicinity, neither of these indications of human habitation having been found in the interior. Stone hatchets and stone arrow-heads, springs rudely built up with stone walls, have been found at no great distance from the shores; one of the latter may still be seen a short distance northeast of the Fresh Pond, or Silver Lake, in Castleton, and is known by the name of the Logan Spring.

The interior of the island was their hunting ground, where deer, bears and other animals of the chase were found. The shores also afforded an abundant supply of water fowls, and thus, all their resources considered, the Indians were well supplied by nature with the necessaries of life. In addition to these, they had wild berries and fruits, and maize, beans, tobacco, and other articles of their own cultivation. The proximity of the island to the mainland, enabled them to extend their hunting expeditions indefinitely. The wild animals which were found on the neighboring continent, were also found here, but they, as well as their human contemporaries, have gradually retired or perished as civilization advanced. Forty years ago, an occasional fox might be detected prowling through the bushes, but now nothing but the timid rabbit, of all the quadrupeds which once roamed over the hills and through the valleys, is left.

CHAPTER II.

Name—Dimensions—Surface—Climate—Geology—The Fur Trade—The First English Claim—The Dutch take Possession—The Brownists.

THERE is no evidence that Hudson ever circumnavigated the island, but that he satisfied himself of its insular character, is evident from the name he bestowed upon it; he called it "Staaten Eylant," the island of the States—that is, the States General, under whose flag he was sailing. To the aborigines it was known as "Aquehonga Manacknong," and in some old documents it is called "Egquahous," another Indian name which is said to signify "the place of bad woods."

The form of the island is that of an irregular triangle. The longest line which can be drawn through it, from the shores of the bay at New Brighton to the extremity of Ward's Point, is a few feet over thirteen and a half miles in length; the longest line which can be drawn across it, from the shore of the Sound near Buckwheat Island, to the shore at the lighthouse near the Narrows, is about two hundred feet over seven and three-fourth miles in length.

The surface of the island is diversified; there is a high ridge commencing at Tompkinsville, and running southwesterly to the Fresh Kills, in the vicinity of Richmond, the highest point of which is at the intersection of the Toad Hill road and Ocean Terrace, and which is the summit of the Island; a branch of this ridge terminating near the Black Horse Corner, is distinguished by the local, and by no means euphonious name of "Toad Hill." To the southeast of this ridge is a level, and probably alluvial, tract of country composed of upland and salt meadow, extending to the ocean. The soil of this upland is of excellent quality, and some of the best farms in the county are located here. To the northwest of this ridge the surface is undulating, gradually declining to level upland and saline meadows. Almost every farm in the county is furnished with several acres of this meadow, from which large quantities of salt grass are taken annually. The soil of the island generally may be considered fertile—in some places unusually so—though in consequence of more than two centuries of cultivation it has become partially exhausted, and requires fertilizing. The island is well watered with springs, some of them very copious, and all of them affording water of excellent quality; these are the sources of numerous rivulets and brooks which irrigate the surface in all directions. Excepting the salt meadows, the whole island was originally covered with dense forests, which have long since disappeared; in most places the woods now growing, occupy lands which were once cultivated.

The climate of the Island has long been celebrated for its salubrity, except for affections of the lungs and throat. There are few localities on the continent where the number of instances of extreme longevity in proportion to the population can be equaled, many of them being more than centenarians.

Staten Island is based upon primitive rock, which rises near its centre into a ridge, running longitudinally through it, with a breadth of from one to two miles. Boulders of green-stone, sand-stone, gneiss, granite, etc., appear in some sections sparingly, but in the northeast part of the Island, in considerable abundance. Steatite, containing veins of talc, amianthus and alabaster covers the granite of the ridge; this approaches in many places within one and a half feet of the surface. Brown hematitic iron ore, of a superior quality, is abundant, as well as granular oxide of iron. Chalcedony, jasper, lignite, crystalized pyrites, asbestos, dolomite, brucite, gurhofite, and serpentine, are the other principal minerals.

The climate of Holland and other countries of Europe, rendered furs indispensable to their inhabitants; hitherto these had been obtained chiefly from Russia, and at great expense. The Dutch had discovered that there were furs in the countries newly discovered, which were easily procurable in exchange for articles of extremely trifling value; the temptation to engage in a traffic so exceedingly profitable, was too strong to be resisted by a people so prompt to promote their own interests. Accordingly, in 1611, a vessel was dispatched to the Manhattans as an experiment, and so successful was this venture, that a spirit of commercial enterprise was at once awakened. Two more vessels, the Little Fox and the Little Crane, were licensed, and under the pretence of looking for the Northwest Passage, sailed direct for the newly-discovered river. This was in the spring of 1613. Having arrived, the traders erected one or two small forts for the protection of the trade on the river. The position of the island of Manhattan for commercial purposes was so favorable as to strike the Europeans at once, and the traders who had scattered in various directions made that island their head-quarters. Hendrick Cortiansen was the superintendent of the business, and with his small craft penetrated every bay or stream where Indians were to be found, in pursuit of furs.

In the autumn of this year, an Englishman, known in colonial history as Captain Argal, a resident of Virginia, touched at the island of Manhattan, to look after a grant of land which he claimed to have received from the Virginia Company, and, it is said, compelled Cortiansen to submit to the English authorities, and to pay tribute in token thereof. When the merchants in Holland who were interested in the fur trade heard of the pretensions of the English, they at once adopted such measures as they deemed necessary to secure both the trade and the country to themselves. They petitioned the States-General for protection and relief, and on the 27th of March, 1614, an octroy or ordinance was issued, granting them the privilege of making six voyages for the purpose of discovering new countries and seas, and trading to them. This octroy awakened the enthusiasm of adventurers, and five ships, viz. the Nightingale, the Little Fox, the Tiger, the Fortune of Amsterdam, and the Fortune of Hoorn, were sent out. Among the commanders of these vessels were Adrian Block and Cornelis Jacobson Mey, the former of whom gave his name to an island, and the latter to a cape on the American coast, which they still retain. Block had the misfortune to lose his ship by fire, but he immediately built a small vessel, with which he penetrated into the unknown waters eastward; he passed through and named the Hellegat, after a river in Flanders, then continuing his course with Metoae or Sewanhacky, now Long Island; on his right, he sailed along the shores of the continent, discovered the Housatonic and Connecticut rivers; the latter he named the Fresh river, and finally discovered the open ocean, thus for the first time demonstrating the insular character of the land on the south of his course; to one of the smaller islands east of Long Island he gave his own name. Continuing his voyage along the coast, he discovered and examined Narragansett Bay, which he called Nassau Bay, and thence to Cape Cod, which Hudson had already discovered and named New Holland, and here he found Cortiansen's ship. While Block was thus examining the north side of Long Island, Mey was similarly employed on its south side, until he also reached its end, when he stood towards the south and entered Delaware Bay, giving his own name to one of its capes, and calling the opposite cape Hindlopen, from a town in Holland.

When the intelligence of these discoveries reached the projectors of the several voyages, at home, steps were immediately taken by them to secure to themselves the benefits of their enterprise and perseverance. All the country lying between the 40th and 45th degrees of North latitude was called "New Netherland." Exclusive privileges to trade to these countries for a limited period were given to them. A trading house was at once erected on an island in the Hudson, near the present site of Albany, and the country on both sides of the river thoroughly explored in quest of furs; and by the time of the expiration of the grant, which was at the close of 1617, some of the merchants engaged in the trade had realized immense fortunes therefrom.

The charter having expired, the trade of New Netherland was thrown open, and adventurers from all parts of the fatherland eagerly enlisted therein; the former traders, however, held on to the advantages they had gained by their prior occupancy.

Thus it will be seen that the first Europeans who visited this part of the Continent, came for the purpose of trading, not of settling permanently, but having become favorably impressed with the soil and climate of the country, they began to entertain the idea of making it the place of their future abode, and to devote to agriculture that part of the season when furs were not obtainable.

During the reign of Elizabeth, certain religionists who had renounced the communion of the established church, had formed themselves into a separate organization under the pastoral care of Richard Brown, from whom they were called "Brownists;" these became the objects of the intolerance of the hierarchy, and the several enactments enforced against them drove them from their homes and country to Holland, as the only refuge in which they might enjoy their religious opinions undisturbed. But they left a seed behind which eventually germinated and fructified, and in turn became the objects both of clerical and regal persecution. These also were compelled to flee to Holland, where they settled in several towns. Those who took up their residence at Leyden were under the pastoral care of the Rev. John Robinson, and after a protracted residence, applied to the States-General for permission to settle on Manhattan Island. The company of traders whose ships were employed in traversing the ocean, and carrying to the old world the wealth of the new, at once perceived the benefits which would result, not only to both countries, but to themselves individually from such an arrangement, seconded the application with great earnestness. But the government, though not averse to the scheme, had matters of infinitely more importance at that juncture to engage their attention. The twelve years' truce which had been arranged between the United Provinces and Spain, was about to expire, and the latter power had already required the former to return to their allegiance. This demand having been indignantly rejected, preparations were made for a renewal of hostilities, and therefore the vessels of war, and the armed protection which the petitioners had requested, was refused. This decision changed the destinies of the emigrants, who subsequently settled on the bleak shores of New England. Different commercial associations had been formed among the Dutch themselves, whose several interests began to interfere with each other, and this led to bickerings and disputes, all of which were finally set at rest by the chartering of the "Dutch West India Company," which absorbed all private interests, and became the controllers of all matters relating to the New Netherlands.

CHAPTER III.

The West India Company—English Claims—Arrival of Settlers—First Settlement on Staten Island—At the Wallabout—Birth of the First Child—Purchase of Manhattan Island—The Patroons—Communipaw—De Vries' Grant—Melyn's Patent—Staten Island Massacre and its Consequences—Still, etc., upon the Island—Indian Murders and Murder of Indians.

The powers and privileges of the West India Company were not confined to the narrow limits of the New Netherlands; they embraced the whole range of the American coast, from the Horn to the Arctic Sea, and on the west coast of Africa from the Hope to the Tropic of Cancer, not previously occupied by other nations. On the American coast settlements had been made by the French at Canada, by the English at Virginia, and by the Spaniards at Florida. The preparations made by the directors of the newly chartered company to improve the privileges granted to them, attracted, in England, the attention of the government, and a strong remonstrance was sent to Holland, insisting that all the territory claimed by the Dutch was embraced in the charter of Virginia, and therefore was under the jurisdiction of England. The matter was from time to time brought before the authorities of both countries, and the discussion protracted by the Dutch for the purpose of gaining time, that the preparations of the new company might be completed. The country was organized into a province, a few settlers were sent out, and a form of government was established, with Peter Minuit at its head as Director; this was in the year 1624. In the same year, and probably in the same ship with Minuit, a number of Walloons arrived and settled upon Staten Island; this is the first settlement on the Island of which we have any knowledge. These people came from the country bordering on the river Scheldt and Flanders; they professed the reformed religion, and spoke the old French, or Gallic language; they were good soldiers, and had done efficient service in the thirty years' war. Two years before their arrival here, they had applied to Sir Dudley Carleton, for permission to emigrate to some part of Virginia, upon condition that they might build a town of their own, and be governed by officers chosen by and from among themselves. This application was referred to the Virginia Company, and met with a favorable response so far as the mere settlement was concerned, but the privilege to elect their own officers was too long a step toward popular freedom, and could not be conceded; the permission to settle upon the Company's land was fettered with so many conditions affecting their civil and religious liberty, that they declined to entertain it, and turned their attention to the New Netherlands, where so many arbitrary conditions were not insisted upon. On their arrival here, they appear to have abandoned the idea of settling in a single community, for they separated and went in different directions, a few families, as we have said, taking up their abode on Staten Island. The precise spot of their settlement cannot now be ascertained, but wherever it was, they did not occupy it long; annoyed by the constant intrusions of the Indians, and apprehensive that in the event of difficulty with them, they were too remote from assistance, in the following year, 1625, they removed to Long Island, and settled at what is now known as the Wallabout, a name supposed to have been derived from them. The name of only one of these Walloons has been preserved, that of George Jansen de Rapelje, who, on the 6th or 9th of June of that year, became the father of a daughter who was the first child of European parents born in the colony.* Some of our local annalists have claimed that the birth of this child took place before the removal to Long Island, but this is a claim which cannot be sustained. The father of this child was the progenitor of the respectable family of that name on Long Island.

Having determined to colonize the country, and the permission of the government having been obtained, the West

* Vide App. N. (8.)

India Company proceeded to extinguish the Indian title by purchase. They repudiated the principle involved in the adage, "Macht maakt recht,"* and entered into negotiations for securing title to the whole of Manhattan Island; this was accomplished during the year 1626, for articles the value of which was about twenty-four dollars. They have been charged with imposing upon the simplicity of the natives, and taking an undue advantage of their ignorance, but it must be remembered that at that time the island was a mass of rocks, swamps and dense forests, unavailable for even the purpose of a residence without great labor and expense; that the Indians were content with their bargain, is evident from the fact that they never after attempted to re-sell it, as they did Staten Island and several other places.

The first great landed proprietors in New Netherland were called "Patroons;" they were Samuel Godyn, Samuel Bloemart, Killian Van Rensselaer and Michael Pauw. The two first named settled in Delaware. Van Rensselaer obtained a patent for a large tract on the Hudson in the vicinity of Albany and Troy, and Pauw became the proprietor of all the country extending from Hoboken southward along the bay and Staten Island Sound, then called Achter Kull, now corrupted into Arthur Kull, including Staten Island; this grant was made to him by the Directors in 1630. At the same time the country was purchased from the natives for "certain cargoes or parcels of goods," and called Pavonia. The name of this proprietor still attaches to a part of his possessions in the locality known as Communipaw—the Commune of Pauw—which has usually been supposed to be a name of Indian origin. It is to be mentioned to the credit of the Company, that they made it a condition in the patents which they granted, that the recipients should extinguish the Indian title by direct purchase, and this was exacted in every instance.† The consideration paid to the natives was not money, which would have been useless to

---

* Ibid (4.)   † Vide App. N. (5.)

them, but cloths of various kinds, culinary utensils, ornaments, etc., but not fire-arms.

The value of the articles paid for the fee of the Island varied at different times, for the Indians sold it repeatedly. Pauw's acquisition was not of much benefit to him; it is not known that he made any effort to colonize it, or that he ever cleared a rood of it, for very soon after acquiring it, difficulties arose between him and the Directors, and he disposed of his territorial rights on the Island and on the Continent to his associate Directors for the sum of 26,000 guilders. He was a man of consequence in his own country; he was one of the Lord Directors of the Company, and among their names we find his set down as the Lord of Achtienhoven.

In 1630, or soon thereafter, David Pietersen De Vries obtained a grant for a part of the Island, and began to make settlements upon it, but the precise locality is not known; it is supposed, however, to have been at or near Old Town, (Oude Dorp). The dwellings of the settlers, on their arrival, were generally constructed as speedily as possible, that their families might be sheltered. Excavations for this purpose were generally made in the side of a hill, or other convenient spot, and lined and roofed with rude planks, split out of the trees; sometimes the roofs were covered with several layers of bark; these were only meant for temporary dwelling places, until better ones could be provided.

De Vries was a literary man, and author of a historical work. There is no evidence that he resided upon the Island permanently; the settlers, however, who were introduced by him, prospered for a time, and until their bouweries or farms were desolated by the savages, as we shall see hereafter.

Peter Minuit having been recalled, in 1633 Wouter Van Twiller was appointed in his stead. The change, on the whole, was not beneficial to the colony. Minuit's faults, whatever they might have been, were succeeded by the new Director's vices, among which inebriety was not the least. The appointment was a sad mistake on the part of the XIX, and though it took nearly five years to convince them of the fact, yet when once convinced, they took prompt measures to repair their error by removing him. There is no historical evidence, that we have been able to discover, that Van Twiller ever set foot upon Staten Island during his administration, or that a single event occurred in connection with the Island, except the actual bickerings and disputes with the Raritans, as well as with other Indians. Notwithstanding, he appears to have had a predilection for islands, for when he perceived indications of the approaching termination of his administration, he hastened to secure to himself the possession of the island called by the Indians Pagganck, which subsequently became known as Nutten Island, and later still as Governor's Island, then estimated to contain 160 acres of land; and two other islands in the Hallegat, the one called Tenkenas, containing 200 acres, and the other called Minnahanock, containing 120 acres. He secured these islands by private purchase from the Indians. The wisest act of Van Twiller's administration was an advantageous peace he concluded with the Raritans, the Indians inhabiting Staten Island and the adjoining shores of the continent; this was in 1634. During this year came over Jan Evertsen Bout and his wife Tryntje Simonz de Witt; he afterwards became a man of considerable note in the colony, and in 1638 purchased a farm and settled upon it; this was the first settlement in the town of Bergen, N. J.

In 1639, Cornelis Melyn, of Antwerp, sailed for America; he is known in the Dutch history of the colony as the patroon of Staten Island. He was a wealthy man, and accompanied by several of his own class. He had obtained from the Directors in Holland authority to take possession of Staten Island, and have it settled, but on the passage his vessel was captured by the "Dunkirkers" or French, by which he lost all, or nearly all his property. Early in 1641 he applied to the Directors for a passage for himself and family, which was granted, and in August of that year he arrived at New Amsterdam. He came over in a ship called the Eyckenboom, (oak tree), and brought with him a small quantity of goods for the Indian trade. On the 19th of June, 1642, he received a patent for so much of Staten Island as was not already occupied by the farms or bouweries of De Vries.

In the spring of 1640, some parties, on their way from New Amsterdam to South river, Delaware, stopped at Staten Island to take in water, and while there stole some hogs from the settlers on De Vries' bouweries. The Indians residing on the Raritan, and who had manifested a hostile disposition, were at once charged with this theft, which from the scarcity and value of the animals was regarded as a serious offence. Kieft, the director of the province of New Netherland, who had been appointed to succeed Minuit, appears to have been an indiscreet and imprudent man, and eminently possessed of the Dutch attributes of obstinacy and self-will. He at once charged the Indians with the theft, and resolved to punish them severely. He sent his secretary, Vantienhoven, and seventy men, some of whom were sailors from the ship Neptune, Capt. Hendrick Gerritsen, and some of them soldiers from the stockade or fort, with instructions to invade the Indian country, capture as many of the natives as they could, and destroy their crops. When the party reached their destination, they became insubordinate, and the secretary lost all control over them; they declared their intention to kill every Indian they could find, and though reminded that that would be exceeding their instructions, they persisted in their resolution, and the secretary becoming disgusted with their conduct, left them. Several of the unfortunate savages were killed, and the chief's brother was barbarously butchered after he had been made a prisoner, by one of the party named Govert Loockermans. Their crops were destroyed, their wigwams burned, and other outrages perpetrated. Having done all the mischief in their power, the whites retired, leaving one of their number, the supercargo of the Neptune, named Ross, dead on the field.

During the same year, 1640, the director erected a still upon Staten Island, and put it in charge of Willem Hendricksen, and thus our Island obtained the unenviable honor of being the place where spirits were first manufactured, not only in the province, but probably in America. Kieft also commenced the manufacture of buckskin on the Island, about the same time. In September of the same year, the director and council caused a staff to be erected at the Narrows, that by the hoisting of a flag the approach of a ship might be telegraphed to New Amsterdam; this was the first marine telegraph in the harbor of New York.

The Indians, goaded to desperation, not only by the unjustifiable destruction of their crops, and slaughter of their brethren, but by a long continued course of frauds practised upon them by unscrupulous men, who first intoxicated and then cheated them in bargaining with them, resolved upon revenge. One of their first acts was to invade Staten Island, where they attacked De Vries' bouwerie, killed four men, and burned two of his houses. This was in 1641.

Not long before, a young Indian, smarting under a sense of wrong, vowed to kill the first Dutchman who crossed his path, and he kept his vow. Kieft, forgetting that himself was the instigator of all these outrages, announced his intention of taking summary vengeance upon the savages. It was in vain that the prominent men of the colony counselled moderation—in vain that they represented to him that his course would be adding fuel to the fire—he replied to all their remonstrances that the law was "blood for blood," and he meant to have it; he recognized the applicability of the law to the whites, but not to the savages. His anger was chiefly directed to the Raritans, and he entered into an agreement with some of the river Indians to assist him in annihilating that tribe; to excite their blood-thirsty dispositions, he offered ten fathoms of wampum for the head of a Raritan, and twenty fathoms for the head of every Indian engaged in the murders upon Staten Island. At this time he built a small redoubt upon the Island.

In the meanwhile, the Indians upon Long Island began to manifest a hostile disposition, and Kieft found himself involved in new troubles. It was evident from some of his measures that he began to regret his precipitancy, and if nothing else had occurred to irritate him anew, he might have consented to forget the past, and to "bury the hatchet," but just at this juncture some traders happened to meet an Indian of the Hakensack tribe, who was clothed in a dress of valuable beaver skins; him they made drunk, and then robbed. On recovering his senses, the savage vowed to shoot the first Swannakin (white man) whom he should meet; he did that, and more; an Englishman, who was a servant of De Vries on Staten Island, was met by him and killed, and shortly after a man named Van Vorst, while engaged in repairing a house in the vicinity of Newark bay, met the same fate. Apprehensive of further trouble, a deputation of chiefs of some of the neighboring tribes, waited upon the Director, whom they found greatly excited, and not disposed to reason with them. He informed them that the only way to keep peace was to surrender the murderer. "We cannot do that," they replied, "because he has fled, and is out of our reach." They offered to make compensation for the crime, according to the customs of their people; nothing, however, could propitiate Kieft but the possession of the murderer. The Indians represented to him, that it was not they who committed the murders, but the white men's rum; "keep that away from the Indians," said they, "and there will be no more murders;" but Kieft was inexorable—he was resolved upon war, unless they surrendered the murderer, who was as far out of their reach as out of his.

An event now occurred which gave a new direction to Kieft's purposes. A band of Mohawks, the terror of all the neighboring tribes, made a descent upon some of the villages of the river Indians, who fled to Manhattan Island to seek the protection of the Dutch. They were hospitably received and protected by them for a fortnight. Half dead with cold* and hunger, they were objects of commiseration; even Kieft appeared to have some sympathy for their wretchedness. Here was an opportunity for reconciling all difficulties and effecting a permanent peace; but an evil

* Vide App. N. (6.)

spirit was abroad in the land; people began to talk about the final disposition of these refugees; they were divided in opinion; the Indians became aware that they had enemies even among those who had afforded them temporary shelter, and they fled the second time, scattering themselves in various directions, and seeking shelter and protection among the neighboring tribes. Van Tienhoven and his associates, some of whom were members of the Council, sought permission to pursue and kill the fugitives, while De Vries, Domine Bogardus and their associates, recommended conciliatory measures and Christian forbearance. Kieft was in a dilemma, but the secretary, taking advantage of the Director's inebriety, presented to him a commission ready drawn, and plied him with such arguments as a drunken man would be likely to appreciate, succeeded in obtaining his signature.

In the dead of the night of the 25th of February, 1643, two companies left the fort on their errand of death—one commanded by Maryn Adriaensen, a man infamous for his bloody deeds, the other by sergeant Rodolph. Both companies were impiously committed to the guidance and protection of Heaven. They went in different directions, but as their proceedings are in no way connected with the task in hand, it must suffice to say that they both accomplished their bloody purposes; the savages were found buried in slumber, and were ruthlessly murdered without discrimination. Over one hundred of them were sacrificed under the most appalling circumstances of barbarity.

CHAPTER IV.

Long Island Indians—Roger Williams—Expedition against the Staten Island Indians—Searches for the Precious Metals—Toad Hill Iron Mine—Misgovernment of the Directors—Bogardus and De Vries—Their policy—Decline of the Fur Trade—Kieft recalled—His Death—The several Sales of Staten Island.

NEW troubles now arose with the Long Island Indians. Thus far they had remained quiet, but the Dutch, with an infatuation utterly unaccountable, suffered no opportunities to pass to excite them to deeds of violence. Matters were becoming worse daily, and an outbreak of Indian fury could not have been suppressed much longer, when, through the unremitting assiduity of the philanthropic Roger Williams, a meeting between Kieft and several Indian sachems took place at Rockaway on the 25th of March, and a reconciliation was effected.

The peace thus concluded was of short duration. The Indians continued to commit depredations upon the property of the settlers, and especially was this the case upon Staten Island. Many of them still held their residence there, and could not resist the temptation to appropriate the products of the agricultural skill and labor of their white neighbors, which were so much superior in quantity, quality and variety to their own. Remonstrances had proved ineffectual, and it became necessary to adopt severer measures. In addition to this, the Raritans, who were the offending tribe, had interrupted the communication between the two shores of the river at New Amsterdam, and it had become perilous to attempt to land on the west shore. Early in 1644 an expedition against the Staten Island Indians was organized. It consisted of forty burghers under Joachim Pietersen Kuyter; thirty-five Englishmen under Lieutenant Baxter, and several soldiers from the fort under Sergeant Peter Cock, the whole being under the command of Counsellor La Montagne. They embarked after dark, and at a late hour landed upon the Island. They marched all night, and when the morning dawned, had arrived at the place where they expected to find the Indians, but there were none there. Secretly as the whole enterprise had been conducted, the savages had discovered it and escaped. The troops, after burning the village, returned, taking with them over five hundred schepels of corn.*

Notwithstanding the successful trade which had been carried on in peltries, and the large amounts which had been realized therefrom, the several successive directors, the patroons, and even the company at home, had men employed in the search after the precious metals; the discovery of one or two places which yielded a substance supposed to be silver, created considerable excitement. The Indians possessed a peculiar substance with which they painted their faces on important occasions, and the Director, having obtained a specimen of it, submitted it to the test of the crucible, and the result was iron pyrites, though he called it gold. An expedition was sent to the Neversink mountains to procure a quantity of a certain metal to be found there, which, together with specimens from various other places, were shipped for Holland, but the ship foundered at sea. An expedition was also sent to Staten Island to examine the iron mine there; this was the mine on Toad Hill, in the vicinity of the Moravian Church. The hill was then known as the Iron Hill, and is alluded to by that name in some of the earliest conveyances recorded in the country, and especially in the patent of Governor Dongan to John Palmer. So important was this mine considered, that the Company at Amsterdam in 1645 proposed to send a qualified person to examine it. It was worked to some extent at a very early period.

The history of New Netherlands under the early Dutch Directors, or Governors, consists of little else than a history of the outrages committed by the whites and savages upon

* Vide App. N. (7.)

each other, the former being in most instances, directly or indirectly, the aggressors. They were also the principal sufferers, because, though they were better armed, they were fewer in number, and had more to lose. They appear to have not remembered that the success of their trading enterprises depended chiefly upon the friendship of the Indians. The Directors of the Company at home were peculiarly unfortunate in their selection of Directors for the colony; none of them, unless we except the last, Stuyvesant, understood the object for which they were sent out; their chief aim and purpose was to annihilate the neighboring tribes, a measure which at the same time would have annihilated the fur trade also. Prominent among the few who comprehended the situation, and understood what course of policy would have been best for the colony, was the minister, Dominie Bogardus, and De Vries, the patroon of part of Staten Island. They were strongly opposed to the course pursued by the Directors in their dealings with the Indians, and the event showed the wisdom of the policy of forbearance and conciliation which they recommended. So persistent were they in pressing their views upon the authorities, that they excited their anger, and were charged with a design of ingratiating themselves into the favor of the Indians for selfish purposes, and to the prejudice of the interests of the colony at large. The Indians understood these men and recognized them as friends, and when, in one of the raids they made upon the settlers on the Island, they had killed some of De Vries' cattle without knowing to whom they belonged, they expressed their regret for the act, calling him the friend of the Indians. At another time, when a difficulty had occurred with some of the Long Island Indians, and Kieft found himself in a dilemma, he was very desirous of making peace with them, but he could find no ambassador who was willing to trust himself in their power, until De Vries offered to visit them for the purpose. He was hospitably received, and when his mission was explained to them, and they were requested to visit the Director at the fort in New Amsterdam, they refused to go until he had pledged himself for their safety.

For many years the traffic with the Indians for peltries had been exceedingly profitable, and large fortunes had been secured by many of the traders, but in the course of time, as the articles of the Indian's traffic became scarcer, and the value of the Dutch commodities depreciated in consequence of their abundance, the trade gradually decreased, until at length the cost of sustaining the colony was greater than its revenues, and the West India Company found itself rapidly descending to the verge of bankruptcy. These misfortunes were charged to the incompetency of the colonial Directors, and Kieft came in for a large share of the censure. He was accordingly summoned home in 1647, to give an account of his stewardship. In obedience to this summons he took passage in the ship Princess, but was shipwrecked on the coast of Wales, and perished.

It has already been said that the Indians were always ready to sell the Island. In 1630 they sold it to Michael Pauw; shortly after they sold a part to David Pietersen De Vries; in 1641 to Cornelis Melyn; in 1651 to August Heermans; in 1657 to Baron Van Cappelan, and in 1670 to Governor Lovelace. To this last sale they were obliged to adhere; there was probably a little more ceremony about it, which rendered the transaction more impressive. It is said that in delivering possession, they presented a sod and a shrub or branch of every kind of tree which grew upon the island, except the ash and elder, some say ash and hickory. In one of these sales, the price was paid in goods as follows: 20 fathoms of cloth, 2 coats, 2 guns, 5 kettles, 10 bars of lead; 20 handsfull of powder, 400 fathoms of white wampum and 200 of black; it has been computed by a local annalist* that the price, in cash, was about one mill an acre, or ten acres for one cent; in this sale was included a large tract in New Jersey.†

* Vide App. N. (8.) † Ibid. (9.)

CHAPTER V.

Appointment, arrival and character of Stuyvesant—His silver leg—Disputes respecting Boundaries—Disputes between Melyn and Kieft—Melyn's Troubles with Stuyvesant—His sentence, and the reversal thereof—Stuyvesant summoned to Holland to answer—Sends his Attorneys—Local troubles—Charges against Stuyvesant by the English—Early condition of the Island.

In 1647, Petrus Stuyvesant succeeded William Kieft as Director-General of New Netherland. He is represented as having been a very honest and brave man. He had served his country before as Vice-Director at Curacoa, and in an attack on the Portuguese at St. Martin's, had lost a leg, which loss was supplied by a wooden substitute, bound with silver bands—hence it was said that he had a silver leg. It is also said that he was a man of more than ordinary literary attainments. His earliest efforts were directed to conciliate the Indians, and in this he was so successful that he excited the jealously of the neighboring English colonies, between whom and the Dutch, unpleasant differences with regard to boundary lines had for a long time existed. The English pretended to believe that the object of the Dutch governor was to attach the surrounding tribes to himself, for the purpose of inciting them to a general massacre of the English colonists. But Stuyvesant, with a sagacity superior to their own, had another object in view; he foresaw trouble with England and a probable war between that country and his own, and consequently between his colony and its neighbors, in the event of which the assistance of the Indians would have been invaluable if not indispensable. Fortunately, however, Cromwell and the States-General arranged all their difficulties, and the war cloud for the time was dispersed. No harm, however, had been done in conciliating the savages; indeed, it was Stuyvesant's desire and policy to live in peace with all his neighbors, civilized or savage.

During the early years of the new Director's administration, the disputes between him and the governors of the several neighboring colonies, respecting boundaries, jurisdictions and various other matters, assumed proportions which bid fair to become serious, but as they form no part of the history of the Island, we pass them by for matters in which we are more directly interested.

During the administration of Kieft, Melyn, the patroon of Staten Island, lived in a state of unremitting hostility with him. Having adopted, in a great measure, the policy of De Vries in the treatment of the Indians, though not as successfully, he found himself in almost constant collision with Kieft, who was prompt to notice and avenge every act of the savages which he could torture into a hostile demonstration, and thus during the whole five years he controlled the destinies of the colony, his hands were reeking with the blood of hundreds of the natives, shed in collisions usually provoked by himself. De Vries had frequently warned him that Heaven would not permit the blood of so many of these children of nature to be thus causelessly shed without condign punishment—words which, with the ex-Director's end in view, were prophetic.

Kieft continued to reside at New Amsterdam for a short time after he had been superseded, and Melyn improved the opportunity to prefer charges against him. Stuyvesant, though on the whole disposed to deal justly with all men, would brook no direct attack upon the dignity of the Directorship, either in his own person or in that of his predecessor, and this was the light in which he chose to regard Melyn's complaint; perhaps, too, Kieft had improved the opportunities offered by a daily intercourse to prejudice the Director against the patroon in advance; it is certain, however, that when Melyn's charges were preferred, they were met by counter-charges from the ex-Director, among which was one that Melyn had said he could get no justice from Kieft; however true the assertion might have been in that instance, it proved quite true in the present, for after a long investigation, the Attorney-General expressed an opinion that both

Melyn and Kuyter, who had also been implicated in the charges, ought to suffer death. The Director, however, knowing that his public acts were likely to be reviewed, was unwilling to inflict a penalty so severe, yet, though he professed to coincide with the opinion of the Attorney-General, he was disposed to deal more leniently with them; he therefore, with the consent of the majority of the counsel, condemned Melyn to a banishment of seven years, and a fine of three hundred guilders,* and Kuyter to three years' banishment, and a fine of one hundred and fifty guilders.

In accordance with this sentence, the defendants were sent to Holland. The attention of the government was immediately called to the manner in which justice was administered in the colony, by an appeal which the banished patroon and his associates had taken on their arrival. An elaborate investigation followed, and the sentence was reversed; the Director was also censured, and required to return home and answer for his arbitrary conduct. Melyn, armed with the necessary documents, returned triumphantly to New Amsterdam, and had the satisfaction of serving them upon the Director in person. The reply was, "I highly respect the authorities of my country, and with all deference I will obey their commands, but I shall appear by attorney, and not in person." Melyn was not content with a verbal reply, but required one in writing. This, however, was refused. These proceedings on the part of the patroon were far from mollifying the Director; and, as he had proved to be a dangerous man to meddle with arbitrarily, he gratified his animosity by acts of hostility to his antagonist's family. Jacob Loper, the son-in-law of the patroon, who had served under Stuyvesant in the West Indies, applied for permission to make a trading voyage to South River, Delaware, but it was peremptorily refused. The council, however, probably apprehensive of another appeal and reversal, favored the application; but the Director obstinately refused, and said, "He shall not go."

Vide App. N. (10.)

Cornelius Van Tienhoven and Jan Jansen were sent to represent the Director before the authorities at home, but Melyn followed them, resolved that they should take no advantage by reason of his absence. Stuyvesant's representatives appeared before the tribunal which had cited him, to answer for and defend the acts of their principal. It was not, they said, so much for remonstrating against Kieft's Indian policy, as for disrespectful words and conduct towards his superior officers, that Melyn was punished. Their arguments in behalf of their principal do not appear to have had much weight; the opinion of the court was that Melyn had been seriously injured in his property and person for no crime, and indeed for no cause whatever, except that it might have been a difference of opinion with the Director.

In the meantime, the trade of the colony having become unremunerative, the government at home involved in political complications with other powers, and Stuyvesant himself annoyed by the encroachments of his English neighbors on the east and the predatory acts of the savages on all other sides, had no time to devote to private grievances. Melyn's matters were left in abeyance. The difficulties which surrounded the perplexed Director were of no trifling character. He was charged by the English colonists with endeavoring to instigate the Indians to massacre them; with giving them arms and ammunition for that purpose; with claiming territory on the Connecticut river as belonging to the Dutch; with prohibiting Englishmen from settling on the South, or Delaware river, on a like pretence; with an intention of poisoning and bewitching them, and that, through the assistance of an Indian he had engaged as an "artist," to practice his art upon them, which would have succeeded had not the conjuror been detected and slain; with furnishing the Indians with wild fire and rum; with instigating the Indians to contemn the English; and many other charges of an equally serious character. It was evident that the English were seeking an opportunity to quarrel with their Dutch neighbors, and all Stuyvesant's disclaimers, explanations and proofs went for nothing; the charges continued to be iterated and reiterated during the whole term of his administration.

We pause here, in the course of our narrative, for a brief space, to take a view of the condition of our Island at this early period. The first dwelling houses erected on the Island, after the removal of the Walloons to Long Island, were in the vicinity of the Narrows, or between that and Old Town, which is so called, probably, from that circumstance, and were not more than five or six in number. There was one, probably, at the extreme south end, and one or two at Fresh Kill. Subsequently, in 1661, when the Waldenses arrived, and, after them, the Huguenots, the settlements at Old Town and Fresh Kill received accessions. Before their arrival there were no roads, except, perhaps, foot-paths through the forest, between the two last-mentioned localities; there was no need of any, for the intercourse of the Islanders was only with New Amsterdam. After the settlements at Old Town and Fresh Kill had received accessions, intercourse between them became more frequent, and, in due course of time, the road from the one to the other was constructed; particularly after the Waldenses had built their church at Stoney Brook, and the Huguenots theirs at Fresh Kill.

The houses were built in clusters, or hamlets, for convenience in mutual defence and protection. Tradition says that one of the first dwellings on the Island was situated on the heights at New Brighton, and was constructed of bricks imported from Holland, and occupied, for a time, at least, by a prominent official of the government. If there is any truth in the tradition, the house was, probably, the residence of De Vries, who, feeling secure in the friendship of the Indians, ventured to erect his dwelling in that beautiful, but remote, locality. That the builder's confidence in the Indians was not misplaced, the same tradition further says that, in 1655, when the great Indian war broke out, and the Island was nearly depopulated, this house, and its occupants, were spared. In the latter part of the last century, and in the beginning of the present, all the territory embraced in the first, and most of the second wards of the present Village of New Brighton, constituted farms owned by the families of the Van Buskirks, Crocherons, and Vreelands; these farms extended from the Kills one mile into the country. Abraham Crocheron, the owner of one of them, erected a grist mill in the valley east of Jersey Street, relying for a supply of water upon the spring now known as the Hessian spring;* but, this not proving sufficient, he converted his grist mill into a snuff mill, for which the supply was abundant. About the same time Captain Thomas Lawrence built a distillery on a small wharf which nows forms a part of the present large New Brighton wharf. Long before this part of the Island was patented to any individual, and laid out into farms, and while it was yet covered with the original forests, there was a deep ravine, extending from the spring mentioned above, to the Kills, into which the tide ebbed and flowed, and which, in the days of the Dutch and early English governors, afforded a place of concealment for the smugglers who infested the coast. The face of the country has now become materially changed, by cutting down the hills and filling up the valleys.

In process of time, as settlers arrived, they located along the shores, and roads became a necessity; these at first were constructed along the shores, until at length cross roads for convenience of communication between the several settlements were constructed. Some of these old roads have been closed, but the Clove road is the only original one now left.

* Vide App. N. (11.)

CHAPTER VI.

A "Hard Winter"—Melyn's Character—His return to America—Sale of the Ship and Cargo—Van Dincklagen—War between England and Holland—Stuyvesant's Perplexities—Ferry Rates—John De Decker—Stuyvesant's Proclamation against Preachers—Indian War of 1655—Staten Island ravaged—Melyn forsakes the Colony—Sells his title to the Island—Waldenses and Huguenots settle on the Island—Dom. Drisius—Defence of Melyn—Kieft's Shipwreck and Death.

The winter of 1650 is noted in colonial history for its severity; the Kills and Sound were frozen; there was also a great scarcity of provisions, and the people suffered for every necessary of life except fuel; that alone was abundant. One writer says that it was so cold that the ink froze in the pen as he was writing. There were other winters also remarkable for their severity, which will be noticed hereafter.

To return to Melyn. He has been called "an unprincipled adventurer," but we have failed to find anything in his public life in the colony to warrant such a conclusion; on the contrary, as a member of the Council he persistently advocated moderate measures in all transactions with the Indians, and in the management of his own affairs he as persistently insisted upon his chartered rights, and adopted only legal measures to defend them. Notwithstanding his successful appeal to the authorities at home—notwithstanding the reversal of the sentence imposed upon him by Stuyvesant, and the censure implied in such reversal, as well as the direct citation to appear and answer for his arbitrary and illegal proceedings, his persecutions still continued. In the Spring, Melyn and some twenty colonists took passage in the ship "New Netherland's Fortune," Captain Adrian Post, the ship and cargo belonging to the Baron Van Capellan. Melyn had no venture of his own in the vessel, but his colonists were supplied with agricultural implements belonging to themselves.

The passage was one of extraordinary length and more than usually boisterous, and they were obliged to put into Rhode Island for supplies; they did not reach Manhattan until in the Winter. Making this stop at Rhode Island the occasion for another prosecution, Stuyvesant seized the ship under the pretext that it belonged to Melyn, and caused it and the cargo to be sold. The harassed patroon immediately withdrew to his "colonie" on Staten Island, from whence he was summoned by Stuyvesant to appear, and answer to new charges which had been preferred against him. This summons he positively refused to obey, and a lot of land, with a house upon it, in New Amsterdam, belonging to him, was declared confiscated, and accordingly was sold. Melyn now fortified himself on the Island and established a manorial court. The ship was sold to Thomas Willet, who sent it on a voyage to Virginia, and thence to Holland, where Van Cappelan replevined it, and after a protracted law suit, the West India Company was obliged to pay a large sum in consequence of the illegal act of its representative and servant in New Netherland.

Among the charges preferred against Melyn were the following: that he had distributed arms amongst the Indians, and had endeavored to excite hostile feelings towards the Director among some of the river tribes. When he left Holland, the patroon had taken the precaution of furnishing himself with a "safe conduct," as it was called, which was a sort of protection against further aggressions on the part of Stuyvesant; to this, however, he paid little regard when he had the patroon in his power; but now that he had proved contumacious by refusing to appear, and putting himself into his enemy's power, the Director scarcely dared venture to arrest by force one who was protected by a document of such authority; he therefore affected to be alarmed for his own personal safety, and applied to the Council for protection, who granted him a body guard of four halbidiers, to attend him whenever he went abroad. Van Dincklagen, the Vice-Director, had been instrumental in assisting both Van Cappelan and Melyn in promoting the successful settlement of Staten Island; he therefore fell under the displeasure of the Director, who ordered him to resign, or the council to expel him from their body, but he refused to resign, and defied the Council to expel him, as they had no more power to deprive him of his office than the Director himself, as both held their commissions from the same authority at home. Nevertheless, he was arrested and imprisoned in the guard-house, and the counsel who had defended him was forbidden to practice his profession in the colony. After the lapse of several days, the Vice-Director was liberated, and immediately took up his residence with Melyn on Staten Island. These events occurred in 1651. War now broke out between England and the States-General, and Stuyvesant found sufficient occupation to engross his time and attention, in preparing to defend himself against the anticipated troubles with the neighboring English colonies, and the treachery of the English residing under his own government, notwithstanding the oaths of allegiance which they had taken. These latter, when they learned that Cromwell intended to send a fleet to America, for the purpose of subverting the Dutch governments there, entered into correspondence with the English colonial authorities, and but for the dilatory proceedings of Massachusetts, something disastrous might have resulted therefrom; but the ratification of a peace between the belligerents in April, 1654, and the consequent proclamation of the Protector inhibiting all English subjects from acts of hostility to the Dutch, put an end to their designs. A heavy burden was thus taken from the shoulders of Stuyvesant, and "Richard was himself again." He was now at liberty to devote himself to home bickerings, in which his soul appeared to delight. Among these were the Long Island ferry troubles, which sometimes proved to be of serious inconvenience to the people residing on either side of the water. After numerous and protracted discussions, regular rates were finally established, and though not connected with our task, we give a list of them as a curiosity. They were as follows: for a wagon and horses, 2 guilders and 10 stuyvers, equal to one dollar; for a single wagon, 2 guilders—80 cents; a horse or horned beast, 1 guilder and 10 stuyvers—60 cents; for an Indian, male or female, 6 stuyvers—12 cents; each other person 3 stuyvers—6 cents.

In the month of April, 1655, arrived Johannes De Decker, a young man of excellent reputation, who had officiated in some public capacity at Schiedam, bringing with him a letter from the Directors of the West India Company, recommending him to the first vacant "honorable office." He came as supercargo of the ship Black Eagle. The Vice-Director, Dyckman, at Fort Orange, having become insane, De Decker was appointed to succeed him, "to preside in Fort Orange and the village of Beaverwyck, in the Court of Justice of the Commissaries, to administer all the affairs of police and justice as circumstances may require, in conformity to the instructions given by the Director-General and Council, and to promote these for the best service of the country and the prosperity of the inhabitants." A responsible situation for a young man and a stranger, but he proved equal to the emergency. Whilst he was discharging these several duties, Stuyvesant issued a proclamation against unauthorized preachers, from whom nothing could be expected but "discord, confusion and disorder in church and state." On the reception of this proclamation, De Decker issued another of a similar character, and rigidly enforced it. This act of the Director, when the knowledge of it reached Holland, was severely rebuked, and he was forbidden thereafter to interfere with the free exercise of religion. The next year, 1656, De Decker returned to Holland, where he married, and in 1657 returned to New Netherland. He had acquired a title to 120 acres of land on Staten Island, but probably by reason of some dispute with Stuyvesant, he was dispossessed, and, it is said, banished; if so, he must either have been recalled, or had his sentence reversed, as in the case of Melyn, for we find him in the colony at the time when the English wrested it from the possession of the Dutch, and acting in the capacity of commissioner for arranging the terms of surrender, by Stuyvesant's own appointment.

This Johannes De Decker is regarded as the progenitor of the numerous and respectable families of the Deckers now residing on the Island, and in many other places. He was a man of a most resolute character, with a disposition almost as obstinate as that of Stuyvesant himself, and of respectable acquirements.

During the year 1655, another and more serious calamity befell Staten Island than any which had preceded it. Hendrick Van Dyck, former attorney-general at New Amsterdam, on rising one morning, discovered a squaw in his garden stealing peaches; in a moment of anger he seized his gun and shot her, killing her instantly. Of this rash act, little, if any notice, was taken by the authorities, but the Indians did not overlook it; immediate measures were taken by them to avenge the outrage. Several of the neighboring tribes united, and early on the morning of the 15th of September sixty-four canoes, containing nineteen hundred savages, suddenly appeared before New Amsterdam. They landed and dispersed through the various streets, while many of the people were still asleep. As soon as they were discoverd, an alarm was sounded. The officers of the colony and city, and many of the principal inhabitants, assembled, and the leaders of the savages were requested to meet with them, which they did; they accounted for their sudden appearance under pretext of searching for some hostile northern Indians, who, they pretended they had been informed, were either in the city or its vicinity. After much persuasion they were induced to promise to leave Manhattan Island at sunset, but when evening came they were still there, and manifested no disposition to leave. They became unruly, and the people became excited, and violent acts were committed by both parties; Van Dyck, the thoughtless author of the trouble, paid the penalty of his rashness by being killed with an arrow, and Paulus Leinderstein Van Der Grist, one of the city officials, was killed by a blow with an axe. The soldiers in the fort and the city guard were called out, and attacked the invaders, driving them back to their canoes. Crossing the river, the savages attacked the settlements there and killed or captured most of the people. Thence they went to Staten Island, which at that time had a population of ninety souls and eleven flourishing bouweries; twenty-two of the people were killed, and all of the remainder who did not escape were carried away captive, and the bouweries were desolated. The Indians continued their ravages three days, during which they killed one hundred whites, took one hundred and fifty prisoners, and ruined three hundred more in their estates. The damages were estimated at two hundred thousand guilders, or about eighty thousand dollars, an enormous sum at that day. The whole country became alarmed, and people from all directions flocked to New Amsterdam for safety, but even here they were not secure, for the Indians prowled over the Island by day and by night, slaying all within their reach.

Stuyvesant, in the meantime, was at South River, Delaware, whither he had gone to remove some Swedish intruders on the Company's lands; but as soon as the news of the outbreak reached him, he returned and adopted such measures as the exigency seemed to require. Ships in port were stopped, and all on board were impressed into service; armed men were sent to the surrounding settlements, and the defences of the fort were enlarged and strengthened. The savages, finding so many prisoners a burden to them, sent Post, who had been superintendent at Staten Island, and whom they had captured, to negotiate for their ransom. Fourteen prisoners were sent in by one chief, who demanded some ammunition in exchange, which was sent; then twenty-eight were returned on the same condition, and finally, after a protracted negotiation, they were all, or nearly all, set at liberty, Three years after this event, Staten Island had not yet recovered from its effects.

Melyn, discouraged by the difficulties which he was constantly doomed to encounter, and despairing of ever coming to terms with Stuyvesant, forsook New Netherland and removed to New Haven, where he took the oath of allegiance. Van Cappelan, however, did what he could to induce the affrighted people to return to their desolated homes, and sent out new colonists. These efforts were made by Van Dincklagen, his agent. To avert the probability of another attack, he negotiated another purchase of the Island from the Indians, and made a treaty with them. These proceedings on his part were disapproved by the Directors of the Company at home, who insisted that all settlers' titles should come through them; Stuyvesant was therefore directed to declare the late purchase void, to secure the Indian title for the Company, and then to convey to Van Cappelan what land he might require.

In 1661 Melyn returned to Holland, and in consideration of fifteen hundred guilders (six hundred dollars), conveyed all his interest in Staten Island to the West India Company; he was also granted an amnesty for all offences which had been charged upon him by either Stuyvesant or his predecessor. Van Cappelan being dead, the Company also purchased all the title he had to any part of the Island during his life-time, and thus became the possessors of the whole of it. Soon thereafter the Company made grants of land to several French Waldenses, and a still greater number of Huguenots from Rochelle, the descendants of whom are still residents here, and in a few instances still occupying the identical grants made to their ancestors. About a dozen families commenced a settlement south of the Narrows. In 1663 they built a block-house as a defence against the Indians, and placed within it a garrison of ten men, and armed it with two small cannons. At the request of these settlers, Dominie Drisius, of New Amsterdam, visited them every two months and preached to them in French, performing also the other functions of his calling. Rev. Samuel Drisius was sent to America by the Classis of Amsterdam, in 1654, at the request of the people, who desired a minister who could preach to them either in Dutch or French, which he was able to do. On his arrival at New Amsterdam he was at once installed as the colleague of the Rev. Johannes Megapolensis, who had resided in the country since 1642. Drisius continued to officiate at New Amsterdam and on Staten Island until 1671.

Before we take our final leave of the patroon of our Island, Cornelis Melyn, it is necessary to say a word or two in his defence. He was charged with many crimes, which are but echoes of the charges made by both Kieft and Stuyvesant against him. In a work entitled, "*Breeden Raedt, aen de verenighde Nederlansche Provintien,*" originally published at Antwerp, 1649, and extracts from a translation of which are printed in the fourth volume of the Documentary History of New York, it is said Cornelis Melyn was charged, in his sentence, with more crimes than Kuyter, and punished more severely, (because Kieft had formerly flattered himself that he should have a part with him in Staten Island; and, finding himself deceived, he had been obliged to make other conditions with other persons; and Kieft played him this trick, as was afterwards proved)—and he was found guilty of *crimen læsæ majestatis, crimen falsi, crimen* of libel and defamation, and, on that account, was to forfeit all benefits derived from the Company, or which he might still claim, a penalty of 300 guilders, and to be banished from New Netherland for the term of seven years; so that those who had accused Kieft were kicked out and sent away by Stuyvesant. It is well known that, when Director Kieft was reminded that these suits would, most probably, have taken another turn in Holland, he replied: "Why should we alarm each other with justice in Holland?—in this case I only consider it as a scare-crow." And Stuyvesant replied: "If I was persuaded that you would appeal from my sentences, or divulge them, I would have your head cut off, or have you hanged on the highest tree in New Netherland." He also inveighed so furiously that the foam hung on his beard. They were brought on board like criminals, and torn away from their goods, their wives, and their children. The Princess (the name of the ship) was to carry the Director and these two faithful patriots away from New Netherland; but, coming into the wrong channel, it struck upon a rock, and was wrecked. And now, this wicked Kieft, seeing death before his eyes, sighed deeply, and, turning to these two (Melyn and Kuyter), said: "Friends, I have been unjust towards you; can you forgive me?" Towards morning the ship was broken to pieces. Among those drowned were Melyn's son, the minister, Bogardus, Kieft, Captain John De Vries, and a great number of other persons. Much treasure was lost, as Kieft was on his return with a fortune of four hundred thousand guilders—160,000 dollars.

CHAPTER VII.

The Province wrested from the Dutch by the English—A change of masters—De Decker banished—New Grants on Staten Island—Elizabethtown settled—The establishment of Courts—Berkley and Cartaret's patent—Nicolls surprised and indignant—Treaty of Breda—Nicolls' resignation, and appointment of Lovelace.

It is not our purpose to approve or disapprove of the seizure of the Dutch territories by the English, to which period we have now in due course arrived; whether it redounded to the benefit or injury of the people, we shall not attempt to demonstrate; Clarendon pronounced it "without any shadow of justice." England, in a time of profound peace, determined to annihilate the Dutch government on the continent of America, and she did it. She was already in possession of all that extensive country lying between the Spanish province of Florida and Delaware bay, and that other large tract lying between the Connecticut river and the French territories on the North, and now the king, with a deliberation as cool as if he owned it, patented to his brother, the Duke of York and Albany, all the intervening territory, which embraced every rod of the Dutch possessions. Being Lord High Admiral of England, the Duke lost no time in despatching four vessels, viz.: the Guinea, of 36 guns; the Elias, of 30; the Martin, of 16, and the William and Nicholas, of 10 guns, with 450 soldiers—the whole under the command of Col. Richard Nicolls—to cross the ocean and take possession of his newly-acquired domain. Nicolls was also to be governor of the territory when he had subjugated it. Commissioners accompanied the expedition, furnished with instructions to the English governors in America to render such assistance as might be required of them. When Stuyvesant heard of the designs of the English, he adopted such measures as the exigency required, so far as his means permitted. In August, 1664, the fleet arrived in the bay, and anchored near Coney Island. The first Dutch property seized by them was on Staten Island, where the block house was taken and occupied. On the 30th of August, a formal demand for the surrender of New Amsterdam was made, but an immediate submission to the demand did not take place. To do Stuyvesant justice, he was disposed to fight it out, but the municipal officers and the people, believing that resistance would be in vain, opposed his wishes, and desisted from working on the defences. Probably for the first time in his life he submitted to the popular will. Nicolls had offered to restore the country if the respective governments agreed upon the boundaries between the Dutch and English territories, an offer which he might safely make, as he well knew that the seizure was not made with a view to the settlement of any territorial limits. Stuyvesant, however, appears to have seen a ray of hope in it, and appointed six commissioners, among whom was Dom. Megapolensis and Johannes De Decker, to meet a like number on the part of the English, to arrange the terms of the capitulation. These were just and reasonable, under the circumstances; no change was to be made in the condition of the people, but all were to be permitted to enjoy their property and their religion to the fullest extent. As no one's rights and privileges were to be molested, the people submitted to a change of rulers, not only with a good grace, but many with satisfaction, as it released them from the overbearing and arbitrary tyranny of the Director.

Though De Decker had been one of the commissioners who agreed to and signed the articles of surrender, yet, when the English began to change the names of places, and appoint new officers in place of those who had become obnoxious to them; in short, when everything began to assume an English aspect, his patriotism began to revolt, and he endeavored in some instances to oppose the work of reform which the conquerors had initiated. This brought him to the notice of

Nicolls, who, to rid himself of a troublesome subject, ordered him to leave the colony within ten days. In the course of a few months everything became quiet, and the people seemed to be content with the new order of things. Unappropriated lands now began to be parcelled out to English proprietors, by English authority. Staten Island, already settled by the Dutch and French, was now to receive acquisition of another nationality. Capt. James Bollen received a grant of land on the Island; the country between the Raritan River and Newark Bay was bought anew from the savages, and settled by people from Long Island, chiefly along Achter Cull, as the Dutch called it, because it was *achter*, or behind the Cull, but now corrupted by the English into Arthur Kull, and four families from Jamaica began the settlement of Elizabethtown. Beside Capt. Bollen, Capt. William Hill, Lieut. Humphrey Fox and ——— Coleman, all officers of the fleet received grants of land on Staten Island, but as the vessels to which they were attached were no longer needed, and were sent back to England, they had little or no opportunity to enjoy their acquisitions.

Under the Dutch rule, the centre of all authority was at New Amsterdam; criminals from all the settlements were brought there for trial, except from Rensselaerwyck, where the patroon assumed supreme judicial authority, an assumption which sometimes brought him into collision with the Director, who always insisted upon his own supremacy in all matters. It was the policy of the Duke of York to make as few changes as possible, and thus reconcile the Dutch settlers, who comprised three-fourths of the people, to the new order of things. As the population was likely to increase by emigration, it became necessary to institute local tribunals, that justice might be conveniently dispensed. A Court of Assizes was created, having both common law and equity jurisdiction; it was comprised of the Governor and his Council, and was the supreme tribunal. This did not differ materially from that established by the Dutch, in which the Director and his Council were supreme.

In organizing the political divisions of the colony, Long Island, Staten Island and Westchester were all comprised in one shire called Yorkshire, and divided into three "Ridings;" the territory now comprising Suffolk County was called the East Riding; Kings County, part of Queens and Staten Island, was called the West Riding, and the remainder of Queens, with Westchester, the North Riding. The Governor and Council retained the right to appoint a sheriff for the whole shire annually, and Justices of the Peace in each Riding to hold their office during the Governor's pleasure. These Justices held Courts of Sessions in each Riding three times a year. In the city the Burgomasters, Schout and Schepens, elected by the people, were replaced by a Mayor, Alderman and Sheriff, appointed by the Governor. Thomas Willett was the first Mayor. (*Vide Appendix D.*)

When it was known in England that New Netherland had been reduced, and was now actually in the possession of the English, Lord William Berkley and Sir George Cartaret, two of the royal favorites, induced the Duke of York, probably influenced by the king, to give them a patent for the territory west of the Hudson and the bay, and as far south as Cape May; this they named Nova Cæsarea, or New Jersey. With thirty emigrants, English and French, Capt. Philip Cartaret, a cousin of Sir George, and governor of the new territory, sailed for New York, but by stress of weather was driven into the Chesapeake. While lying there he forwarded despatches to Bollen, who was commissary at the fort in New York, and also to Nicolls. This was the first intimation the Governor had received of the dismemberment of the extensive territory over which he ruled; he was both astounded and chagrined; he had already conveyed several parcels of land within the limits of the new grant, and regarded the whole as the best part of the Duke's domain. He remonstrated, but his remonstrances came too late; the Duke evidently thought he had been too precipitate, but as he could not well retrace his steps, he suffered matters to remain as they were. Cartaret arrived in New York about midsummer, 1665, and immediately took possession of his government. He chose Elizabethtown as his capital. It is said that when he first landed on the soil of New Jersey, he carried a hoe upon his shoulder, in token of his intention to devote his attention to the promotion of agriculture.

It is not to be supposed that the Dutch quietly submitted to be robbed of a territory which they had occupied so long, and which had cost them so much. Remonstrances, of course, followed the perpetration of the outrage—for as such it was regarded throughout Europe,—but they availed nothing. War was declared. Louis, of France, though disposed to friendship with Charles, of England, was under a treaty obligation to assist Holland in the event of a war with England, and he, accordingly, declared war against England also. This step was followed by vigorous preparations for the defence of the French territories in America. It is not our province to follow the events of this war, which lasted until the summer of 1667, when a peace was concluded between the belligerents, by what is known in history as the Treaty of Breda. By the terms of this treaty, the Dutch lost New Netherland, but obtained what they regarded as fully equivalent, valuable possessions in the East Indies.

In 1668, Nicolls, by his own request, was relieved of the government of the province, and was succeeded by Colonel Francis Lovelace. Thomas Lovelace, whose official signature is appended to so many of the old documents connected with the conveyance of property on Staten Island, and otherwise, and who at one time was sheriff of the county, was a brother to the Governor, and a member of his Council; there was also another brother, named Dudley, likewise a member of the Council.

CHAPTER VIII.

Tradition and legitimate History—Doubts as to the proprietorship of the Island—Circumnavigated—Christopher Billop—The Bentley Manor—The Billop family—Tomb-stone Records—Errors of Dunlap corrected—Col. Billop's capture and imprisonment.

WE have now arrived at an interesting period in the history of Staten Island, and in presenting it we shall be under the necessity of mingling, in some measure, tradition with legitimate history, and of correcting some errors into which some of the prominent historians of the State have fallen.

As the history of one of the most prominent families of this period is involved, we shall also be under the necessity of anticipating, in some degree, the chronological order of events.

After the Duke of York had conveyed the territory of New Jersey to Berkley and Cartaret, a doubt arose whether Staten Island was not included in the grant, by the terms of the charter. Cartaret, the governor, not the proprietor, laid no claim to the Island; on the contrary, he tacitly admitted that it did not belong to his jurisdiction, by accepting a conveyance for a tract of land on the Island from Nicolls the Duke of York's agent; this he would scarcely have done, had he considered his brother the proprietor. In 1668 the Island "was adjudged to belong to New York," because one of the outlets of Hudson river ran around the Island; while Berkley and Cartaret, by the terms of their patent, were bounded by the river and bay. The Dutch always appear to have regarded the inner bay or harbor as a mere expansion of the river, and the Narrows as its mouth. In their documents, Staten Island is frequently described as lying in the river. If this view was correct, the Island evidently belonged to New Jersey, because it was embraced within its limits.

The Duke of York himself appears to have had his doubts about the matter, for it is said, that when this question of jurisdiction was first agitated, he decided that all islands lying in the river, or harbor, which could be circumnavigated in twenty-four hours, should remain in his jurisdiction, otherwise to New Jersey.

Christopher Billop, being then in the harbor in command of a small ship called the Bentley, which it is also said he owned, undertook the task of sailing around the Island, and accomplished it within twenty-four hours, thus securing it to the Duke, who, in gratitude for the service rendered him, bestowed upon Billop a tract of 1163 acres of land in the extreme southern part of the Island, which was called the "Manor of Bentley," after the ship which had accomplished the task. Here Billop built his Manor house, which has withstood the storms of more than two centuries, and is said to be in good condition at the present day. Important events, not only in the history of the Island, but in that of the country, have transpired in this house, to some of which we shall have occasion to refer hereafter. In 1674 the Duke of York, by permission of the king, organized a company of infantry of one hundred men; of this company Christopher Billop was commissioned second lieutenant. He had served his king before his arrival in America, but in what capacity is not known; his father, however, was not well spoken of. In 1677 Billop, while residing on his plantation on Staten Island, was appointed by Governor Andros, who had succeeded Lovelace, commander and sub-collector for New York, on Delaware bay and river. While occupied with the duties of these offices, he "misconducted" himself by making "extravagant speeches in public;" but of the subject of these speeches we are not informed; they were probably of a political character, and must have been peculiarly offensive, for Andros recalled him the next year, and deprived him of his military commission. This action of the Governor was approved by the Duke, who directed that another should be appointed to fill the vacant lieutenancy.

Billop now retired to his plantation on Staten Island, there to brood over the ingratitude of princes, or perhaps over his own follies and indiscretions. We hear nothing more of him for two years, when he again appears as one of a number who preferred complaints or charges against Andros, to the Duke, some of which must have been of a serious nature, as the Duke thought it necessary to send an agent over to investigate the matter, and on receiving his report, Andros was summoned to appear in person in England to render his accounts. This was probably in 1680 or 1681, when Brockholst succeeded Andros; in 1682 Dongan succeeded Brockholst. In 1684 the question of the proprietorship of Staten Island was again agitated, and many of the landholders became apprehensive of the validity of their title, and some of them, among whom was Billop, were desirous of selling, but as no purchasers could be found for a dubious title, the property remained in the family. Dongan was directed, if the Billop estate was sold, to find some purchaser for it in New York, and not to suffer it to pass into the possession of a resident of New Jersey. Here we lose all further historical trace of Christopher Billop; tradition says that in the latter part of the seventeenth, or the beginning of the eighteenth century, he sailed for England in his ship, the Bentley, and was never heard of after: he left no male issue, but he had at least one daughter.

"Christopher Billop lived on Staten Island, opposite Perth Amboy, and from him Christopher Farmar took the name and estate, and *he* was the noted Colonel Billop, of the revolutionary war."—(*Dunlap's Hist. New York, vol. II. App. p.* 158.)

There are two errors in the above extract; the name of the person who took the "name and estate" of Billop was *Thomas* Farmar, and it was he who married Billop's daughter, and thus acquired both the "name and estate," for the one was conditional on the other. He was *not* the Colonel Billop, of the revolutionary war; if Thomas (Farmar) Billop had lived until the war had broken out, he would have been nearly seventy years of age, but he did not live until then. The following inscriptions are still to be seen on his tombstone and that of his wife.

"Here lies the body of Thomas Billop, Esq., the son of Thomas Farmar, Esq., Dec'd August y° 2d, 1750, in the 89th year of his age."

"Here lies the body of Evjenea (Eugenia,) y° wife of Thomas Billop, aged 23 years, Dec'd March y° 22d, 1735."

Tombstones are usually reliable records as to dates. Thomas (Farmar) Billop's wife was born in 1712; therefore her father, Christopher Billop, was still residing on the Island, at or about that date; and if, as tradition affirms, he was lost at sea, it could not have been prior to that date.

The Colonel Billop, of revolutionary notoriety, evidently was not the one who married the daughter of Billop, for when the war commenced he had been dead more than a score of years, and as this was the only family of the name on the Island at that time,* it was his son, named Christopher, after his grandfather, who was so prominent during the war, at which time he was more than forty years of age. He married the daughter of Judge Benjamin Seaman, and both their estates were confiscated after the war.

We note here, in passing, that both father-in-law and son-in-law were members of the New York Assembly in 1775, and on the 23d of February of that year they both voted with the tories against sending delegates to the Continental Congress—the tories, on that occasion being successful, casting 16 votes against 9 Whigs.

The stones from which the above inscriptions were copied, no longer occupy their places at the heads of the graves of those whose names they bear; they have been removed, and the enclosure once sacred to the memory of this young couple, is now an undefined part of a cultivated field in the town of Westfield.

Colonel Christopher Billop rendered himself obnoxious to many of the people of Staten Island by the intensity of his

---

* Vide App. N (12.)

loyalty to the British crown during the war. His commission was that of a Colonel in the British army, and he commanded a regiment of native loyalists, or tories, composed chiefly of residents of the Island. Communication between Staten Island and New Jersey, having been prohibited, he was very active in enforcing the prohibition. The patriots of New Jersey were exceedingly bitter in their hostility to him, and took him prisoner twice. On one of these occasions, some of them, by means of a telescope from a church steeple in Amboy, still standing, saw him enter his own house. Boats were immediately manned and sent over, and he was captured and taken to New Jersey, and incarcerated at Burlington. Elias Boudinot, who had been appointed by Congress Commissary-General of Prisoners, issued the following order:

"To the keeper of the common jail for the county of Burlington, greeting: You are hereby commanded to receive into your custody the body of Col. Christopher Billop, prisoner of war, herewith delivered to you, and having put irons on his hands and feet, you are to chain him down to the floor in a close room in said jail, and there to retain him, giving him bread and water only for his food, until you receive further orders from me, or the Commissary of Prisoners for the State of New Jersey for the time being. Given under my hand at Elizabethtown, the 6th day of November, 1779.

       ELIAS BOUDINOT,
       Com. Pris. New Jersey."

While enforcing these severe measures, the Commissary informed his prisoner that his treatment was in retaliation for the sufferings of John Leshler and Capt. Nathaniel Randolph, two patriots who had been captured by the British, and that as soon as the severity of their sufferings was mitigated, his should be.

CHAPTER IX.

Purchase of the Island in 1670—Indian Reservations—De Decker restored to his rights—Death of Stuyvesant—Preparations for war—War between England, and France, and Holland—Capture of the Province by the Dutch—Restoration to the English—Manning's punishment—Duke of York's new patent—Staten Island separated from the Long Island Courts—Excise—The dreadful Comet Star—Dongan's administration—His patent to Palmer—Dongan's Manor House—Historical errors corrected—Papist alarms—Dongan's Mill—Leisler's administration—Officers of the County—Sloughter—Plowman's lawsuit.

ON the 13th of April, 1670, Staten Island was purchased from the Indians, for the Duke of York, by Governor Lovelace. This act has been termed "the most memorable" of his administration, and the Island was described as "the most commodiousest seate and richest land" in America. The year previous, the principal sachem had confirmed the former bargains made with the English, but several other inferior sachems now presented their claims, insisting that they were the owners. To quiet them, a new bargain was made; they executed another deed and received their payment in wampum, coats, kettles, guns and ammunition, axes, hoes, knives, etc., and as before related, possession was given by "turf and twigg." This was the last sale made by the Indians. It will be remembered, as it was stated before, that the Indians reserved two sorts of wood, and within the memory of people now living, several small parties of Indians, at long intervals have visited the Island, and exercised their reserved right of cutting such wood as they required for the purpose of making baskets. In the same year Lovelace made Love Island, the property of Isaac Bedlow, an alderman of the city, and now known by his name, a sort of "city of refuge," by decreeing it a privileged place where warrants of arrest should be inoperative.

It will be remembered that during the administration of Nicolls, Johannes De Decker, by reason of an imprudent display of his Dutch patriotism, was banished from the province, and that previous to this Stuyvesant had not only banished, but dispossessed him of his estate upon Staten Island. Some time after the peace of Breda, he applied to the Duke of York for a redress of his grievances and a restitution of his property. This application the Duke referred to Lovelace, with instructions to do in the premises what might be just and proper; the result was that De Decker was restored to all his rights and privileges, and he retired to private life on his farm on Staten Island.

Governor Lovelace also owned a plantation on the island, on which he built a mill for grinding cereals. The next year, Stuyvesant, who, after the conquest of the country, had also retired to private life on his bouwerie, died at the age of eighty years.*

Rumors of anticipated troubles in Europe reached America, and Lovelace immediately began to make preparations for the worst, so far as his means permitted; he strengthened the defences of the fort, organized several military companies in the metropolis, and other places in the province, repaired arms and laid in a large quantity of ammunition and other warlike stores. In April, 1672, England and France declared war against Holland; in Europe, the war was chiefly naval, and the English and French fleets suffered severely at the hands of De Ruyter and Tromp. On the 7th day of August, 1673, a Dutch fleet of twenty-three vessels arrived in New York bay, and anchored under Staten Island. Soon after their arrival they made a raid upon the plantation of Lovelace, and carried off sufficient cattle and sheep to make a breakfast for the 1600 men on board the ships of the fleet. This arrival produced the greatest consternation in the city and neighboring villages. Lovelace being absent in Connecticut, the fort was in command of Captain John Manning, who was in a state

* Vide App. N (18.)

of dreadful perplexity; he caused the drums to be beaten for volunteers, but none came; he sent to the Long Island villages for re-inforcements, but none responded to his call; many of the Dutch inhabitants were "assuming airs," many had gone on board the Dutch ships to welcome the arrival of their countrymen, while others on shore manifested their joy, and "talked threateningly." Manning was bewildered with his responsibilities, and fervently prayed for the Governor's return, but Lovelace, had he been present, could not have averted the fate of the city and its dependencies; he could only have assumed the responsibilities which now devolved upon the unhappy captain of the fort. To endeavor to procrastinate in the hope of his superior's return, was all that he could do. He sent a deputation to open a correspondence with his unwelcome visitors, but the Dutch, having learned the precise strength of the fort, and the amount of resistance that Manning was capable of making, were not disposed to delay, but while the deputation were on their way to the Commodore's ship, they had sent a trumpeter with a peremptory demand for surrender. To the inquiry of the deputies, What was the object of the Dutch in coming to the city ? the commodore replied, "To take it, and get our own back again." To the trumpeter's demand for surrender, Manning replied that he would send an answer when his messengers returned from the ships. When they did return, they reported that the Dutch were altogether too strong to be resisted successfully, and would grant only a delay of half an hour. In the meantime the vessels had been brought up within musket shot of the fort; another messenger was sent to ask a delay until the following morning, but the request was refused, only another half hour being allowed. At the expiration of the time, a broadside was opened on the fort which killed and wounded several of the garrison. The fort replied and struck the commodore's ship. In the meantime a detachment of 600 men were landed above the "Governor's Orchard" on the east shore of the Hudson, which was in the rear of the present Trinity Church burial ground, the water then coming up nearly to that place. About 400 of the Dutch citizens met the detachment, and gave them a hearty welcome, assuring them that the fort could make no serious resistance. Manning raised a flag of truce, and three men were sent to meet the approaching enemy, two of whom were detained, but the third ran away out of the city. He then sent another messenger with a proposition to surrender the fort and garrison "with the honors of war," which was accepted.

Before the sun set on the 9th day of August, 1673, the Dutch flag once more occupied its old elevation, at the top of the staff within the fort. Nine years before, the English, during a time of profound peace between the two nations, had secretly and treacherously fitted out an expedition for the express purpose of seizing a place comparatively defenceless. The Dutch retook it during a state of war between the two nations, by a fleet fitted out for another purpose. The Dutch squadron consisted of two separate fleets, the one under the command of Admiral Cornelis Evertsen, the other under the command of Commodore Jacob Binckes, or Benckes, and after their union they took alternate weeks in the command. The conquest having been consummated, Captain Anthony Colve was appointed Governor until further directions were received from "fatherland." The name of the city was changed to New Orange, and the following record or memorandum was made of the event: "On the 30th day of July, stilo vetery, ano 1673, was the fort and city of New York taken by the Dutch." At the time of the capture a vessel from a Connecticut port was also taken; the governor of that colony indignantly remonstrated with the Dutch admirals against the seizure of the vessel, oblivious of the fact that war existed between the two nations; the Dutchman, however, reminded him of it, and informed him further that they meant to do the English all the harm they could, unless they submitted.

Colve was not disturbed in the performance of the duties which had devolved upon him as governor, during the few months the province remained in the possession of the Dutch. On the 9th of February, 1674, peace was concluded between England and the States-General, by the treaty of Westminster, and according to its terms the colony reverted to the English. Major Edmond Andros, of Prince Rupert's dragoon regiment, which had been disbanded, was selected as the proper person to proceed to America and receive the province from the Dutch. Armed with the proper authority from the Dutch government, which had been furnished at the request of the English king, he arrived in the Diamond frigate in October, 1674, and anchored under Staten Island. A correspondence was at once opened between him and Colve, which resulted in a surrender of the province on the 10th day of that month. Manning, the commander of the fort at the time of the surrender to the Dutch, was arrested and tried for treason and cowardice, and sentenced to be cashiered and have his sword broken over his head, which sentence was carried into effect, after which he retired to his island, now known as Blackwell's.

The Duke of York, apprehensive that the validity of his title might be called in question, in consequence of the province having been in the possession of a foreign power, received a new patent from the king.

In 1675, at a Court of Assizes held in New York, among other things it was ordered, that "by reason of the separation by water, Staten Island shall have jurisdiction by itself, and have no further dependence on the courts of Long Island, nor on its militia." From this time forward, the Island has been an independent judicial district, and the first record, which soon after began to be kept, is still in existence in the office of the County Clerk; it is a small square volume, bound in vellum, and besides many quaint records of "sewts," contains the descriptions of the ear-marks on domestic animals, to distinguish the ownership, the animals probably running at large through the woods and unappropriated lands.

The regulation of the Excise received the early attention of the government, and the following rates were established throughout the province, which "tapsters" were allowed to charge; French wines, 1s. 3d. per quart; Fayal wines and St. George's, 1s. 6d.; Madeira wines and Portaport, 1s. 10d. Canaryes and Malaga, 2s. per quart; brandy 6d. per gill; rum, 3d. per gill; syder, 4d. per quart; double beere, 3d. per quart; meals at wine-houses, 1s.; at beere-houses, 8d.; lodgings at wine-houses, 4d. per night; at beere-houses, 3d.

Among the residents of New York at that time, we find several familiar Staten Island names, such as Matthew Hillyer, a schoolmaster, whose salary was £12, ($30) per year; DeHart, Garrison, Blake, &c.

Andros having received his commission as governor, caused the oath of allegiance to be administered to the people; the English government was once more established, and so continued for a century thereafter.

Towards the close of the year 1680, the people throughout the whole colony were greatly alarmed by the appearance of a "Dreadfull Comett Starr," which was visible in broad daylight, and had a "very fyery Tail or Streamer." It was at once universally accepted as an omen of "Dreadfull Punishments." and the authorities were requested to appoint a day of fasting and humiliation, that by the penitence of the people Heaven might be induced to avert the impending calamities. The lieutenant-governor Anthony Brockholst, in reply to the application, informs the petitioners that the terrible star had been observed, and that it "Certainly threatens God's Vengence and Judgments," but recommends each individual to keep his own day of fasting and humiliation, and to perform his duty by prayer, &c., as became good Christians.

Andros having been recalled, Brockholst administered the government until the arrival of Colonel Thomas Dongan, who, though commissioned September 30th, 1682, did not arrive until the 25th of the following August. He was a professed papist, but is said to have been a "wiser man than a master." The people of Staten Island are more directly interested in him than in any other governor of the province under either nationality; having the whole country before him, from which to select his residence, he judiciously made choice of Staten Island, and the evidences of his residence here are still, in some measure, perceptible. We anticipate the order of events in the history of the Island, that we may complete that of this governor, the two being almost identical.

At the time of Dongan's arrival, there dwelt in the city of New York a gentleman named John Palmer, by profession a lawyer, who, at the time of the separation of Staten Island from the Long Island towns, was appointed "ranger" for Staten Island. He had formerly lived on the island of Barbadoes, and had emigrated thence to New York. In 1683 he lived on Staten Island, and was appointed by Dongan one of the two first judges of the New York Court of Oyer and Terminer. He was also a member of the Council, and generally an active and prominent man in the affairs of the province. To this man Dongan executed a patent, known in the Island history as the Palmer or Dongan patent. The small brook which forms a part of the boundary between the towns of Castleton and Northfield, and which runs to the Mill Pond, is still known by the name of "Palmer's Run," because it also formed a part of the boundary of the land conveyed by the patent.

The document is dated March 31st, 1687, and the following is a description of the territory conveyed. "Beginning at a cove* on Kill Van Cull, on the east bounds of the lands of Garret Cruise, (Cruser) and so running in the woods by the said Kill to a marked tree, and thence by a line of marked trees according to the natural position of the poles, south and by east two degrees and thirty minutes southerly according to the compass south, there being eight degrees and forty-five minutes variation ffrom the north westward, and from thence by the reare of the land of Garret Cruise & Peter Johnson, east & by north two degrees and thirty minutes to the line

* Vide App. N. (14.)

of Peter Johnson's wood lott, & by his line south and by east two degrees and thirty minutes south sixty-one chains, and thence by the reare of the aforesaid lott & the lott of John Vincent northeast & by east one degree northerly to the southeast corner of the land of John Vincent thirty three chains & a halfe, from thence by his east line south & by west two degrees thirty minutes northerly to a white oak tree marked with three notches, bearing northwest from the ffresh pond,* from thence to a young chesnutt tree the southwest corner of the land of Phillip Wells & so by a line of marked trees east nine degrees & fifteen minutes southerly by the south side of a small ffresh meadow to the north & to the north of the ffresh pond including the pond to the land of Mr. Andrew Norwood & so by his land as it runs to the reare of the land of Mary Brittaine & so by the reare of the Old Town lotts to the land of Isaac Bellew & Thomas Stilwell & from thence upon the Iron Hills † to the land of William Stilwell & by his land to the land of George Cummins & ffrom his northeast corner to the southeast corner of the land of Mr. James Hubbard at the head of the ffresh kills & so round by his land to the reare lotts at Karles neck & so by the lotts to the highway left by Jacob pullion & the great swamp‡ to the land of John ffitz Garrett including the great swamp, thence by the soldier's lotts and the reare lotts of Cornelis Corsen & company to the southwest corner of theire ffront lotts & so by the runne which is theire bounds to the mill pond including the mill pond to the sound or Kill Van Cull & so by the sound to the cove where ffirst begun. Containing with all the hills, valleys, ffresh meadows & swamps within the above specified bounds five thousand one hundred acres be the same more or less.——Also a great island of salt meadow lying near the ffresh kills & over against long neck not yet appropriated—and all the messuages, tenements, fencings, orchards, gardens, pastures, meadows, marshes, woods, underwoods, trees, timber, quarries, rivers, brooks, ponds, lakes, streams,

---

* Vide App. N. (15.)   † Ibid. (16.)   ‡ Ibid. (17.)

creeks, harbors, beaches, ffishing, hawking & ffowling, mines, minerals, (silver and gold mines only excepted) mills, mill dams, etc.—The same shall from henceforth be called the Lordship & manor of Cassiltowne,—Yielding rendering and paying therefore yearly and every yeare one lamb and eight bushels of winter wheat."

On the 16th day of April, 1687, John Palmer, and Sarah, his wife, conveyed the territory described above to Thomas Dongan, "for a competent summe of lawfull money," after an ownership of about a fortnight.

Being unable to convey this property to himself, the astute governor invented and adopted this plan to obtain a lawful title thereto. It is now quite impossible to trace the lines described in the patent, as the most of the land-marks mentioned therein have disappeared. If, by the terms "great swamp," is meant that extending from Graniteville to New Springville, and which is so designated in a variety of other ancient documents; and if, by "Ffresh Kills," is meant the waters now known by that name, and which are, also, frequently alluded to by that name in similar documents, it is evident that the territory conveyed embraced not only the greater part of the present towns of Castleton and Middletown, but a large proportion of Northfield also.

In the following year, 1688, Dongan erected his Manor House, which still remains, externally modernized in some degree; but the oak frame, hewn out of the adjacent forest, is the identical one erected by him, the date of its erection having been marked upon one of the timbers with white paint. The house alluded to is the one standing in the middle of the square bounded by the Shore Road on the north, Cedar Street on the south, Dongan Street on the east, and Bodine Street on the west, at West New Brighton. There is now a gradual descent of the surface of the land from the house to the Shore Road; but, originally, the earth was as high on the southerly side of the road as it now is at the house, forming a sand hill between the house and the road, and which entirely concealed the house from view when standing in the road in front of it. When this sand bank was removed, several skeletons, evidently of Indians, besides numerous other Indian relics, were unearthed, indicating this spot as having been one of their burial places.

There is a conveyance on record, in the office of the County Clerk, dated May 9th, 1715, from Thomas Dongan, Earl of Limerick, to Thomas, John, and Walter Dongan, and others, from which we make the following extract: "And the said Thomas, Earl of Limerick, being willing to preserve, and uphold, and advance, the name and family of Dongan, and *having no issue of his own to continue the same,* he, therefore, in consideration of natural love and affection to his kinsmen, the said John, Thomas, and Walter Dongan," &c.

This extract is made to show, by his own authority, that he had no descendants.

One of our State historians says: "The last of his descendants had reduced himself, by vice, to be a sergeant of foot or marines in 1798, '99." And again: "A Colonel Dongan was wounded on Staten Island in August, 1777, and died Sept. 1st; was he a grandson of the governor?"

The "kinsmen" mentioned in the conveyance, alluded to above, were nephews of the governor. The grave of one of them is marked by a tombstone, still standing in the churchyard of St. Andrews Church, in Richmond, and the following is the inscription thereon: "Walter Dongan, Esq., died July 25th, 1749, aged 57 years." Consequently, when the estate was conveyed to him by his uncle, the Earl of Limerick, he was about 23 years of age. His wife, Ruth, interred by his side, died July 28th, 1733, aged 32 years.

The late Walter Dongan, who owned an extensive property at the Four Corners, Castleton, where he died February, 1855, at the age of 93 years, was a descendant, either son or grandson, of Thomas, another of the nephews. John C. Dongan, who was a supervisor in 1785, and several times Member of Assembly, was the son of the nephew Walter, who was surrogate in 1733, and was generally known as "Jackey Dongan." He succeeded by some means, in obtaining a very large part of the governor's estate; he was a free-liver, and what in modern parlance is known as a "fast man." He disposed of much of his property in small parcels, at low prices, and finally the residue passed into the McVickar family, with which, it is said, he was connected by marriage. The Dongan family name is now extinct in the county, notwithstanding the governor's anxiety to perpetuate it.

Governor Dongan, though a professed papist, was a decided enemy to the French, whose schemes of aggrandizement on the northern frontier he persistently opposed, even against the expressed wishes of his master, the Duke of York, afterwards James II. The people of the province, and especially of the Island, where he resided, lived in constant dread of his religion. It was generally believed that Dongan had been appointed to his high trust for the purpose of forcing his religion upon the people of the province, and the fact that he selected his co-religionists, of whom there were some in the province, for the highest official positions, gave an aspect of probability to the suspicion. In 1689 the apprehensions of the people on Staten Island culminated in a panic. Fear reigned supreme for a while; they dared not remain at night in their own dwellings, but in the deepest recesses of the forest they constructed temporary shelters, to which they resorted after dark, that they might not be observed and their retreats discovered; they preferred to encounter the perils of the darkness and the forests, than trust themselves to the tender mercies of their fellow men. Some took their families upon the water in boats, which they anchored at a distance from the shore, and thus passed the nights; and various other expedients were resorted to for concealment and security. Reports of various kinds were spread, which added fuel to the flame, and kept it burning for some length of time; among these were, that a number of papists who had been driven out of Boston, had been received into the fort at New York, and had enlisted as soldiers; that the papists on the Island had secretly collected arms, which they kept concealed and ready for use at a moment's notice; that the Governor's brigantine had been armed, and otherwise equipped for some desperate enterprise, and the refusal of the commander of the vessel to permit it to be searched, was not calculated to allay the alarm. He admitted that the vessel had been armed, but not for the purpose alleged, but, as she was bound on a voyage to Madeira, she was in danger of being attacked by the Turks, and she had been armed for the defense of her crew and cargo. However plausible this reason might have been, it was not generally credited. The excitement at length subsided, and not a Protestant throat had been cut.

Tradition says that several pieces of cannon were afterwards found in the cellar of the Governor's mill, which it was supposed had been concealed there, to be in readiness when they might be required. This mill stood on the South side of the recently constructed public road in West Brighton, called Post Avenue, which is in fact part of an old road reopened, for, prior to the construction of the causeway which now connects West New Brighton and Port Richmond, the only communication between Castleton and Northfield, near the shore, was round the head of the cove or pond now known as the mill pond. After the construction of the causeway, and its adoption as a public road, the old road ceased to be used, and was enclosed as a part of the Post farm, though the Post family did not own the farm until a subsequent period. This pond is alluded to in the Palmer patent, and the tide flowed and ebbed in it, so that boats, at high water, could reach the door of the old mill. This mill was largely patronized by the people of Bergen Point and its vicinity, as well as by the people of Staten Island. When the present avenue was constructed, the foundation stones, and some of the decayed oak timbers of the old mill, were unearthed, but no cannon. In the latter part of the last century, a flouring mill was built on the present steamboat wharf at West New Brighton, and the most of the water which had propelled the old mill, was diverted from its natural course by a canal which led it into the large pond at the foot of the present Water street, which pond was then constructed to hold the water in reserve for the use of the new mill; this was built by a McVickar, though it subsequently passed into the hands of the Van Buskirk family, and was better known as Van Buskirk's mill. This mill was burned a few years ago, and the wharf, the pond and the canal for more than half a century have belonged to the New York Dyeing and Printing Establishment. After the construction of the causeway, and the diverting of the water, the pond has gradually filled up, until now it can scarcely be utilized for the purpose to which it was once devoted.

It is not certain when Dongan returned to Europe, but it was probably in 1691, when he took up his residence in his native country, Ireland, and died, as is said, in 1721. He was the first Governor of the province who suffered an election by the people for Member of Assembly.

It has been said that the apprehensions of the people in all parts of the province, on the occasion mentioned above, were entirely unfounded; but if we glance at the condition of England at that time we shall find reason to believe that their fears were not altogether chimerical. James II, formerly Duke of York and Albany, had abdicated the throne, and was then, 1689, a fugitive. William of Orange, and Mary his wife, the daughter of James, had just been proclaimed in England as William III and Mary II. Andros, the Governor of New England, had superseded Dongan, and had appointed Nicholson his deputy in New York, himself being an appointee of James. Dongan, Andros and Nicholson were known as professed Roman Catholics, and as such sympathized with James in his exile. Throughout England the new king and queen had been proclaimed, and the colonists of New York and New England were disposed to do so also, but were restrained by the Governor and his deputy, who were suspected, and not without reason, of a design of seizing the fort at New York, with a view of overawing the people and preventing any demonstration in favor of William and Mary, who were the professed champions of Protestantism.

In such a state of affairs it would have been surprising indeed if the apprehensions of the people had not been aroused. Early in the summer of that year a report was circulated, which obtained credence, that the papists intended to attack the people on Sunday, while at church in the fort, massacre them, and declare for James. So well were the people convinced of the truth of this rumor, that they assembled in great numbers, anticipated the intentions of the governor and his deputy, and their adherents, and seized the fort themselves. This they held until Nicholson had left the country, and William and Mary had been proclaimed by the exultant populace. Notwithstanding the reiterated assertions made at the time, that neither Andros nor Nicholson were friendly to the papists, there were affidavits and other proofs of a convincing character to contradict them.

Jacob Leisler, a prominent character of that day, exercising both civil and military authority, was intrusted by the magistrates with the administration of affairs, after the departure of Nicholson, and one of his first acts was to cause William and Mary to be proclaimed in the counties of Richmond, Westchester, Queens, Kings and Ulster, and the city and county of Albany and East Jersey; the order to Richmond was dated December 17th, 1689. On the 30th of the same month, he issued an order requiring all persons who held commissions, warrants, "or other instruments of power or command, either civil or military," derived from either Dongan or Andros, forthwith to surrender the same to a justice of the peace of the county wherein they resided, except the counties of New York and Richmond, who were to surrender at the fort in New York.

After the burning of Schenectady, and the massacre of its inhabitants by the French and Indians, in February, 1690, he issued another order to the military and civil officers of several counties, Richmond County being one of the number, that "fearing too great a correspondency hath been maintained between ye s^d ffrensch & disaffected P^{r}sons among us," to secure all persons reputed papists, or who are inimical to the government, or who continue to hold any commissions from Dongan or Andros, and bring them before him.

In the same year, 1689, Leisler commissioned the following civil and military officers in Richmond County:

Ely Crossen, high sheriff.	Jaques Puillion, Captain.
Jacob Corbett, clerk.	Cornelis Corsen, do.
Obadiah Holmes, justice.	Thomas Morgan, Lieutenant.
Jaques Poullion, do.	John Theunis Van Pelt, do.
Thomas Morgan, do.	Seger Geritsen, Ensign.
Jacob Gerritse, do.	Cornelis Nevius, do.
Cornelis Corsen, do.	

The following persons from Staten Island were members of a company commanded by Capt. Jacob Milborne, which was sent to Albany to establish Leisler's authority, the government of that city having refused to recognize it, viz.: "Jean Marlett, Francis Maurisa, Hendrick Hendricksen, Jean faefre, John Rob, John doulier and Peter Henkesson."

Leisler's administration was far from being peaceful; other places in the province besides Albany disputed the validity of his appointment, but none were so decided in their opposition. Milborne's expedition to Albany resulted in nothing.

In July, 1690, Leisler issued an order directed to the "Constable at Elizabethtown, & so foreward requiring and desiring the arrest of 'five armed frenchmen,' who were seen on Schutter's Island, having a watch out on trees, & being assured that peter deumont & Andrew ffallourdell" were amongst them, having fled *out of this province* from the hands of justice. We have no means of learning whether any of these men were ever arrested, nor whether they were guilty of any other crime than that of being Frenchmen; but from the tenor of the order, we infer that he did not recognize Shooter's Island as being a part of the province of New York.

There is no evidence that the people of Staten Island took any decided stand with regard to Leisler's administration, nor in what light it was regarded by them; generally, they submitted quietly to the authorities placed over them.— Further than commissioning some officers, and issuing some general orders, he does not appear in connection with the history of the Island.

After the arrival of Governor Sloughter, Leisler and Milborne, his son-in-law, together with several members of his Council, were arrested for treason and condemned to death, but all were reprieved except the two first named, who were executed by hanging on Saturday, May 16th, 1691. On the 28th of April, preceding, a letter was presented to the Council in New York from the Sheriff of Richmond County, "Giving an Account of severall Riotts and Tumults on Staten Island, and that they are subscribing of papers"; the sheriff was ordered to secure the ring-leaders that they might be prosecuted. The papers which were "subscribed" were petitions in favor of the two condemned men; the people of Westchester also sent a petition for the same purpose, but the Council did not recognize the right of petition in such cases; therefore some were cited to appear before that body, while others were imprisoned as promoters of "riots and disturbances."

During Dongan's administration, Leisler, having imported a cargo of wine, refused to pay the duties thereon to Matthew Plowman, the collector of the port, because he was a papist; he was, however, compelled to do so, and ever, thereafter, was a bitter enemy of Plowman. During his brief arbitrary administration, to gratify his spite, he charged Plowman with being a defaulter to the government; and, learning that he was the owner of a quantity of beef and pork, stored at Elizabethtown, he ordered Johannes Burger, a sergeant at the fort, to proceed to Staten Island, and compel such individuals as he might require to go with him, and assist in the removal of the provisions. Burger obeyed the order, and the property was brought to Leisler in New York, who sent it to Albany for the use of the soldiers he had sent to that place. After Leisler's execution, Plowman prosecuted all who were concerned in the removal of his property, to recover its value. Amongst the number were the following residents of Staten Island, viz., John Jeronison, Thomas Morgan, Lawrence

Johnson, John Peterson, Dereck Crews, (Cruser) Chauck (Jaques) Pollion and John Bedine." These individuals, soon after the arrival of Major Richard Ingoldsby, as president of the province addressed an "humble Peticon" to him and the Council, in which they admit having assisted in the removal of Plowman's property, but that they did so under compulsion, believing that they were doing a service to their majesties; that they considered it unjust to compel them to pay for the provisions when the whole country had the benefit of them; they therefore pray that they may be relieved from the whole responsibility, or if that may not be done, that every person engaged in the removal be compelled "to pay their equall proporceons of the same." This petition was presented by Plowman himself, who thereby recognized the justice of their cause, but what the result of the application was does not appear.

In 1693 the following persons were civil officers of Richmond County:

Ellis Duxbury, Esq., Judge of the Common Pleas. Abraham Cannor (Cannon,) Abraham Lakeman (Lockman,) Dennis Theunisse and John Shadwell, justices; John Stilwell, Esq., Sheriff. The militia of the county consisted of two companies of foot, 104 men in all, under the command of Capt. Andrew Cannon.

CHAPTER X.

Complaints against the Sheriff—Census from 1698 to 1771—Slaveholders—Civil and Military Officers—Disappearance of old Families—Cold Winter of 1740-'1—Traveling in the Olden Time—A Traveler's Adventure in the Woods—Cold Winters of 1761 and 1768—Baron De Kalb—Domestic Life of the Olden Time.

It has been stated above, that the sheriff of Richmond sent a letter to the Council in April, 1691, with information that riots and tumults had taken place in the county, and directions were returned to him to secure the ringleaders, that they might be punished. Thomas Stilwell, the sheriff, was not dilatory in obeying the order, and arrested several of the citizens of the county, among whom were John Theunison, John Peterson and Gerard Vechten, each of whom he compelled to pay three pounds; others were obliged to execute bonds for the payment of that amount, and one refused to do either, and him he imprisoned. When information of the sheriff's proceedings reached New York, orders were sent down to have the bonds cancelled, whereupon the three individuals who had paid their money, demanded that it should be refunded; the sheriff, probably conscious that he had exceeded his powers, promised that it should be done, but delayed so long, that the aggrieved parties appealed to the Council. At the same time, the same three individuals presented a complaint against the assessors, who exempted themselves and some others from the payment of the tax for "negers," and that poor people who have no "negers" must pay "as much accordingly like Them that Has many negers. Therefore your petitioners humbly crave That your Ex^{ll}y will be pleased To signify Them iff s^d negers should be Excluded ffor paying Tax." What the result of these petitions was, we are not informed further than that they met with a favorable reception.

It must be admitted that Leisler, during the time he exercised his authority, had many friends upon the Island, though they were not very demonstrative. His appointments to office were usually from among its best citizens, which operated in his favor; no decided steps were taken in his behalf during his imprisonment and trial, but after his condemnation petitions for his pardon were extensively signed, which had no other effect than to bring upon the signers the displeasure of the government, who regarded the act as disloyal. Further than the imposition of fines, which appear to have been remitted, and the brief imprisonment of a few individuals, no punishment was inflicted upon the culprits.

For the remainder of the century nothing appears to have transpired, within the limited area of the county, of sufficient importance to be considered as of historical interest. Whatever may have taken place in the more densely populated parts of the province, Staten Island, in its secluded position, was left to pursue its own course as a separate and distinct community. In lieu of other materials, we present a few statistics which will prove of interest. They are arranged from tables in the Documentary History of the province.

Years.	Men.	Women.	Children.	Blacks.	Total.
1698	328	208	118	73	727
1708					505
1712					1279
	White Males.	*White Females.*			
1723	640	611		255	1506
1731	686	827		304	1817
1737	777	763		349	1889
1746	856	835		382	2073
1749	887	858		409	2154
1756	862	805		465	2132
1771	1150	1103		594	2847

Notwithstanding the assertion made in the complaint against the assessors, that poor people had no "negers," the number of slaves owned by a single individual was not always an indication of his wealth, for many of the residents appear to have been remarkably prolific, and had many children of both sexes to assist them in their agricultural labors, thus rendering the assistance of slaves unnecessary. The following is a list of the slave holders in the "North Company" of Staten Island, as returned by Jacob Corsen, Jun., in 1755. The names are spelled as in the original, but are readily recognized.

SLAVEHOLDERS.	No. Slaves. Male.	Female.	SLAVEHOLDERS.	No. Slaves. Male.	Female.
Thomas Dongan	7	3	Barent marteling	1	
Jacob Corssen, Seneor	3	2	Richard Merrel	2	2
Jacob Corssen, Juner		2	Otto Van tuyl	2	2
John Vegte	2	2	Bastian Ellis	1	
Gerardus Beekman	1	1	John Veltmon	1	
In care of G. Beekman, but belonging to John Beekman of New York	3		Abraham Prall	2	
			Charles Mecleen	1	
			Margaret Simonson	1	1
Henry Cruse	1	3	Joseph Lake	1	1
Antony Walters	2	2	John Roll	3	
Cornelius Cruse		1	Elenor haughwout		1
Simon Simonson	1		Abraham Crocheron	1	1
Johannis de Groet	1	1	Barnit De Pue	1	1
John Rolf	1	2	John Crocheron	1	
Christiaen Corssen	2		David Cannon		
Joshua Merseral	1	1	Aron Prall	1	
John Deceer	1	1	Charyty Merrill	1	
Garret Crussen		2	Joseph Begel	1	1
Garret Post	1	1	Cornelius Korsan		1
John Roll, Juner	1	1			

The following are the names of the Civil and Military officers of the county of Richmond for the year 1739:

Judges of the Court of Common Pleas.
John Le Conte, Judge.
Christian Corsen, 2d Judge.
Gozen Adrians, 3d Judge.
Nicolas Britton, Justice.
Richard Stilwell, do.
Joseph Bedell, do.
John Veghte, do.
Rem Vander Beek, do.
John Latourette, do.
Thomas Billop,* do.
Cornelius Corsen, do.
Joshua Mersereau, do.
Abraham Cole, do.
Barent Martling, do.
Nicholas Larzelere, Sheriff.
John Hillyer, Coroner.
Danial Corsen, Clerk.

Jacob Corsen, Colonel.
Christiene Corsen, Lt. Col.
Thomas Billopp, Major.

North Division.
John Veghte, Captain.
Frederick Berge, Lieutenant.
Jacob Corsen, Jun., Ensign.

South Division.
Cornelius Stoothoff, Captain.
Jacob Berge, Lieutenant.
Aris Evertse (Ryerss), Ensign.

West Division.
Nathaniel Britton, Captain.
Marthias Johnson, Lieutenant.
Abraham Maney (Manee), Ensign.

The Troop.
Peter Perrin (Perine), Captain.
Garret Crosse, Lieutenant.
Wynant Wynants, Cornet.
Danul Wynants, Qr. Master.

* Vide App. N. (18.)

By examining the lists of names given above, the reader will perceive that a large proportion of the families who were once prominent and influential in the county, have either removed or become extinct by natural causes.

The winter of 1740–'1 was unusually severe; whenever it was alluded to, it was designated as "the hard winter," and it maintained its character until that of 1779–'80 proved decidedly "harder." Its extraordinary severity continued from the middle of November to the end of March. Snow fell to the depth of six feet on a level; fences were buried out of sight; domestic animals were housed during the whole period, and many of them perished; intercourse between neighbors was suspended for several weeks; physicians were not able to reach their patients because the roads were utterly impassable; many families suffered for bread while their granaries were filled, but grain could not be ground because the mills were inaccessible; the roofs of dwelling and out-houses in many cases were crushed by the superincumbent mass of snow; churches remained closed, and the dead unburied. At length a day or two of moderate weather, with a light misty rain, softened the surface of the snow, which froze hard again, forming a thick, firm ice, sufficient to sustain a horse. This for a time afforded great relief to the imprisoned people, and enabled them to procure fuel and other necessaries.*

The conveniences for traveling in the days of our ancestors presents a striking contrast to those of the present day. The following public notice appeared in 1753:

"A commodious stage-boat will attend at the City Hall slip, near the Half Moon battery, to receive goods and passengers, on Saturdays and Wednesdays, and on Mondays and Thursdays will set out for Perth Amboy Ferry; there a stage-wagon will receive them and set out on Tuesdays and Fridays in the morning, and carry them to Cranberry, and then the same day, with fresh horses to Burlington, where a stage-

* Vide App. N. (19.)

boat receives them, and immediately sets out for Philadelphia." Thus the journey between the two cities was accomplished in three days, and was called "an improvement." The stage-boats of those days were the periauguas, or pirogues of the present; they were vessels without keels, heavy lee-boards, two masts and two large sails; the improvement consisted in substituting these boats for the small sloops used before. When wind and weather permitted, the "outside passage" was made—that is, through the Narrows and around the eastern side of Staten Island; at other times they passed through the Kills and Sound. Another route, frequently taken, was across the bay to Staten Island, across the Island to the Blazing Star Ferry,* which was crossed in a scow, then to New Brunswick, where the Raritan was crossed in another scow, thence to Trenton, where the Delaware was crossed in a third scow, and thence to the end of the journey. A third route was by way of Paulus Hook, now Jersey City, which was reached by a periaugua, and thence by stage-wagons and scows. This last route was the safest, as the journey by water was shorter, though that by land was somewhat longer. Three days, however, were occupied by either route if everything was favorable, but if any mishap occurred, or if the man and boy, who usually formed the crew of a periaugua, were intoxicated, as often happened, a fourth day must be devoted to the journey. The perils of crossing the bay in these boats in a gale of wind, was sometimes serious. There were other perils which beset travelers in those days, as may be seen by the following narrative, which we borrow from Dunlap:

"1765, January 10th. A traveler passing from Albany to Boston, put up at a tavern and gave his bags, with money, in charge of the landlord. Next day proceeding, he found his horse lame, and stopped at a blacksmith's, who found the horse had been cut just above one of his hoofs, and some of the hair drawn through the wound. He inquired where the

* Vide App. N. (20.)

traveler lodged last night, and being told, shook his head and advised him not to pursue his journey through the woods alone. 'I have good pistols.' 'Examine them.' He did, and found that the charge had been drawn, and supplied with dirt. This confirmed suspicion, and the blacksmith advised him not to go on. The traveler persisted, and cleaning and reloading his pistols, pursued his way. The blacksmith, anxious for his safety, mounted his horse and followed. Before he overtook the traveler, he heard two pistols discharged, and soon met the traveler returning, who said, 'I have done the business for two of them.' It being near night, he returned to the blacksmith's, and remained until morning, when they both entered the wood, and found the landlord and his son dead—the victims of their own plot to rob the wayfarer."

In January, 1761, the weather became exceedingly cold, and continued so till March; the Narrows were frozen over.

Another severe winter occurred in 1768; it is related of Baron De Kalb that he, with eight other persons, attempted to cross over to Staten Island at the Blazing Star Ferry, but that the scow sunk, leaving them all night upon a sand island. Some died from the cold, while others lost some of their limbs. De Kalb was the only person uninjured; he, after they were rescued, instead of warming himself by the fire as the others did, stood bare-footed in cold water, then took some refreshments and went to bed, and in the morning arose uninjured.

A glance at the domestic life of the olden time will be of interest to the modern reader.

The dwellings of our ancestors, at first, were unavoidably rude and inconvenient, as the necessity of an immediate shelter, upon their arrival, compelled them to erect their houses without regard to anything but that. Log cabins were built by almost every family, and when properly constructed, were comfortable and durable. In process of time, as their means increased, many of them erected spacious, and in some instances costly houses of stone, some of which may still be seen in various parts of the Island, but they were almost, without exception, in the Dutch style of architecture—long, low and massive. The kitchen, which was usually a separate structure, but connected with the main house, was furnished with a spacious fire-place—in some instances occupying one entire end of the apartment. It is said that some of these kitchens were furnished with doors, in front and in rear, large enough to allow a horse and sleigh loaded with wood, to be driven in at one door, the wood to be unloaded into the fire-place, and driven out at the opposite, but we will not pledge our historical veracity for the truth of the assertion. Usually a "back-log," of green wood, too large to be managed without the aid of bars and levers, was rolled into the house and placed against the back wall of the fire-place, then smaller materials were built up in front of it and ignited, and soon a bright and glowing fire was kindled, giving heat, and at night light enough for ordinary purposes. The materials for these houses were abundant on almost every man's farm; stones were either quarried or found upon the surface; timber grew in his own woods, where it was felled and dressed; shingles were cut and split in the same place, and the boards and planks were sawed at some neighboring mill. Of these saw-mills there were several on the Island; the ruins of one or two of them are still to be seen. The nails were made by the hands of the neighboring blacksmith. Lime of the best quality was made by burning the shells, which were found in many places near the shores in large quantities, deposited there by the aborigines. It required much labor, and occupied much time to build a house of this description, but it was built to be occupied by generations. With few exceptions, the people were agriculturists, and their method of cultivation did not differ materially from that of the present day. Their implements of husbandry were usually brought from the old country, and, compared with those of the present day, were clumsy and ponderous. Prior to the introduction of harrows, which is of comparatively recent date, branches of trees were used in their stead, and are still used in many parts of the country at the present day.

Every farmer whose necessities required it, was the owner of one or more slaves, the males being the assistants of the master in the fields, and the females of the mistress in the kitchen. They were invariably treated with kindness by the Dutch, but the French, and especially the English settlers, were disposed to draw the line of social equality more rigidly. Slaves, however, were generally well taken care of, perhaps not always so much from motives of humanity as of interest. They always had their own sleeping apartments and their own separate tables. As the life of a slave was doomed to be one of labor, intellectual cultivation was deemed unnecessary; some, few, however, were taught sufficiently to enable them to read the Bible, and as they were admitted to be responsible hereafter for the deeds done in this life, religious instructions in pious families were not neglected. It was not unusual to see master and slave working together in the fields apparently on terms of perfect equality, but there were lines drawn, beyond which neither males nor females dared to trespass. In the kitchen, especially in the long winter evenings, the whites and blacks indiscriminately surrounded the same huge fire, ate apples from the same dish, poured cider from the same pitcher, and cracked nuts and jokes with perfect freedom.

In the construction of houses of the better class, the chimneys were made of bricks imported from Holland, frequently as ballast, but when it was discovered that an article quite as good could be manufactured from American earth, importation ceased. Ovens were usually built outside of the house, and roofed over to protect them from the weather. The barns were low in the eaves, but very capacious, and some farmers had several of them, according to the size of their farms. One of the most important of a farmer's out-of-door arrangements, was his hog-pen; the number of swine which he fattened annually was proportioned to the number of the members of his family. Beside swine, every farmer fattened a "beef," and when the season for slaughtering came round, which was in the Fall, after the weather had become cold, there was a busy time both without and within doors; what with the cutting up and "corning" of the meat, the labor of making sausages, head-cheese, rollitjes, and many other articles, even the names of which are now forgotten, both the males and females of the family were occupied for a fortnight or more. After the work of "killing time" was over, the long Fall and Winter evenings were devoted to the manufacture of candles, "moulds" and "dips." Every farm has its smoke-house, in which hams, shoulders, pieces of beef, and various other articles of diet, were hung to be cured with smoke. With his corned and smoked meats, his poultry, mutton and veal, the farmer's family was not without animal food the year round. Game of various kinds abounded in the forests for a long time, and was usually hunted by the younger members of the family.

Early in the Spring, every householder made one or more visits to the beach, to procure a supply of fish, both scale and shell; but, more particularly, to lay in a supply of shad for summer consumption. This practice is continued, with many families, to the present day.

Every house was furnished with two spinning wheels: a large one, for the manufacture of woolen thread, and a small one for linen. A thorough, practical knowledge, of the use of these instruments, was deemed an indispensable part of a young lady's education; let her other accomplishments be what they might, without these she was not qualified to assume the care of a family. After the thread had been spun, it was dyed; sumach, the bark of the black oak, chestnut, and other trees, furnishing the materials for that purpose. Large families had looms of their own, with which the cloth for family use was woven, though there were professional weavers, whose skill was in demand when bed-spreads, and other articles with fancy patterns, were required to be made. Girls, at a very early age, were inducted into the mysteries of knitting, and were the recipients of many a boxed ear for "dropping stitches." Provident families were well supplied with woolen and linen garments, and quantities of cloth of both materials laid aside, to be manufactured into household articles when they might be required. The prudent housewife made it her care to provide an ample supply of clothing, not only for the living, but she had also, laid aside, grave clothes for the members of the household, to be ready at hand when they might be required.

There were itinerant tailors, who went from house to house, spending several days at each, making overcoats, and such other garments as the women of the family could not make; and itinerant shoemakers, who, once each year, went on their circuit, making and repairing boots and shoes.

People sometimes lived at great distances from each other, yet social intercourse was not neglected. On Sundays they met at church, and, both before and after service, family and neighborhood news was communicated and discussed. On court days the men from all parts of the county met at the county seat, where they talked over their agricultural experiences, and other matters of interest. But the most cheerful of all social assemblages, especially for young people, took place in the winter, when the sleighing was good; then it was that those who were yet unmarried sought each other's society, and met at Richmond to indulge in the merry dance until the waning hours admonished them to return to their homes. The attractions of these meetings have proved too powerful to be entirely abandoned, and they are still continued by the same class in society. But the *pater et mater familias* were not without their social enjoyments; the long winter evenings were frequently spent in visiting or receiving visitors, in the course of which a sumptuous repast formed one of the pleasant features of the meeting.

The early Dutch settlers on Staten Island, though not a literary, were a pious people; the greatest part of them were able to read and write, as the Dutch family Bibles, and the beautiful chirography in many of them, testify. The Waldensian and Huguenot elements, which amalgamated with them, served to intensify their religious sentiments; indeed, it could not well be otherwise, for it was to enjoy the peaceful exercise of their religion that these latter had forsaken the homes of their childhood and the graves of their fathers, and cheerfully submitted to the inconveniences and sufferings of a life in the wilderness; religious duties had a claim paramount to all others, and long before they were able to erect churches for themselves, their dwellings were thrown open for the accommodation of their neighbors, when the ministers from the city periodically visited them. The language of Holland was, of course, the first in use, the Huguenots brought their French with them, but as the several nationalities mingled and intermarried, it gradually died out, and the Dutch became the prevailing tongue until after the conquest, when in its turn it succumbed to the language of the conquerors. The Dutch, however, continued to be used in social intercourse, and the services of the sanctuary for a long time after the conquest, and less than half a century ago, its uncouth accents were still heard in some dwellings.

The Dutch were never addicted to the observance of holidays; Custydt, or Christmas and Nieuw Jaar, or New Year, were about the only ones of a religious character in which they indulged; Paas, or Easter, was surrendered to the children, and Pingster or Whitsunday to the negroes. Children have not yet resigned their claim to their especial holiday in Dutch communities. Religious services were regularly held on Christmas, and on the first day of the New Year, on which occasion the newly elected church officers were formally inducted into their respective offices, and this ceremony was called being "married to the church."

CHAPTER XI.

Gov. Hardy—The Delanceys—Expedition against Louisburg—Gen. Amherst—Conquest of Canada—Moncton's Army on Staten Island—Amherst invested with the order of the Garter on Staten Island—Extracts from old papers—Beginning of the Revolution—Tories on Staten Island.

SIR Charles Hardy arrived September 2d, 1755, as Governor of the province; he was an English admiral, and on account of his lack of knowledge and experience in civil affairs, was unfitted for the position which he was sent to occupy. He suffered himself, however, to be guided and directed in a great measure by his Council, and especially by the two Delanceys, James and Oliver. When the provincial expedition against the French at Louisburg was being organized, he was appointed to the command, and embarked July 20th, 1757, leaving the government in the hands of James Delancey, who had been appointed Lieutenant-Governor in 1753. On the 29th of July, 1760, the Lieutenant-Governor, with General Provoost and several other prominent gentleman, visited Staten Island, and dined there; it is said to have been a very jovial party, and that he indulged in eating and drinking to excess, the penalty for which he paid the following day, when one of his children found him expiring, seated in a chair in his study. His house was in the Bowery. He was buried on the 31st, under the middle aisle of Trinity Church.

The war between the English and French had been carried on for several years with great activity, but Abercrombie, the English commander-in-chief, though he had the reputation of being a consummate general, was unfortunate in most of his efforts against the enemy, probably because he relied more upon his English regulars, who were not accustomed to fighting in a wild country, than upon the provincials, who accompanied him and formed an important part of his army, and who were perfectly familiar with the country, and the manner of fighting the French and their Indian allies; a mistake into which other British generals than Braddock and Abercrombie have fallen. In 1759, Abercrombie was superseded by General Amherst, and affairs on the Northern frontier soon began to assume a more favorable aspect.

One of the most important services during this protracted war, was the capture of the French fort Frontenac, on the 27th of August, 1758. With 3,000 men, mostly provincials, Colonel Bradstreet, himself a provincial, traversed the wilderness between Albany and Lake Ontario, carrying with him eight pieces of cannon, and three mortars. Among these troops was a regiment commanded by Colonel Corse, of Queens county, and in that regiment was Captain Thomas Arrowsmith's* company of Staten Islanders. This regiment contributed materially to the success of the expedition. Corse volunteered to erect a battery during the night of the 26th, and effected his purpose under a continuous fire from the fort. On the morning of the 27th, this battery opened on the enemy, who at once deserted the fort and fled. The material captured with the fort consisted of forty-six pieces of cannon, sixteen mortars, and a very large quantity of military stores, provisions and merchandise.

In September, 1760, Canada was surrendered to the English, and the provincial forces engaged in its reduction turned their faces homeward.

The revolutionary army of Howe was not the first British army that had occupied Staten Island; in 1760, General Moncton encamped here for several months. During his occupancy an important ceremony, as it was regarded at that time and by that people, was performed here. Amherst, after the conquest of Canada, returned to New York, where he was received with salutes and illuminations. Móncton had been deputed to invest him with the order of the Garter,† which was done upon Staten Island, in the presence of all

---

* Vide App. N. (21.) † Ibid. (22.)

the dignitaries of the province, and a large concourse of spectators. The government of the province had been committed to Doctor Cadwallader Colden, of Ulster county, who administered it until the commission of Moncton as Governor arrived, which was on the 19th October, 1761. He, however, did not remain long, for on the 15th of the succeeding month he embarked with all his army for Martinique in a fleet consisting of one hundred transports and two line-of-battle ships.

Early in the Summer of 1764, the light-house on Sandy Hook was lighted for the first time. Holt's *New York Gazette*, or *Weekly Post Boy* of June 18, of that year, gives the following as items of important news:

"The long-wished for ferry is now established from the place called Powles's Hook (Jersey City) to the City of New York."—Also a ferry established across the Kill Van Kull from Staten Island to Bergen.

There is no evidence that the political questions of the day, which even at this early period began to agitate the minds of the people throughout the several provinces, produced much excitement on Staten Island; the people were an isolated community, holding little intercourse with the world around them, and taking comparatively little interest in matters not of a strictly local character. There were, however, some intelligent men among them who kept themselves informed on the topics which began to agitate the country, and who well understood their merits. The great majority of the people, however, if not indifferent, were opposed to the patriotic doctrines which found so many advocates elsewhere. This is evident from the political character of the men sent by them as their representatives to the provincial assemblies, such as Benjamin Seaman, and his son-in-law, Christopher Billop, and later, Abraham Jones, who subsequently was refused his seat on account of his known sympathies with the British.

The geographical situation of the Island gave a direction to the political sentiments of the people. Commanding the approach to the metropolis and the province, whatever nation possessed it, took advantage of its natural facilities in a military point of view. The Dutch had a battery on the heights at the Narrows at one time; the English enlarged the military works at the same important point, and the United States have not failed to improve its advantages. Whoever, then, possessed this important point, before the revolution, to a certain extent might be said to possess, or at least to control the Island and the metropolis. Whilst the English held the government of the province, the people naturally imbibed English sentiments; freedom of opinion on political subjects, so far as the nature and character of the government was concerned, was not tolerated. It is not to be wondered at, then, that a people who for more than a century had been taught to believe that it was little short of treason to doubt the divine origin of monarchy, and especially of the English monarchy, should be conscientiously opposed to a change which was calculated to overturn all their most cherished institutions. More than half of the population on the Island, at the dawn of the revolution, were either of English birth or descent, and few, perhaps none, entertained the idea that the rebellion could by any possibility succeed, and even among the whigs themselves there were probably thousands who hoped against hope.

CHAPTER XII.

Military Value of Staten Island—British take possession of Staten Island—Skinner and Billop—Col. Mersereau—Battle of Long Island—Brutality and insolence of the British Soldiers on Staten Island.

LYING between the ocean and the metropolis, and on the highway from the one to the other, Staten Island, early in the war, was regarded as an important location in a military point of view. Its importance was enhanced by the fact that it was situated in a bay more than half surrounded by the main land of New Jersey, and commanded not only a great part of Long Island, but New York city, and a large extent of country, embracing nearly all the northern part of New Jersey; the possession of it therefore became a matter of importance to both belligerents.

In 1776, General De Heister, with his army of German mercenaries in the pay of George III, arrived at Halifax, where the British fleet and army had for some time been awaiting re-inforcements. Washington had driven the British out of Boston, and soon thereafter, (April 14,) arrived in New York, on his way to Philadelphia, to meet Congress. During the absence of Washington, the American army in New York was under the command of Putnam and Lee, and numbered in all 10,235 men, a force not at all comparable with that of the British, but which Clinton, with his cautious policy, considered too great to molest; so, giving New York a wide berth, he sailed for Charleston, South Carolina.

When he arrived, he found Lee there before him, and again he judged it prudent not to attempt to land his army until after the fleet had removed the obstacles. Sir Peter Parker,[*] the British admiral, attacked the fort on Sullivan's Island, but was repulsed.

In the meanwhile General Howe, after being driven from Boston, had awaited the arrival of his brother, Lord Howe,

[* Vide App. N. (28.)]

at Halifax, sailed from thence. and, on the second of July, landed on Staten Island without opposition.* His army amounted to 9,000 men. Not long after, Lord Howe, with a large fleet and 20,000 men, arrived, and also landed on the Island. Howe had now the command of nearly 30,000 troops, who were well armed, well disciplined, and, in every other respect, prepared for the work they had to do. Washington's army consisted of about one-third of that number, raw, undisciplined, and but partially armed; new levies, however, were coming in daily. Clinton, after his repulse at Charleston, also came north, and united his fleet, or, what was left of it, and his army, to that of the Howes, thus increasing the number of the British army on Staten Island by 3,000 men.

The first object to engage the attention of General Howe, was the conciliation of the American loyalists, and, to this end, he had numerous interviews with Governor Tryon, and other prominent individuals in New York and New Jersey, all of whom led him to believe that large numbers of the people were anxious to flock to his standard the moment it was unfurled. Delancey, of New York, and Skinner, of Perth Amboy, were made Brigadier-Generals, and Billop, of Staten Island, Colonel, of the native loyalists, or tories. Proclamations were issued, promising protection to the people, so long as they remained peaceably at home, and manifested no sympathy for the rebels, or their cause. These, however, had little effect; the people knew what British protection meant; proclamations had been issued by other British commanders, in other parts of the country, promising the same thing, and the protection which had been afforded was that which the wolf gives to the lamb. Misled by the specious promises which Howe had promulgated, hundreds of the whig inhabitants of Staten Island remained peaceably at home, to reap the fruits of their credulity in having soldiers quartered upon them—in enduring, submissively,

* Vide App. N. (34.)

the insults and outrages committed upon themselves and their families, their houses and barns openly and defiantly plundered, their cattle driven away or wantonly killed, their churches burned, and, not unfrequently, some of their own number barbarously, and without provocation, murdered.

There were some, however, who had no faith in the protestations of the British commander, and too much manhood to conceal their sentiments; to these the political atmosphere of the Island was decidedly unhealthy, and these had to escape for their lives.

Among these was Col. Jacob Mersereau. He was the son of Joshua Mersereau and Maria Corsen his wife; by the records of the Ref. Church, Port Richmond, he was baptised May 24th, 1730, and died in September, 1804, in the 75th year of his age. He resided in the old stone-house in Northfield, not far from Graniteville, now occupied by his son, the venerable and Hon. Peter Mersereau. Soon after the beginning of the war, he became apprehensive for his personal safety, and fled to New Jersey. During his protracted residence there, he made occasional stealthy visits to his family by night, and on one of these occasions had a very narrow escape from capture. Having crossed the Sound, and concealed his boat, he took his course for home across fields, avoiding the public roads as much as possible. It was while crossing a road from one field to another, that he was met by a young man whom he knew well, but as neither spoke, he imagined the young man did not know him; in this, however, he was mistaken, for he was recognized at once. There was no British post just then nearer than Richmond, and thither the young tory hastened and informed the commanding officer, probably Col. Simcoe, of his discovery. Preparations were made immediately to effect the arrest of the Colonel, but it was near daylight in the morning before the party set out. They were in no haste, for they supposed he intended to remain concealed at home during the day. The family, as was their custom, had arisen early, but they did not discover the soldiers until they were within a few rods of the house. The alarm was immediately given, which, being perceived by the approaching party, a rush was made, and as they reached the door, the Colonel sprang out of the upper northwest window of the house, upon a shed beneath it, and thence to the ground. A few rods west of the house is a small elevation, and it was while crossing this that he was discovered. On the other side of the hill was a hedge row, terminating at a swamp, along which he ran on all fours, to keep himself out of sight, until he reached the swamp, in the middle of which he found a place of concealment. When he was discovered crossing the hill, those who had begun a search within were called out, and pursuit was made, but when the top of the hill was reached, the colonel was nowhere to be seen. The swamp was discovered, and it was at once concluded that he was there concealed, but as the pursuers were ignorant of its intricacies, they could proceed no further. Dogs were then put upon the track, which they followed to the edge of the swamp, where they chanced to scent a rabbit, and away they went in chase of the new game. Here the pursuit terminated, and the colonel, after remaining concealed the whole day, escaped during the following night to New Jersey. For a week thereafter a close watch was kept upon the house by day and by night. It is some consolation to know that the treacherous young tory did not receive the reward which had been offered for the patriot's capture.

Immediately preceding the battle of Long Island, or Brooklyn, as it is sometimes called, the American forces were posted in New York and on Long Island. General Greene commanded at the latter place, but being confined to his bed by illness, his place was temporarily supplied by General Sullivan. This, for the Americans, was unfortunate, as the former general was intimately acquainted with the country, while the latter, being almost a stranger, knew very little of the advantages of the surroundings.

On the 22d of August, Howe, having determined to commence active operations, crossed the Narrows from Staten Island to Long Island, and landed without opposition between New Utrecht and Gravesend. There is no need of recapitulating the story of the battle and its unfortunate result—they are well known; the British succeeded in gaining posssesion of New York, which was their main object. To keep possession after having obtained it, required a strong force, and, in consequence, the greater part of the British forces on the Island were withdrawn; enough, however, were left to defend it against any force the Americans might be able to bring against it.* The result of the battle, on the whole, was beneficial to the people of Staten Island, as it left fewer soldiers there to depredate upon them, and rob them of their substance. If the history of the sufferings of the people of Staten Island during the war could be written, it would present a picture too dreadful to contemplate. Neither age, sex nor condition were exempt from insults and outrages of the grossest character; no home was too sacred to protect its inmates from injury; the rights of property were not recognized, if the invader coveted it; even the temples of God were desecrated; the law of might alone prevailed. Proclamations and professions of good will and protection had been promulgated repeatedly, but those who relied upon them usually reaped disappointment. It was useless to appeal to those high in authority, for the complaints of the people were unheeded, and redress for injuries, except under peculiar circumstances, could not be obtained. If a British officer's horse was in need of hay or oats, a file of soldiers was sent to any farmer who was known to have a supply, to seize and take it away. If the officer himself needed a horse, the same method was adopted to procure one. Money, provisions and even bedding and household furniture were taken by force; sometimes promises of payment were made, but seldom fulfilled. The course adopted by the British while in possession of the Island, effectually alienated many of the friends of the royal cause, and hence it was that so many of them, at the close of the war, eagerly took the oath of allegiance to the new government, and so few adhered to the cause of the king, and followed its fortunes.

* Vide App. N. (25.)

CHAPTER XIII.

The Tories and Whigs of Staten Island—Submission of Kings County—Interview between Howe and the American Commissioners at the Billop House—Richmond—Great fire in New York—Howe's Expedition into New Jersey, and attempt to reach Philadelphia by land—Knyphausen's expedition into New Jersey—Murder of Mrs. Caldwell—Invasion of the Island by Americans—Stirling's Invasion.

The population of Staten Island, at the beginning of the revolution, consisted of the descendants of the early Dutch settlers, and English and French emigrants and their descendants. Of these, nearly all the former were whigs, or patriots; those of English descent were loyalists, or tories, and the French were divided in their sympathies: the two latter classes, however, considerably outnumbered the former. Many of the French having settled here before the conquest of the province by the English, had intermarried with the Dutch, who were then the dominant class, and had imbibed Dutch opinions, manners and customs, and had even fallen into the use of the Dutch language. In some of the families bearing French names and of French descent, at the present day, are to be found family records, such as they are, written in the Dutch language. There was, however, another and more marked difference between the people of the several nationalities than mere political sentiments and opinions; the Dutch were imbued with a deep religious feeling; they were not generally as well educated as the English, but they could read and write, and keep their own accounts: the English had their religion, too, but they were more formal and less earnest and devoted than their neighbors; the French in this, as in other respects, accommodated their religion to that of the class with which they had amalgamated. The whig cause throughout the country was calculated to foster religious enthusiasm, for, being conscious of their own weakness as compared with the mighty power and resources of Great Britain, they naturally looked to a higher power than that of man to sustain them in what they conscientiously believed to be the cause of right.

In speaking of the battle of Long Island, a British officer writes as follows:

"The Hessians and our brave Highlanders gave no quarters; and it was a fine sight to see with what alacrity they despatched the rebels with their bayonets, after we had surrounded them so they could not resist. We took care to tell the Hessians that the rebels had resolved to give no quarter—to them in particular—which made them fight desperately, and put to death all that came into their hands."

Another officer, of high rank, possessed of some humanity, of which the former appears to have been destitute, writes: "The Americans fought bravely, and (to do them justice) could not be broken till they were greatly outnumbered and taken in flank, front and rear. We were greatly shocked at the massacre made by the Hessians and Highlanders after the victory was decided."

Shortly after the battle of Long Island, over 400 of the citizens of Kings County, besides over 40 of its civil officers, voluntarily offered their submission to Gen. Howe and Gov. Tryon, having first taken the oath of allegiance to the king.

Howe, who was undoubtedly sincere in his oft-expressed desire for peace, sent General Sullivan, who had been taken prisoner at the battle, with a verbal message to Congress, requesting that body to appoint some of its members in a private capacity, to meet him for the purpose of adopting such measures as might be agreed upon for the restoration of peace in the country, intimating that he was clothed with sufficient power for that purpose. By the same messenger Congress returned answer that they could not send any of their number, except in their official capacities as members of their body, and a committee of that character they would send for the purpose expressed in the message. Accordingly, on the 6th of September, Benjamin Franklin, of Pennsylvania; John Adams, of Massachusetts, and Edward Rutledge, of South Carolina, were appointed as such committee. On the 14th they met Howe on Staten Island; the interview took place in the "Old Billop House," still standing. It had been occupied as a barrack for soldiers, and was in an exceedingly filthy condition; but one room had been cleaned and purified, and furniture placed therein, for the purpose of the meeting. Howe met the committee in a courteous manner, and at once proceeded to explain the nature of the power with which he had been invested, which were simply to extend the royal clemency and full pardon to all repentant rebels who would lay down their arms and return to their allegiance. The committee informed him that they were not authorized to entertain any propositions which did not recognize the political independence of the colonies. Howe replied that he had a great regard for the Americans as a people, but that recognition of their independence was a matter beyond his authority, and could not for a moment be entertained, and that their precipitancy was painful to him and perilous to themselves. Franklin answered that the people of America would endeavor to take good care of themselves, and thus alleviate as much as possible the pain his lordship might feel in consequence of any severities he might deem it his duty to adopt. This terminated the brief interview, and the committee rose to depart. Howe politely accompanied them to the shore, the party walking, both in coming and returning, between long lines of grenadiers, who, to use the language of Mr. Adams, "looked as fierce as ten furies, and making all the grimaces and gestures, and motions of their muskets, with bayonets fixed, which, I suppose, military etiquette requires, but which we neither understood nor regarded." On the way down, his lordship again expressed his regret that he was unable to regard them as public characters, to which Mr. Adams replied, "your lordship may consider me in what light you please, and indeed, I should be willing to consider myself for a few moments in any character which would be agreeable to your lordship, except that of a British subject." To this Howe replied, "Mr. Adams appears to be a decided character."

The consequence of this exhibition of Mr. Adam's independent and fearless spirit was subsequently apparent, when the list of unpardonable rebels was published, prominent among which was the name of John Adams. It must have been humiliating in the extreme to the pride and arrogance of the British government to be obliged to receive this proscribed rebel as the first minister plenipotentiary of the new government of the United States of America. The remark of Mr. Adams did not prevent Lord Howe continuing his courtesy, for he sent them over to Perth Amboy in his own barge. A native annalist,* speaking of this interview, says, "This momentous interview at the old Billop House, between the old world and the new, was an event regarded with extreme solicitude by the people of both at that day. With the developments of time, it rises into the grandeur of a great battle-point and monument of history. The interview was brief. There was no agreement, no reconciliation. Independence was maintained. The result was limned by the hand of God, and is seen in the progress of a continent and the achievements of a century all over the world."

When the British took possession of Staten Island, they immediately threw up strong intrenchments. Simcoe says: "In the distribution of quarters for the remaining winter, Richmond was allotted to the Queen's Rangers. This post was in the centre of the Island, and consisted of three bad redoubts, so contracted, at various times and in such a manner, as to be of little mutual assistance; the spaces between these redoubts had been occupied by the huts of the troops, wretchedly made of mud;" these Lieut. Col. Simcoe had thrown down, and his purpose was to build ranges of log houses, which might join the redoubts, and being loop-holed, might become a very defensible curtain. Other fortifications were erected in other parts of the Island—one at New

* Vide App. N. (8.)

Brighton, on the height now know at Fort Hill, which commanded the entrance to the Kills; another was built at the Narrows, near the site of the present national fortifications, and in several other places. Many remnants of British occupancy have been found in and around these old fortifications, such as cannon balls, bullets, gun locks, &c.

On the 21st of September, 1776, a great fire occured in New York; it begun on the wharf at the foot of Whitehall street, and was driven by a southeast wind towards the North river, consuming in its course the Lutheran Church and Trinity Church, and did not stop until it reached Mortlike street (now Barclay;) the number of buildings destroyed was 493.

Later in the autumn of this year, the British began to make predatory excursions from Staten Island into New Jersey along the Raritan, and these were continued through the war with various successes. Howe, having determined to make an effort to obtain possession of Philadelphia, left Clinton in command at New York, and began his march across New Jersey.

Washington was strongly entrenched at Morristown, and had made preparations to dispute Howe's passage across the State, whenever a fitting opportunity presented itself. Small detachments were sent out for the purpose of reconnoitering and annoying the British, while Howe resorted to various feints to draw Washington out, in all of which he failed. Thwarted in his purpose of crossing the State, the British general turned towards Amboy on his retreat to Staten Island, and committed terrible devastation on his way, which so exasperated the people that even his retreat became perilous. General Greene hung upon his rear, striking whenever opportunity permitted. On the 22d of June, 1777, the British general, having arrived at Amboy the day before, sent all his heavy baggage and other incumbrances, together with a part of his troops, over to Staten Island; but before he had time to transport the whole of his forces across the water, he received information that Washington had left his strong position, and was advancing to meet him. On the 25th, in consequence of this information, which, however, proved to be unfounded, he recalled all his forces, and on the morning of the 26th advanced from Amboy to meet the American army. He sent Cornwallis with a strong force to cut off a detachment of the Americans, under Lord Stirling and General Maxwell, who were advantageously posted on some high grounds, but who were obliged to abandon the advantages of their positions, being greatly outnumbered by the British. They did not retreat, however, until a severe skirmish had taken place.

Having by this time learned that the report of the advance of Washington was premature, and abandoning all hope of drawing him out of his intrenchments, Howe turned his face once more towards Staten Island.

Being foiled in his effort to reach Philadelphia by land, Sir William Howe resolved upon going thither by water. Accordingly he commenced the embarkation of his army on the 5th of July, but it was not until the 23d of that month that the fleet, consisting of 267 sail, passed Sandy Hook. His movements, after putting to sea, greatly perplexed Washington; if, as was reported, it was his intention to return and sail up the North river to the relief of Burgoyne, it was necessary that an effort should be made to prevent him; if, however, on the other hand, he was aiming at Philadelphia, it was necessary that he should be met in that direction. There was one of two opposite courses to be pursued, and it was not until he learned that the British fleet had attempted to pass up the Delaware, but had been prevented by obstructions to the navigation of that stream, and was then actually coming up the Chesapeake, that his perplexities were removed.

When Howe sailed for Philadelphia he left General Knyphausen in command at Staten Island.

In the early part of the year 1780, among the thousand reports which were rife throughout the country, and which reached his ear, was one that the American army in New Jersey was in a mutinous condition, and that the people of that State were desirous of returning to their allegiance to the British crown. To give the mutinous soldiers an opportunity for desertion, and the disaffected citizens the facilities for submission, Knyphausen determined to invade the State. Accordingly, on the 6th of June, he crossed over from Staten Island to Elizabethtown with an army of 5,000 men. From this place he marched towards Springfield by way of Connecticut Farms, where he halted. Before reaching that place, however, he discovered that the reports of disaffection among the people were entirely without foundation; instead of being received with open arms, as he had expected, the hostile demonstrations of the people were more decided than ever; out of every ditch, from every hedgerow, from behind every tree in orchard or forest, in the line of his march, he was met by "the leaden messengers of death." Though the people almost without exception did what they could to oppose his progress, they were not sufficiently numerous to combine and make a stand. The German general's disappointment was not only great, but he was exasperated to such a degree, that he caused the village, with its church, to be burned, before he attempted to retrace his steps. The minister's wife, who had remained at home, supposing that her sex would be her protection, was deliberately shot through a window; permission, however, was graciously given to remove the body before burning the house. This cold-blooded murder of Mrs. Caldwell produced a thrill of horror throughout the country, and no one act of British brutality more excited the indignation and hatred of the people towards their enemies, than this. Notwithstanding the weakness of Washington's army, preparations were hastily made to meet the invaders, and if possible, to drive them back, but their precipitated retreat prevented a battle.

The British affected to believe that it was was the désire of Washington to obtain possession of the post at Richmond, though what peculiar value either he or they attached to it in a military point of view, except that it commanded one of the entrances to the Island through the Fresh Kills, is not apparent. To give the rebels, as well as his own semi-barbarous Hessians, employment, Knyphausen sent out frequent expeditions from the Island into the Jerseys, where the most horrid atrocities were sometimes committed.

These were not usually sent forth on their errands of robbery and murder, unless they were known to be much superior in number to the patriots, who were likely to meet and oppose them, or had same other important advantage. These predatory excursions, however, were not confined to the British, the Americans, on their part, sadly annoyed their enemies by striking at them whenever the opportunity offered. The first of the hostile demonstrations on the part of the patriots occurred on the 17th day of October, 1776. General Hugh Mercer, who was in command of the American forces in that part of New Jersey contiguous to Staten Island, planned an attack upon the British entrenchments at Richmond; the forces sent on this expedition were under the command of Col. Griffin. They were so disposed as to make the attack upon all the available sides simultaneously. They succeeded in reaching the place before daylight, but the enemy had been informed of their approach; a skirmish ensued, which resulted in the retreat of the British, leaving two or three men dead, some wounded and dying, and seventeen prisoners in the hands of the Americans, beside a standard or two, and arms.

On the 8th of August, 1777, a party of Americans crossed the Kills and landed somewhere on the shore at West New Brighton, and directed their course for Richmond. As they approached that village, they were met by a party of British, who, after a slight resistance, retreated slowly until they reached St. Andrews Church, which they entered; the Americans fired at the windows until every pane of glass had been broken; they then approached, and fired through the broken windows until the British were driven out; a reinforcement from the vicinity of the quarantine had been hurried forward, who reached Richmond just as the church had been vacated. It was now the turn of the Americans to retreat, which they did by the Fresh Kill road, keeping the prisoners which they had taken in their rear. These consisted, not of soldiers only, but of citizens also, whom they had captured on their way; this prevented the British from firing, lest they should kill their own friends, or at least non-combatants. After the Americans had descended the hill and crossed the bridge at the locality now known as Laforge's Store, Westfield, they concealed themselves in a cornfield, where they waited until their pursuers were within reach, when they fired a volley at them, and the British colonel in command was killed. Continuing their retreat until they reached the shore of the Sound, they drove their prisoners, some thirty in number, into a large hog-sty, while they themselves seized what boats they required, and effected their escape. While they were crossing, the British reached the shore and opened upon them with their artillery, which they had not yet had opportunity for using, and killed several of them.*

Another blow was struck at the British on Staten Island by Lord Stirling in the winter of 1779, which was afterwards spoken of as "the hard winter." The Kills and the Sound were frozen over so that communication between the Island and the mainland was easy; the bay was also bridged with ice, but a passage for boats was kept open until the bitter cold closed that also. With about 2,000 men, the American commander crossed the Sound, designing to surprise "Skinner's New Corps," but the tories on the Island did not permit their friends to be surprised. Notice of the expedition was at once sent to the nearest post, and preparations were promptly made to meet the invaders. Tradition says that the Americans crossed at Elizabethtown, and marched along the shore to Port Richmond, where they were met by the British, and after a sharp skirmish, were driven back. An eye-witness said that a detachment of the Americans attempted to pass up the Mill Road, now known as

* Vide App. N. (34.)

Columbia Street, but the snow was so deep they were obliged to return.* This was the *invasion* alluded to in the old records, where Bedell and Micheau,† were paid "for powder delivered by Clonell Bilop's order, when the Island was inwaded."

The winter of 1779–'80 was remarkably severe; the waters surrounding the Island were firmly frozen over, so that troops, cannon and military stores of all descriptions were conveyed from New York to the Island on the ice. An old resident, now some years deceased, informed the writer that on one occasion during that winter he visited some of his relatives on Long Island; he entered his sleigh at his own door on Staten Island, and did not leave it until he reached his relative's door at New Lots, in Kings County.

Rivington's Gazette (New York) of that year has the following items:

Jan. 29, 1780. This day several persons came over on the ice from Staten Island.

Feb. 1. A four-horse sleigh came over on the ice from Staten Island.

* Vide App. N. (87.)   † Ibid. (28.)

CHAPTER XIV.

Lt. Col. Simcoe—His Adventures in New Jersey—His Capture—Negotiations for Peace—Was Washington ever on Staten Island ?—His Opinion of the People—Dwellings of the Hessians.

ONE of the most active of the British officers, and if his biographer is worthy of credit, one of the most bitter and relentless of the enemies of America, stationed upon Staten Island during the revolution, was Lieutenant-Colonel John Graves Simcoe. When the British army first took possession of Staten Island, a provincial corps, called "The Queen's Rangers," was then newly raised, and Simcoe solicited the command of it, but did not succeed in obtaining it until after the battle of Brandywine in October, 1777. He was then about 24 years of age. His biographer says, "he knew that common opinion had imprinted on the partisan the most dishonorable stain, and associated the idea with that of dishonesty, rapine and falsehood," and apologizes for his eagerness to obtain this command by saying that he considered it the best source of instruction, and a means of acquiring a habit of self-dependence for resources. To judge from his subsequent exploits, and the egregious misrepresentations of his "Journal," "common opinion" was justified in its estimate both of the corps and its commander. He began his career by publishing the following advertisement in *Rivington's Royal Gazette*, printed and published in New York.

"ALL ASPIRING HEROES
Have now an opportunity of distinguishing themselves by joining
THE QUEEN'S RANGERS,
Commanded by
LIEUTENANT COLONEL SIMCOE.

Any spirited young man will receive every encouragement, be immediately mounted on an elegant horse, and furnished with clothing,

accoutrements, etc., to the amount of FORTY GUINEAS, by applying to Cornet Spencer, at his quarters, No. 1033 Water Street, or his rendezvous, Hewitt's Tavern, near the Coffee House, and the defeat at Brandywine on Golden Hill. ☞ Whoever brings a Recruit, shall instantly receive Two GUINEAS.
Vivant Rex et Regina."

That such an officer, whose malignity was so often and so barbarously manifested wherever he served, should be lauded by British officers and writers, is not to be wondered at. The services of this corps were not confined to Staten Island and its vicinity—it followed in the wake of the British army when it went South, and partook of all its vicissitudes there. Sir Henry Clinton said of it, "the Queen's Rangers have killed or taken twice their own numbers," and adds, "they had not met with a single reverse," totally oblivious of its commander's capture and imprisonment by the Americans in New Jersey, and some other mishaps which befel him elsewhere. These assertions were made by Clinton in 1780; if he had delayed only one short year longer, he would have qualified, or totally omitted his extravagant laudations, for Lafayette, describing Simcoe's retreat in Virginia, says, "the whole British army came out to save Simcoe. They retired next morning when our army came within striking distance."

The general return of officers and privates surrendered prisoners of war on the 19th of October, 1781, the day of the surrender of Cornwallis, enumerates among the officers of the Queen's Rangers, one lieutenant colonel: this was Simcoe. He was the coadjutor of Colonel Billop in enforcing with great severity the regulations of the military police, while serving on Staten Island. In the "Journal" referred to above, mention is made of an armed vessel stationed at Billop's Point, which undoubtedly was the "gun-boat" so often alluded to in the old county records, and the maintaining of which was a charge upon the people of the county. The design of this vessel was to prevent intercourse between the people of the Island and those of New Jersey, a measure of great severity, when it is remembered that before the war there was a considerable commercial as well as social intercourse between the two places. Allusion is also made in the Journal to a gun-boat at Richmond, which is probably the same vessel stationed in the Fresh Kills under the protection of the fort on the heights near Ketchum's mill, when not in active service elsewhere. Simcoe desired to be furnished with two gun-boats, twenty batteaux, and a sloop, the batteaux to be mounted on wheels, that they might readily be conveyed from Richmond across land, to the south beach, with which he proposed to keep the patriot forces in a state of constant alarm from Sandy Hook to Newark Bay, and force Washington to give up the coast from Middletown to Brunswick, but the Commander-in-Chief did not appear to appreciate the value of the suggestion.

On the 22d of June, 1780, Simcoe and his Rangers were sent into New Jersey to join Knyphausen in an attack on the Americans, who were stationed beyond Elizabethtown. They crossed the Sound on a bridge of boats, and on the same day made an unsuccessful attack upon the Continentals. The next day they marched towards Springfield, where a small party of Americans were also temporarily stationed, and attempted to surround them; this was also a failure. After various marchings and counter-marchings, during which nothing of importance was achieved, they retired, and by the same bridge re-crossed the Sound to Staten Island.

There were numerous marauding expeditions sent from the Island into various parts of New Jersey, which were not led by Simcoe, but by other officers almost as savage and brutal in their treatment of such Americans as were so unfortunate as to fall into their hands.

Towards the end of October, 1780, there was a great excitement among the British on Staten Island, caused by a rumor that Lafayette had arrived in the vicinity of Elizabethtown with a large force, and furnished with boats on wheels, and that he meditated an attack upon the British posts on the Island. Every precaution was taken to prevent a surprise; the defences were all strengthened, and defects which they supposed would not be observed by the inexperienced and uneducated eyes of the American officers, but which the more cultivated observation of the French would readily detect, were repaired so far as time and means permitted. Simcoe marched his Rangers down from Richmond to Billop's Point toward the close of the day, in full view of the people on the opposite shore, to create the impression that an inroad into New Jersey was about to be made, and then marched them back again through the interior after dark. Reinforcements were sent from New York city, and Simcoe issued the following proclamation:

"The Lt. Colonel has received information that M. Lafayette, a Frenchman, at the head of some of his majesty's deluded subjects, has threatened to plant French colors on the Richmond redoubts. The Lt. Colonel believes the report to be a gasconade; but as the evident ruin of the enemy's affairs may prompt them to some desperate attempt, the Queen's Rangers will lay in their clothes this night, and have their bayonets in perfect good order."

He also had orders from the Commander-in-Chief to abandon his post, "if the enemy should land in such force as to make, in his opinion, the remaining there attended with risk." Nothing, however, came of this alarm..

The most serious of Simcoe's experiences, while stationed here, occurred in October of the previous year. A rumor had reached the British Commander-in-Chief, that preparations were being made to attack the city of New York; that fifty boats, each capable of holding seventy men, were on the way from the Delaware to Washington's army, and that they were all collected together at a certain point on the Raritan river. Simcoe proposed to go there and burn them, and Clinton approved the plan, and directed him to carry it into execution. He had, however, a wholesome dread of Lee's cavalry, who, he had heard, had recently been at Monmouth, and sent to Clinton for information concerning this corps. Clinton replied that, according to the last intelligence, Lee was no longer in that part of the country, nor were there any other troops in the way, except a few Jersey militiamen. Simcoe, however, knew that these were not to be despised, for they were partly composed of such refugees from Staten, Long and York Islands, as had been driven from their homes by the British; besides, he had before come in contact with these "virulent principled" characters, who had an execrable custom of attacking British foraging parties from their coverts, "and insulting their very outposts, and had thus acquired a great degree of self-confidence and activity." After obtaining the aid of one Sandford, a Jersey tory, captain of a troop on Long Island, who was supposed to be familiar with the topography of that part of the country, as a guide, and sending Major Armstrong to South River, where he was to ambuscade his troops, Simcoe started at eight o'clock in the evening from Richmond, and marched to Billop's Point. The boats which were to be at the Point at twelve o'clock to convey them over, did not arrive until three in the morning, when the crossing was effected. His plan was to reach the place where the American boats were said to be collected, burn them, and then return by way of New Brunswick, and thence to South Amboy, where Armstrong's ambuscade was to be placed, into which he proposed to lead the American forces who might follow him; but, in the event of any mishap, Armstrong was directed to give credit to any one who could give the countersign of "Clinton and Montrose." On their way they overtook a man named Crow, who said, upon being questioned why he was out so late, that he had "only been sparking;" the poor fellow was very communicative, believing that he had fallen in with a party of Americans. When they arrived at Quibbletown, a party of men with knapsacks came out of a tavern, whom the Rangers prepared to attack; but Simcoe, to carry out the delusion that they were a part of Washington's army, cried out, "These are not the tories we are in search of;" and the presence of Crow among them, who was well known, confirmed the people collected together in the idea that they were what they pretended to be. There was one man among the people, however, who was not so easily deceived; he knew Simcoe by sight, and as soon as the party had left, sent an express to Governor Livingston, then at New Brunswick.

The British were then guided by a boy, who believed Sandford to be a French officer, because he was dressed in red. This lad was anxious to communicate all he knew, which was not a great deal, but among that little was the unwelcome intelligence that all the boats except eighteen had been sent on to Washington's camp. This information proved to be correct. Simcoe proceeded at once to burn the boats, lamenting, however, that he had not arrived earlier, that he might have captured the whole of them, and taken them down the river; this he could not do now, as the people were collecting from all directions, and his situation was becoming hourly more perilous. Alarm guns were heard all over the country, and the people, who had already collected, fired at them as they passed, wounding several of the soldiers. Shots were also fired at them from the front, and fearful of an ambuscade, he attempted to lead his troops across some fields, and "found himself, when he recovered his senses, prisoner with the enemy, his horse having been killed with five bullets, and himself stunned by the violence of his fall."

In the haste of their retreat, some time elapsed before Simcoe's absence was discovered. A halt was immediately ordered, and the surgeon, Kellock, was sent back with a flag of truce to inquire for the missing officer. The Americans went forward in confidence to meet the flag, when Sandford, the Jersey tory, ordered a file of men to fire upon them, and Captain Voorheis, of the Continental army, was killed. The party thus treacherously attacked fell back, and the British were compelled to return without obtaining the information they had come to seek. When they reached South River where Armstrong had ambuscaded, the two parties united and returned to Staten Island.

Simcoe, at the time of his capture, had some narrow escapes; a boy was prevented from bayoneting him by being told that he was dead already;[*] a man declared he would

[*] Vide App. N (29.)

have shot him if he had known he was a colonel, but as he imagined that "all colonels wore lace," and this man wore none, he was deceived; the people were furious at the death of Captain Voorheis, who was a favorite with them, and loud threats were made to assassinate the captive. Simcoe's reputation had preceded him, and the people were inclined to balance accounts with him, and put it out of his power to do them any more mischief; the intervention of Governor Livingston alone saved him from the popular fury. He was immediately taken to prison, where he remained until the 31st day of December. Permission was given to his servant, and surgeon Kellock, to attend him, an indulgence which was persistently denied to American officers, prisoners with the British. On the 28th, he was permitted, on account of his health, to take up his abode in a tavern in Bordentown, on parole. This place, being on the opposite side of the State, and therefore at a distance from the scenes of his former incursions, the people were not so embittered against him, though his reputation had reached even there, and a few manifested their dislike to his presence among them, yet the majority conducted themselves towards him with forbearance, and sometimes with kindness.

When Colonel Christopher Billop was captured and committed to the jail of Burlington County, Simcoe was released from his parole, and taken to prison with him. The reason for this step will appear presently. The mittimus of Elias Boudinot, Commissary of Prisoners, which will be found in another place, commanded Billop to be ironed, chained down to the floor, and fed on bread and water; the same treatment was ordered for Simcoe. The Commissary expressed his regret that he was compelled to resort to such severe measures, and advised Billop to write to New York to procure a relaxation of the sufferings of two American officers confined there by the British, and concluded by saying, "It seems nothing short of retaliation will teach Britons to act like men of humanity." This was the reason why Billop was dealt with so severely, and one of the reasons why the same treatment was meted out to Simcoe. Another reason is given in a letter from Governor Livingston, to whom he had written for permission to go to Staten Island on parole, to effect the exchange of Billop and himself. The Governor says, "Your counteracting the express terms of your parole at Bordentown, and your having been heard to say that whenever you should apprehend yourself in danger of being insulted by the people, you should think yourself at liberty to effect your escape (of which danger you doubtless intended to be the judge,) not to mention that your present situation is your best security against all popular violence, in case there were any grounds for such apprehension," and this extract gives the other reason for the severity with which he was treated. In reply to an inquiry in Simcoe's letter, the Governor further says: "To your question whether private resentment is harbored against you, 1 answer, sir, public bodies are not actuated by private resentment, but the actions of individuals of a public nature, such as cruelty to prisoners, may nevertheless properly occasion towards such individuals a line of conduct very different from what is observed towards those of an opposite character, and this with as little color for complaining of personal resentment, as of the civil magistrate's punishing a public offender; but as no such charge has been proved (though many have been alleged against you,) I have no reason to think that such reports have influenced this government in the measures hitherto directed concerning you."

Simcoe, in his reply to the Governor, assumes a deal of indignation, and says, "You cannot *force* yourself to believe, sir, that I ever harbored a thought of violating my parole," and at the close of his letter, remarks—and the Governor must have smiled when he read it—"cruelty is contrary to my nature, my education, and my obedience to my orders."

He continued to write to the Governor, who probably became weary of his importunities, and at length ceased to reply. He then addressed himself to General Washington, who also made no reply, but he probably did what was better; an exchange was effected, and Billop and Simcoe were both released. Several plans were contrived by the friends of the two prisoners to effect their release, but they were all thwarted in various ways.

After the arrest and confinement of Major Andre, Simcoe offered his services and that of his Rangers to the Commander-in-Chief, to effect his release, but his offer was not accepted. He termed the execution of Andre a "useless murder."

We have now done with Simcoe in connection with Staten Island and the war of the revolution. In consideration of his valuable services, his government, after the war, rewarded him with the appointment of governor of Upper Canada, where he continued to manifest his hostility towards the United States by tampering with the Indians, a disposition which was probably considered a qualification for the office.

On the 19th of October, 1781, Cornwallis capitulated at Yorktown; this virtually terminated the war. Both countries were weary of it. The people of Great Britain complained bitterly of the expenses of the war, which were annually increasing; they had been encouraged to bear these, sustained by the hope of ultimate reimbursement by the exclusive trade of the subjugated colonies. The campaign in Virginia was regarded by both parties as probably the last of the struggle; the English knew that the resources of America were well nigh exhausted, and the Americans were well informed of the discontent prevailing in England, and the apprehensions of the government of a revolution at home; therefore each party regarded the campaign of 1781 as the decisive. When the capitulation took place, it produced the most unbounded joy in America, but consternation in England. The government, it is true, were making preparations for carrying on the war with renewed energy, but the popular feeling was strongly in favor of its discontinuance; public meetings were held in various places, attended with demonstrations which it would have been imprudent to disregard, and towards the close of February, measures were introduced into Parliament which eventually resulted in peace. In the interim, however, both army organizations were maintained, though both remained passive; "there was no war, there was no peace." The soldiers of both armies, having nothing else to occupy them, organized predatory expeditions in the neighborhood where they happened to be stationed.

In this respect, Staten Island was peculiarly unfortunate. Occupied by a hostile army, the people of the Island were preyed upon by desperadoes living in their midst, while the patriots on the opposite side of the Sound regarded them as tories, and therefore legitimate objects of plunder. They were thus, as it were, placed between two fires, and powerless to defend themselves against either.

Was General Washington ever on Staten Island? The only evidence of the fact which is attainable at this day is contained in the extract from his carefully kept accounts with the government of the United States, which we here present.

"1776.
Ap^l. 25th, To the Exp^s of myself and party reco^g the sev^l landing places on Staten Island............ £16 10 0."

It may be said that the reconnoitering, which is almost unintelligibly abbreviated in the original account, might have been done on the water, and quite as efficiently as on the land. The following objections, however, exist to this view of the subject:

First.—The object of Washington was to erect fortifications and other defences on the most eligible sites, as the British did when they took possession on the following July; and some parts of the shores—perhaps the most important—could not be examined with such an object in view, from any position attainable on the water.

Second.—The Commander-in-Chief expresses himself in the above extracts, in terms similar to those used in other parts of his accounts for similar services in places not accessible by water, and

Third.—There were two or three British vessels-of-war lying near the Island, on one of which Governor Tryon had taken up his quarters, and from which he kept up an intercourse with royalists on the Island, and a reconnoitering of the shores by water would not have been permitted, to say nothing of the danger of capture.

Washington was as prompt to perceive the natural advantages of Staten Island in a military point of view as were the British. Within a week after his personal visit to the city, he established a look-out at the Narrows, which, when the British made their appearance, sent a message by express that forty of the enemy's vessels were in sight. This information was at once forwarded to the several posts on the Hudson, with instructions to prepare to give them a warm reception if they should attempt to ascend the river. But the ships, upon their arrival, anchored off Staten Island, and landed their troops, and the hill sides were soon covered with their white tents. Military works were at once erected upon every available point, thus intimating their intention of taking a permanent possession.

The opinion which Washington had formed of the people of Staten Island, as well as of their immediate neighbors at Amboy, may be learned from the following extract from one of his letters:

"The known disaffection of the people of Amboy, and the treachery of those of Staten Island, who, after the fairest professions, have shown themselves our inveterate enemies, have induced me to give directions that all persons of known enmity and doubtful character should be removed from these places."

After the British had entrenched themselves upon Staten Island, several expeditions were planned against them by the patriots, some of which were carried out with various degrees of success, as has elsewhere been stated, but others died almost in their inception. Of these latter the following was the most daring. One Ephraim Anderson contrived a plan for destroying the enemy's fleet in the harbor by means of fire ships, the effort to be seconded by a descent upon the British forces stationed upon the Island. General Putnam approved of the proposed attempt, and communicated the particulars in a letter to General Gates. The scheme was not carried into effect, because time failed to construct the number of vessels which were deemed necessary to its success. Several night attacks were also planned, but which for various reasons were never made.

There is tradition that an attempt was made by a small party of patriots from New Jersey, to land at night, upon the Island, in the small cove on the shores of the Kills, immediately west of the Pelton house; they were met, however, by a party of British, and a skirmish ensued, during which a General Skinner* was either killed or mortally wounded.

The enemy's forces on the Island, both native and foreign, were exceedingly troublesome to the people of New Jersey. John Jay, in writing to Gov. Morris, said that if he had been invested with the power, he would have desolated all Long Island, Staten Island and New York, and withdrawn the Continental troops into the interior, and thus rendered the occupation of these places by the British of no advantage to them.

As late as 1832 the remains of some of the dwelling places of the Hessian soldiers were still distinctly to be seen along the Richmond Road, at the foot of the hill in the rear of Stapleton. These consisted of excavations in the side of the hill, eight or ten feet square, covered with planks of pieces of timber, upon which earth or sods had been placed to form roofs; the fronts had been boarded up, and probably the sides. How they had been warmed in winter, or whether they had been warmed at all, was not apparent. They must have been miserably dark, damp caves, but probably, in the opinion of their English masters, good enough for Dutch mercenaries.

* Vide App. N. (30.)

CHAPTER XV.

Capt. Hyler's Adventures—Nathaniel Robbins—The Prall families robbed—Futile attempt to rob John Bodine—Insolent conduct of two British officers—A soldier scalded with boiling soap—Soldiers stabbed with hay forks—Attempt to kidnap a young lady frustrated—Instance of prompt decision—Soldier shot by a boy—Attempt to rob a farmer of his horse—Burglars discovered by means of a button—Evacuation of the Island—An eye-witness' account of it.

THE *New Jersey Gazette* of Sept. 25th, 1782, contains the following obituary notice: "Died Sept. 6, 1782, after a tedious and painful illness, which he bore with a great deal of fortitude, the brave Capt. Adam Hyler, of New Brunswick. His many enterprising acts in annoying and distressing the enemy endeared him to the patriotic part of his acquaintance. His remains were decently interred, with a display of the honors of war, in the Dutch burial ground, attended by a very numerous concourse of his acquaintances." We learn, further, from *Rivington's Royal Gazette*, that "Hyler died of a wound in the knee, accidentally given by himself some time ago."

This Capt. Adam Hyler was an active partisan in and about that part of New Jersey where he resided. As his expeditions against the enemy were chiefly conducted by water, and in small boats, it is probable that he held his title of Captain by courtesy, and not by commission. The following are some of his exploits, as related in the papers of that period.

In April, 1781, two rebel whale boats, one commanded by Hyler, the other by Dickie, attacked and captured a sloop from New York; after plundering the vessel of goods of considerable value, she was ransomed for 500 hard dollars. This took place off Coney Island.

On Sunday night, the 15th of the same month, just one

week after the capture of the sloop, Hyler went over to Gowanus, L. I., and brought off a Hessian Major and Ensign, with their servants. They were in the centre of two picket guards, yet the address of Hyler was such that the guards were not alarmed till he was out of their power. The prisoners were carried safely into New Jersey.

During a Saturday night in May, of the same year, Hyler captured a pilot boat and two other boats between Robin's Reef* and Yellow Hook with a single whale boat. The pilot boat was plundered of valuable articles, and then redeemed for four hundred dollars.

On a Thursday night in June, of the same year, the house of Nicholas Schenck, three miles south of Flatbush, was surprised by the crews of two rebel whale boats. The family were at supper, and not prepared to make resistance. They wounded a man named Bogart with a bayonet, and took what valuables he had on his person; they then relieved the family of the plate they could find, and decamped.

About the same time Hyler entered a house at Canarsie, where a sergeant's guard were at supper, seized their arms, which were standing in the hall, borrowed their silver spoons, and sent the guards to report themselves to their officer.

In August of the same year, Hyler, with his companions went three and a half miles into the country on Long Island, and captured Colonel Jerome Lott, who was notorious for his cruelty to American prisoners. They also secured about £600 in cash, and a bag supposed to contain guineas. On their passage up the Raritan, the bag was opened for the purpose of dividing the contents, and found to contain only half pennies, being the church collections. The Colonel was obliged to ransom his negroes, two of whom had also been taken, and he was then released on his parole.

In January, 1782, a party of infantry from Staten Island in six boats went up the Raritan to New Brunswick, and before daylight succeeded in capturing all Hyler's boats. In less

---

* Vide App. N. (31.)

than a month thereafter Hyler launched a large new boat built for 30 oars.

The following, taken from a paper published in New York, in the interests of the royalists, is another instance of the enterprise and indomitable resolution of Hyler. The date is July 15, 1782.

"Last Tuesday night Mr. Hyler took 2 fishing boats near the Narrows, and ransomed them for $100 each. One of them has been twice captured."

The same day "a little before sunset, Mr. Hyler, with 3 large 24-oared boats, made an attack on the galley stationed at Prince's Bay, south side of Staten Island. There being little or no wind, he came up with a good deal of resolution, but Capt. Cashman gave him an 18-pounder, which went through the stern of one of the boats, and obliged Hyler to put ashore on the Island, where, after a smart combat, he was obliged to leave one of his boats and make the best of his way home with the other two."

"John Althouse, with 12 men, was on board a guard-boat at anchor in Prince's Bay, when two whale-boats were descried under South Amboy shore. It was calm. The cable was sprung and a 24-pounder brought to bear, which sent a shot through Hyler's boat. His crew were taken in the other boat, (Dickey's,) and all made off for New Brunswick with Gen. Jacob S. Jackson, whom they had captured in South Bay, and kept prisoner till he was ransomed."

The mantle of Capt. Hyler appears to have fallen on other shoulders after his death. The *New Jersey Gazette* of November 13, 1782, says: "The brave Capt. Storer, commissioned as a private boat-of-war, under the States, and who promises fair to be the genuine successor of the late valiant Cayt. Hyler, has given a recent instance of his valor and conduct in capturing one of the enemy's vessels, and in cutting out a vessel lying under the flag-staff and within half pistol shot of the battery of 14 guns, at the watering-place, Staten Island."

Numerous instances of suffering are preserved in the traditions of some of the old families of the Island. There was one man of local notoriety whose name is still remembered and mentioned by the descendants of those whose misfortune it was to suffer at his hands; his name was Nathaniel Robbins; he resided at what is now known as New Springville, but the house which he occupied was demolished many years ago. It stood near the corner of the roads leading to Richmond and Port Richmond, fronting on the former, but several rods therefrom. He was an Englishman by birth, dissolute in his habits, and the terror not only of those who dwelt in his neighborhood, but of the whole county. His wife was a native of Staten Island, and a daughter of the widow Mary Merrill. The opinion which his wife's mother entertained of him, may be inferred from a clause in her will, which was dated January, 10th, 1789, and in which she bequeaths to her daughter Mary Robbins the sum of £40, "so as never to be in the power or at the command of Nathaniel Robbins, her present husband." His depredations were generally committed under some disguise, which he supposed effectually concealed his identity, though he was often betrayed by his voice or some circumstance, which rendered his identity a moral if not an absolute certainty. He had his associates, who were also well known, some of whose names might be mentioned but for the respectability of their descendants, but Robbins was regarded as the leader and soul of the gang.

Those families residing near the Sound, or "the lines," as it was called, suffered more from marauders than those who dwelt in the interior, because the opportunities for escape were more convenient. As part of the local history of the Island, though authenticated chiefly by family traditions, but not therefore the less reliable, several instances are subjoined.

At or near Chelsea dwelt several families of the name of Prall, some of whose descendants are among the most respectable of our citizens at the present day. Among them were two brothers, Abraham and Peter, both prosperous farmers and men of substance. The house in which the former resided is still standing, though considerably modernized, on the Chelsea road, at no great distance from the Richmond Turnpike. The Chelsea road at that time was little better than a private lane leading to these residences from the main road, and passing through dense woods. On one occasion a man who was indebted to him called upon him and paid him a considerable sum in gold. The next evening the family were surprised by the approach of two men, who were evidently disguised; their errand was at once suspected, and the old man had just time enough to take the money he had received out of the cupboard in which he had deposited it, and put it into his pockets. When the strangers entered, one of them presented a pistol at him, and said, "Prall, we know you have money, so deliver it up at once." He was very much alarmed, and his wife, perceiving his agitation, said, "Father, don't be alarmed, these men are our neighbors." She had detected the speaker by his voice, and knew him to be the same person who had paid the money the previous evening, and had seen it deposited in the cupboard. "Do you suppose," said the old man, "that I am so unwise as to keep any large sum of money in my house in times like these? You are welcome to any money you may find in the house." They took him at his word, and the cupboard was the first place visited; the rest of the house was also searched, but without success. They then turned to go, but directed the old man to go before them through the lane to the public road. The path through the woods was intensely dark, and he managed, as he went along, to drop his guineas, one by one, upon the ground, until by the time they had reached the highway he had none remaining in his pockets. Here another effort was made to compel him to tell them what he had done with it, but all the reply they could extort from him was, "the money I had in my house yesterday is not now in my possession." He was then searched, and he was made to solemnly swear that he would never divulge the circumstances of their visit, nor mention any names he might suspect.

This oath, though by no means obligatory, he scrupulously kept. The next morning he retraced his steps of the previous night, and recovered every piece of his money.

A younger member of one of these families, while on his way homeward, at a late hour, on horseback, when near the corner of the Port Richmond and Signs roads, New Springville, was suddenly stopped by a man, who rushed out of his concealment in the bushes, seized his horse by the bridle, and ordered him to "deliver up." The horse was very spirited, and with a touch of the rider's spur suddenly sprang forward, throwing his assailant violently to the ground. Then, at the utmost of his speed, he made for home, springing over every fence or other obstacle, until he reached his stable door in safety.

At another time, two of these young men, each one of whom owned a horse, put their horses together in a team, and took a sleigh ride to visit some of their relatives on the south side of the Island. When they returned, and before removing the harness from their beasts, they ran into the house for a moment to warm their hands, the weather being intensely cold. They were scarcely seated at the fire when one of the females of the family came running into the room, and informed them that somebody was taking their horses away. Rushing out together, they saw two men in their sleigh driving rapidly in the direction of the Sound. Pursuit was useless; they stood still, and saw them crossing the Sound on the ice, until they reached the Jersey shore, and then disappeared in the country. They never saw their horses after.

Mr. John Bodine* having received a considerable sum of money, suspected that the fact was known, and if so, that an attempt would be made to rob him; he therefore buried it under the step-stone at his back door. His suspicions proved to be well founded; his expected visitors made their appearance the following evening, and demanded all the money he had in the house. It was in vain that he protested there was

* Vide App. N. (32.)

no money in the house; they insisted upon searching for it, but before doing so, bound him hand and foot, and then proceeded with their villainous work. Nothing, however, was found. But they were not discouraged; if the money was not in the house, he had concealed it, and must reveal the place. He concluded that if prevarication was ever justifiable, it was under just such circumstances as those in which he was then placed, so he persisted in his denial of having any, or having concealed any. They threatened to shoot him; he told them to shoot away, he could not give them what he had not. Perceiving that the fear of death did not intimidate him, they resorted to torture; they heated a shovel, and proceeded to burn him on various parts of his body, but all in vain, he persisted in his denial, and they finally desisted, supposing it to be improbable if not impossible for any man to endure so much agony for any amount of money.

It was not money only that satisfied the rapacity of these thieves; household furniture, clothing, linen, anything that had value in their eyes, was ruthlessly carried away. One family had a vault constructed under the flooring of a cider-mill, in which beds, bedding and other articles, except some of the most common description, and in constant use, were concealed. Several years after the war a man who resided near "the lines," being on business in New Jersey, discovered in one house a mirror and several pictures belonging to himself, and of which his house had been robbed.

We are indebted for the following incident to a man who died more than a quarter of a century ago, then in his ninetieth year.

One afternoon, late in the fall, two British officers on horseback rode into his barn-yard, and having dismounted, entered the barn, and perceiving his two horses in their stalls, peremptorily ordered him to take them out and put theirs in. They then directed him to see that their beasts were well fed and otherwise cared for. From the barn they went into the house, and ordered the mistress to show them her best room; this was done; then they proceeded to the upper part of the house, and after having examined every apartment, selected one, and directed her to prepare two beds in that room, and to see to it that they were clean and comfortable in all respects, and that the best room was furnished with everything suitable for the accommodation of gentlemen. They then descended into the cellar, and examined the family stores there, and in the out-houses. Having ascertained the conveniences of the place, they ordered their supper to be prepared and served in the best room, informing her that they intended to reside there for some time, and expected to have their meals served regularly every day when they were at home. They brought no luggage with them except what was contained in two large valises strapped to their saddles.

They remained in that house until Spring. Their clothes were thrown out every week to be washed, and by their order a supply of fire-wood was constantly ready at their door; they did not always take the trouble to put the wood upon their own fire, frequently calling upon some one of the family to do it for them. One of them was a tory officer from Amboy, the other was an Englishman. Said the old man, "they lorded it over our house for that whole winter, and all we had to do was to obey them; there was no use in complaining or remonstrating; if we had done so, we should have been requited with a curse and a blow of their swords. I felt like poisoning them, and verily believe I should have done so, if it had not been for fear of the consequences. They left us as unceremoniously as they came, without even a 'thank you' or a 'good bye.'"

It is related of a young woman, the daughter of a farmer residing in the vicinity of the Fresh Kills, while engaged one morning in boiling soap, two soldiers entered the kitchen and ordered her to prepare breakfast for them; she declined to do so, as she was otherwise engaged, and could not leave her employment to oblige anybody. This reply excited their wrath, and one of them approached her with an intention of striking her. Seizing a large dipper, she filled it with the boiling liquid and dashed it at him; perceiving her intention, he wheeled suddenly around and thus saved his face, but received the whole charge upon the back of his head and neck. His companion, fearing a similar reception, escaped as quickly as possible, but the scalded ruffian, in endeavoring to remove the hot soap, took all the hair off with it, which never grew again, and left the back half of his head bald ever after.

Another farmer in the same vicinity, while he and one of his sons were engaged in the barn one morning, were suddenly alarmed by a shriek and a cry for help from the house. Each seizing a hayfork, they ran in and found three soldiers in the house, one of whom was holding one of the young women of the family by the arm. They both rushed at him, first one stabbed him in the shoulder, and the other in the thigh, disabling him at once. With the same weapons they attacked the other two, driving them all before them out of the house, and pursuing them for some distance down the road; they escaped, however, without further injury, by superior speed.

The following romantic incident, though traditional, is well authenticated:

Thirty years ago, perhaps more, there stood an old stone house nearly on the site now occupied by the residence of Capt. R. Christopher, in West New Brighton. For many years before it was demolished it was owned and occupied by the late Nathaniel Britton, Jr., but the name of the occupant during the early years of the revolution had entirely escaped the memory of the narrator; he was, however, a prominent tory, and the father of a daughter said to have possessed more than an ordinary degree of personal attractions; before the commencement of the war she was affianced to a young man named Mersereau, who resided at Holland's Hook, or its vicinity. A young British lieutenant had seen and admired her, and, probably from the outset, had marked her for a victim. He had succeeded in becoming acquainted with her, and, to the gratification of her father, became very assiduous in his attentions. She, however, repulsed his advances. After several months' efforts, finding he had utterly failed in impressing her with a sense of the honor of his alliance, he resolved to possess himself of her person at all hazards. The same young tory who attempted to betray Col. Mersereau's presence with his family, and who, it would appear, was somewhat noted for his unscrupulosity, and who, for a suitable reward, was ready to lend himself to the perpetration of any outrage which did not actually imperil his own precious life, was applied to by the lieutenant. The plot concocted between them will develop itself as the narrative progresses. Almost directly opposite the junction of the road from Garrison's Station, on the Staten Island Railroad, with the old Richmond Road, (or the King's Highway, as it was called in colonial times,) is a deep ravine, penetrating some distance into Toad Hill, at the farthest extremity of which is a spring of water, near which, before the war commenced, a solitary individual had built himself a rude hut or cabin, in which he dwelt for several years a veritable anchorite. When hostilities began, he disappeared, but the cabin still remained. The approach to it was by a foot-path through the dense forest which lined the hills on either side of the ravine. One evening the young tory called at the residence of the young lady, and informed her that he had been sent to convey her to the residence of her aunt, near Richmond, who had been taken suddenly ill, and had requested her attendance. Suspecting no evil, and being much attached to her relative, she was, soon ready to accompany him. Springing into the wagon which he had brought, she was rapidly driven away. When they reached the entrance to the ravine, two men rushed out of the bushes, seized the horse by the bridle, and ordered the occupants of the wagon to alight. One of them pretended to take possession of the driver, while the other led the young lady up the foot-path into the ravine, cautioning her that her safety depended upon her silence. So far the plot had been carried out successfully, but there was an avenger nearer than they suspected; they had taken but a few steps in the direction of the cabin, when several men rushed out of the bushes and seized the lieutenant, for it was he who had possession of the lady. One of them took her hand, assuring her that they were her protectors, and that she need be under no apprehensions. Though they were all disguised, she at once recognized Mersereau by his voice. Those who had possession of the lieutenant proceeded to tie his hands, informing him that they intended to do him no further harm than the infliction of a severe flogging; and if he attempted to cry out, they would gag him. A bundle of supple rods was at hand, and two of them, one after the other, inflicted the chastisement which they had promised. Having punished him to their hearts' content, they released him, with the warning that if, after the expiration of a week, he was found upon the Island, they would capture him again and cut off his ears. The young lady was safely returned to her home by the same conveyance, but not the same driver, for he had, by some means, disappeared. The lieutenant also saved his ears by his absence before the week expired. How the villainous plot was discovered was never positively known, but it was shrewdly suspected that the young tory had played into the hands of both parties, and for a consideration had betrayed his military employer. The horse and wagon remained in the possession of Mersereau unclaimed for several weeks, but was finally stolen one night, and never heard of after.

There is an instance of extraordinary self-possession and prompt decision related of a young man named Housman, which probably saved his life. He resided in the vicinity of the Four Corners, and one morning, after a slight fall of snow during the night, he went out with his gun in quest of rabbits. Though the people of the Island, during its occupancy by the British, were prohibited from keeping firearms of any description in their houses, some few had succeeded in concealing guns, which, from the associations connected with them, or from some other reasons, were valuable to them; such was the gun carried by young Housman on this occasion. While tramping through the woods, a sudden turn in the path brought him in sight of two soldiers, who were out, probably, on the same errand. They saw each other simultaneously, and each party stopped. The young hunter thought of the loss of his gun, and probably of his life also, but suddenly turning his back to the soldiers, he waved his hand as if beckoning to some other persons as he stepped back round the turn, and shouted out, "Hurry up, here are two Britishers; three of you go round to the right, and three to the left, and the rest of you follow me; hurry up, before they run away." What the "Britishers" had to fear we know not, but hearing these directions, and fearing there might be a small army about to surround them, turned and fled, throwing away their arms to facilitate their flight. What report they made when they reached their quarters is not known, but a detachment was sent out to capture the young man and his army. Their surprise and mortification must have been extreme, when at the turn in the path they could only find the tracks of a single individual in the snow.

This same Housman, in after years, conceived the idea that there was great mineral wealth in the hills about the Four Corners, and with the aid of a negro commenced mining operations in the side of the hill, in what is called "Dongan's wood," now the property of Cornelius Dubois, Esq. The excavation which he made in the solid rock in search of gold, may be seen at the present day.

A farmer whose name has passed into oblivion, residing "in the Clove," was called from home late one day to visit a near relative in some other part of the Island, who had been taken suddenly ill, leaving his wife and only child, a lad of seventeen or thereabouts, alone at home. It was after dark before the boy completed his work about the barn, but just as he was coming out he saw a soldier enter the house with a musket in his hand. Before he had time to reach the house, he heard his mother shrieking for help; he rushed forward, and as he entered he saw the soldier holding his mother by the throat with his left hand, while his right was drawn back to strike her. When he entered, the soldier had placed his musket by the side of the door in the passage;

the son seized it, and at the imminent risk of shooting his mother, levelled it at the ruffian's head, and sent the ball crashing through his brain; of course he was killed on the spot. But here was a dilemma; if the shot had been heard, and should attract any person to the spot, an exposure must necessarily follow, and the lad would have been executed, for no circumstances would have been admitted as a justification for killing a soldier. Fortunately, however, the noise had not been heard, or at least had attracted no attention. All that could now be done was to conceal the body until the return of the husband and father in the morning; this was done by dragging it under the stairs, where it was not likely to be seen by any person but themselves. The next morning, when the farmer returned, and had learned what had taken place in his absence, he also became alarmed, but while his wife and son kept watch, he removed a part of his barn floor under which he dug a grave, and after dark the evening after, the body was thrown into it, and the musket also, and buried, and there they probably remain to this day. The family kept their own secret until after the close of the war, and the evacuation of the Island by the British.

A man named Cole, residing in Southfield, was the proprietor of a remarkably fine gray horse. Several of the officers of the army had offered to purchase him, but he declined to part with him at any price. He had before sold a horse to an officer, who had promised to pay for him within two months, but two years had passed, and the debt was not yet discharged. At another time a Hessian officer, who had been quartered upon him for a short time, when he left, forcibly took away another horse, and Cole had repeatedly vowed that no other officer should have another horse of his unless he stole him; he would shoot him first,—the horse, not the officer. Early, one bright winter evening, he heard a commotion in his stable, and, always on the alert, he thrust two pistols in his pockets and hastened out. At the stable door he saw two soldiers attempting to put a halter upon the head of his favorite horse. "Hi, there," he cried, "what are you going to do with that horse?" "Going to take him away," replied one of them; "Colonel —— wants him, and sent us to get him." "Well," said Cole, "you just make up you minds that neither you nor the Colonel shall take that horse away without my consent." "Stand aside, you d—d rebel," said one them, as Cole attempted to take the horse from them, at the same time pointing a bayonet at him, "or I'll make a hole through your heart." Without further reply, he drew one of his pistols and shot the horse through the head; "there, you infernal thieves," he exclaimed as he threw the pistol down, "now you may take him." For a moment the soldiers were amazed as they gazed upon the struggles of the dying animal, but soon recovering themselves, they prepared to rush upon him with their bayonets, when Cole, presenting the other pistol, exclaimed, "Come on, you thieves and robbers, with your bayonets, and I'll drop one of you at least." The soldiers considering discretion, in this instance, the better part of valor, turned and walked away, threatening him with the vengeance of the Colonel. "Go tell your master," said Cole, as he followed them to the gate, "that I'll serve him, or you, or any other thief who comes upon my premises at night to steal my property, as I served that horse."

The majority of the English, of all ranks, regarded the colonists as physically, intellectually and morally inferior to themselves; in their social intercourse with them they made but little distinction between loyalists and rebels, and, in plundering, none whatever. But there were exceptions; among the officers of the British army, were some who were gentlemen by nature and by culture, and a few were eminently pious men, who found no difficulty in reconciling their obligations to their king with their duty to their Maker; these two latter classes were ever ready to listen to the complaints of the oppressed, and, as far as laid in their power, to redress the wrongs of the injured.

Of this class was Captain John Voke,* of whom the fol-

* Vide App. N. (88.)

lowing anecdote has been preserved. He was billeted upon a farmer in the vicinity of Richmond for some two or three months, and, unlike many other officers, regularly paid for his board and lodging. A few days after he had removed his quarters, the farmer came to him and informed him that during the previous night his house had been entered and robbed of a sum of money, and that he suspected that it had been done by soldiers, because beneath the window through which the house had been entered, and which had been left open, he had found a button, by means of which, perhaps, the culprits might be detected. The Captain took the button and promised to give the matter his immediate attention. The button indicated the regiment as well as the company to which the loser of it belonged. During the parade that same day, he closely scrutinized the company indicated, and found a soldier with a button missing on the front of his coat. After parade he communicated his suspicions to the colonel of the regiment, and the soldier was sent for. When he had arrived, the colonel, using a little artifice, informed him that he suspected him of being implicated in a drunken brawl the night before at a tavern a mile or two distant. This the soldier denied, saying that he could prove he was nowhere near that tavern, or even in that direction, during the night previous. "Were you out last night?" inquired the colonel; "Well—yes," answered the soldier, "but not in that direction. "Where were you?" "In various places, but not at that tavern." "By whom can you prove that you were not at that tavern?" The name of another soldier was mentioned, and the colonel sent for him. When he arrived, he corroborated all that the first soldier had said, adding that they two had been together all the night. "Then," said the colonel, "you two are the burglars who entered the house of Mr. ——— through a window last night, and robbed him of twenty guineas; lay down the money upon this table, or you shall both be executed for burglary and robbery." The affrighted soldiers, taken by surprise, confessed their crime, and each placed ten guineas upon the table. What punishment was meted out to the culprits is not related, but Captain Voke had the satisfaction of returning the money to the owner thereof in less than twenty-four hours after it had been stolen.

On the 25th day of November, 1783, the British finally evacuated New York and Staten Island. Eight years before, they had entered the country with the expectation that, in less than as many months, they would overrun it from North to South, and trample out the rebellion. The people should be made to bow with abject submission before the invincible power of Great Britain, and humbly sue for the privilege of lying in the dust and having her foot placed upon their necks. The march of the army through the land, from its beginning to its end, was to be an uninterrupted triumph. But they now returned overcome and crestfallen; the rebellion which they came to conquer, had conquered them, and their overweening arrogance and pride had received a blow such as it had never received before, nor since. An eye-witness of their departure described the scene as in the highest degree impressive. Several days before the 25th had been occupied in conveying the troops, cannon, tents, etc., from the land to the vessels, both in New York and on Staten Island. When all was ready, they passed through the Narrows silently; not a sound was heard save the ratling of the cordage. "We stood," he said, "on the heights at the Narrows, and looked down upon the decks of their ships as they passed; we were very boisterous in our demonstrations of joy; we shouted, we clapped our hands, we waved our hats, we sprang into the air, and some few, who had brought muskets with them, fired a *feu-de-joie*; a few others, in the exuberance of their gladness, indulged in gestures, which though very expressive, were neither polite nor judicious. The British could not look upon the scene without making some demonstration of resentment. A large seventy-four, as she was passing, fired a shot which struck the bank a few feet beneath the spot upon which we were standing. If we had had a cannon, we would have returned it, but as we had none, we ran away as fast as we could. A few rods from us stood another group, composed of men and women, who gazed silently, and some tearfully, upon the passing ships, for some of the females had lovers, and some husbands on board of them, who were leaving them behind, never, probably, to see them again. It was long after dark when the last ship passed through the Narrows."

But they did not all go ; many of the soldiers, especially Hessians, who had no home attractions across the water, when they learned that peace had been declared, and that the army would shortly leave the country, deserted, and sought places of concealment, from which they emerged when the power to arrest them had departed. Many had formed attachments which they were unwilling to sunder. But many more were detained by admiration of the country, and a desire to make for themselves a new home in a new world. From some of these have descended men whose names are written in the country's history.

In proportion to its population, Perth Amboy contained more tories than any other place within the limits of the State of New Jersey. Many of these enlisted in the regiment known as the Queen's Rangers, and in the several companies composing Col. Billop's regiment. We have been able to obtain the names of but two of the captains of these companies, viz.: Abraham Jones, a native Staten Islander, and David Alston, an Englishman or Scotchman by birth, but for years before the war a resident of New Jersey, in the vicinity of Rahway, and, after the war, of Staten Island.* Many of the British officers, in all parts of the country, remained after the cessation of hostilities, but many more of the rank and file ; this was so particularly on Staten Island, and many of the families now residing here are the descendants of these officers and soldiers. There were not, by any means, as many tories on the Island at the close, as at the beginning of the war. The injustice and cruelty of the British during the

---

* Vide "Alston," App. L.

whole term of their domination, and the repeated flagrant breaches of their promises in their numerous proclamations, as well as the inhumanity with which the American prisoners in their hands had been treated, had caused many to regret the step they had taken in publicly advocating the cause of the crown, and gradually they became converts to the cause of their native country, so that when the end came, there were few left who declined to take the oath of allegiance to the new government, and fewer still who were so infatuated with royalty as to abandon their property and the land of their nativity, to follow its fortunes. Of this latter class we have been able to find but two families, the Billop and the Seaman. The property of these families was confiscated and sold by Isaac Stoutenburgh and Philip Van Courtland, Commissioners of Forfeiture for the Southern district of New York. On the 16th day of July, 1784, they sold to Thomas McFarren, of New York, the Manor of Bentley, containing 850¼ acres for £4,695 ($11,737.50) forfeited to the people of this State by the attainder of Christopher Billop.

On the same day, the same Commissioners sold to the same individual, for £1,120.16 ($2,802), about 170 acres of land, in the town of Castleton, forfeited to the people of this State by the attainder of Benjamin Seaman.

On the 30th day of April, 1785, the same Commissioners sold to Cornelius Rosevelt, of New York, 200 acres of land, more or less, for £3,000 ($7,500), forfeited to the people of this State by the attainder of Benjamin Seaman.

The remainder of the Billop estate, except about 100 acres, came into the possession of two brothers, Caleb and Samuel Ward. Caleb subsequently sold 100 acres to ——— Coddington for $700; this eventually came into the possession of Garret Garrison, who married a daughter of Coddington. Subsequently, Isaac Butler came into possession of 200 acres of the original estate, and James Butler, Gilbert Totten, James Totten and Thomas Storer each 25 acres.

The policy of the Government of the United States appears always to have been of a pacific and conciliatory character towards its enemies, after they have been subdued and rendered powerless for evil. All tories, as well as foreign foes, were permitted to take a position among the citizens of the country upon taking the oath of allegiance. All animosities were buried, and the descendants of a great number of these repentant royalists, now residing on the Island, are ignorant of the position their ancestors took in the great political questions which agitated the country a century ago.

At the close of the war, Staten Island, New York Island, and a part of Long Island, were peculiarly circumstanced; throughout the country the several State governments, and the minor county and town governments under them, had been organized, and were in full operation, except in the counties mentioned; these had been under the control of the British military authorities, and whatever civil government they had, continued to be under the English laws; any attempt to organize a government which had the least tincture of republicanism, would not have been tolerated a moment; therefore, when the English evacuated the country, the government which had directed the destinies of the country for a century, was, so far as these counties were concerned, annihilated, as it were, in a day, and the people, without any previous instruction or experience, were suddenly brought under the influences not only of another, but of a new code of laws. It would be interesting to trace the steps taken by the people of the Island to acclimate themselves, as it were, to the political atmosphere which they were thereafter to inhale, but here resources fail us; there is nothing in the county archives to direct, or even to aid us. Except the records affecting the title to property, and the barren monetary records of the successive boards of supervisors, from which we have elsewhere culled all that is available for our purpose, there is nothing left; all else has disappeared, especially the records of the courts held in the county. Of these there are none, from the beginning of the 18th century to 1843, or thereabouts, a period of nearly a century and a half. This is to be regretted, because there is no method by which the blank can be filled. It is in documents like these that are missing, that many items of local interest are to be found. The few events of a historical nature which have transpired in the limited area of our county since the formation of the government, and which are here recorded, have been drawn from the memories of individuals still living, and from various other sources.

Note.—Since the above was written, the compiler has succeeded in discovering two old books containing the proceedings of the Courts of Common Pleas and General Sessions from 1710 to 1775, and a few cases after 1784. Between these dates no courts appear to have been held in the county, martial law prevailing during that time. The above books are of but little value in a historical point of view, as they contain little else than entries of suits for debts in the Common Pleas, and for assaults and batteries in the Sessions.

CHAPTER XVI.

The Quarantine—Murders.

As the commerce of the port of New York extended itself, and vessels from all parts of the world visited its harbor, and sometimes brought infectious diseases with them, it became an imperative necessity that the authorities should establish a quarantine for the protection of the people dwelling within its limits. Accordingly, the Colonial Legislature, in 1758, enacted a law creating a quarantine establishment, and located it upon Bedloe's Island, where it remained thirty-eight years; it was then removed to Nutten, or Governor's Island. In 1799, three years after its removal, the yellow fever was brought to New York, and it was decided that the establishment was altogether too near the metropolis to be of any service in protecting the people, by preventing the spread of malignant diseases. Commissioners were then appointed by Act of Legislature to procure a site upon Staten Island. They selected a parcel of land containing thirty acres, belonging to St. Andrew's Church, beautifully located on the northeast shore of the Island. Strong opposition was made not only by the owners of the land, but by the people of the Island generally, to its location among them, but it was taken, notwithstanding, by what in law is termed "the right of eminent domain." Hospitals and other necessary buildings were erected, and during the first year of its existence on the Island, twenty-five cases of yellow fever occurred among the people residing outside of its boundaries, all but one of which proved fatal. Almost every year thereafter contagious diseases, in some form, found victims among the people. In 1848, the number of persons sick from infectious diseases outside of the quarantine, amounted to one hundred and eighty. In that year an earnest petition for relief was presented to the Legislature by the people of the Island, supported by powerful influences from New York and Brooklyn, and a committee was appointed by the Legislature to examine into the matter, and report at the following session. This committee at once proceeded to the performance of the duty assigned to them, and in 1849 "unhesitatingly recommended the immediate removal of the quarantine." While the committee were engaged in performing their duty, the yellow fever again broke out, and extended itself to various other places. In April an act was passed for the removal of the quarantine establishment from Staten Island to Sandy Hook. The measure had its opponents among the shipping merchants and others in New York, who were not idle; the State of New Jersey also interposed its objections, and the persons appointed by the Legislature of New York to carry out its intentions, took no action whatever, so that the removal act remained a dead letter upon the statute books.

The fearful visitation of yellow fever in 1856, once more aroused the people of the Island, and another application for relief was made. In March, 1857, another act was passed for the removal of the quarantine from Staten Island, but the opposition of the Commissioners of Emigration, the Board of Underwriters of New York, and the shipping interests of that city, again thwarted the beneficent designs of the Legislature. The precautions adopted by the local authorities to protect the citizens and their families from infection, were opposed by the health officer, and every possible obstacle was thrown in the way of the local officers to obstruct them in the performance of their duties. At length patience ceased to be a virtue, and the Board of Health of the town of Castleton, within which the quarantine was situated, passed a resolution, declaring the institution to be an insufferable nuisance, and called upon the citizens to "abate it without delay." Those residing in the vicinity required but slight encouragement to take the matter into their own hands, and at once to effectually remove the establishment, which had legally been pronounced a nuisance. On the nights of the first and second of September, 1858, they forcibly entered the enclosure, and after carefully removing the patients from the several hospitals, set fire to, and burned down every building connected with the establishment. That some excesses should be committed by an exasperated populace, was to be expected; there was so much system, however, in their mode of operation, that it was evident everything had been previously arranged, and that the people were carrying out instructions previously received. During the continuance of this intense excitement, it was remarkable that not a single life was sacrificed, nor any one seriously injured.

These summary proceedings of the people of Staten Island produced great excitement, not only in the city of New York, but throughout the State, and indeed throughout the country. They were termed in the public prints barbarians, savages, incarnate fiends, sepoys, and in fact no epithets were considered too vile to be applied to them. But they were all borne with equanimity, sustained by the consciousness that sooner or later there would be a revolution in public opinion. After all the mischief had been done, the Governor of the State declared the Island to be in a state of revolt, and sent over several regiments of militia, who were for some time encamped upon the grounds immediately north of the quarantine.

A matter of a character so serious, could not, of course, be passed over in silence. Legal proceedings were at once instituted, and Messrs. John C. Thompson and Ray Tompkins, who were regarded as the instigators and ringleaders of the incendiaries, were arrested on a charge of arson, and arraigned before the County Judge, Hon. H. B. Metcalfe, for examination. His opinion, which was extensively copied and read, had great influence in changing public opinion. His closing remarks merit repetition and preservation.

"Undoubtedly the city of New York is entitled to all the protection in the matter that the State can give, consistently with the health of others; she has no right to more. Her great advantages are attended by correspondent inconveniences; her great public works, by great expenditures; her great foreign commerce, by the infection it brings. But the Legislature can no more apportion upon the surrounding communities her dangers, than her expenses; no more compel them to do her dying, than to pay her taxes; neither can be done."

Thus ended the charges brought against the prisoners; no person was punished for any complicity in the matter, but the county, very unjustly in the opinion of many, was compelled to pay for the value of the property destroyed, both public and private; nevertheless, the people consoled themselves with the reflection, that even at that price, they had cheaply, as well as effectually, rid themselves of a grievous nuisance, which had not only depreciated the value of their property, and exposed themselves and their families to contagion in its worst forms, but had actually been the direct cause of the death of hundreds of their relatives and neighbors.

Towards the close of October, 1815, the community was startled by a report that a murder had been committed in the town of Southfield. The circumstances of the case proved to be as follows:

On the 27th of that month, Bornt Lake, residing on the Amboy,* a few rods south of the Black Horse Tavern, while returning from his father's house, on the same road to his own, was shot and killed on the public road in front of his own premises, by his next door neighbor, a man named Christian Smith. Immediately after the commission of the deed, Smith went to another neighbor, Mr. John Jacobson, and informed him of what he had done, and asked his advice whether to surrender himself, or attempt to escape. What advice his neighbor gave him is not known, but Smith did neither the one nor the other, but wandered about in the woods, where he was found later in the day, and taken to prison. He did not deny having committed the murder, but

* Vide App. N. (85)

justified himself by the plea that Lake was committing a trespass upon his property; that he had frequently done the same thing, and had been warned repeatedly what the consequence would be if he did not desist. He was indicted and brought to trial. The prosecution had an easy task, for the offence was not, and could not be denied; it stood admitted, but the defence was justification. It was proved that a feud had for a long time existed between the parties, and that they did what they could to aggravate and annoy each other. Judge Spencer, who presided, charged strongly against the prisoner, for the law was against him. "If," he said, "the murdered man had trespassed upon the property of the prisoner, the law afforded ample redress, and he had no right to take the law into his own hand and redress his own wrongs." The jury, however, took a different view of the matter; they acquitted the prisoner. The people were everywhere surprised at the result, and perhaps none more so than the prisoner himself. The judge was indignant, and in discharging the prisoner from custody, indulged in some remarks which were bitterly severe. He said, in effect: "The jury have seen proper to find you not guilty; how they have arrived at such a conclusion, in the face of the law and the facts, surpasses my comprehension, but I warn you that there is another tribunal before which you must appear hereafter to answer for your crime, and where you will not have the benefit of a Staten Island jury." It was said, probably more in jest than earnest, that the jury arrived at their verdict by the following argument of one of their number: "If we convict the prisoner, the judge will give him two or three months more of life, during which time the county will be obliged to feed him, and to keep his cell warm, which will cost a good sum of money; if to this is added the cost of building the gallows, the sheriff's fee for hanging him, the cost of burying him, the expenses will amount to a hundred or a hundred and fifty dollars, and all of which will have to be raised by taxation; but if, on the other hand, we say "not guilty," every dollar of this amount will be saved," and therefore they said "Not Guilty." Others said that the jury suffered their sympathies for the prisoner to control their verdict, as it was evident that he had suffered much mental torture during his incarceration.

On Christmas morning, 1843, the community was again startled by the rumor that a double murder had been committed at Graniteville. A woman and her child, named Housman, had been found dead in an apartment of their dwelling house, evidently killed by violence. Suspicion soon was fixed upon a relative of the deceased persons, but who, after several trials, in one or more of which the jury failed to agree, was, upon a change of venue, finally acquitted. The matter still remains shrouded in mystery.

APPENDIXES.

1

"A."

CIVIL LIST, &c.

CIVIL OFFICERS, RICHMOND COUNTY.

Members of the Provincial Congress.

Adrian Bancker, 2d Prov. Cong., 1775—'6.
Richard Conner, 1st and 3d Prov. Cong., 1775—'6.
Aaron Cortelyou, " " " " " "
John Journeay, " " " " " "
Rich'rd Lawrence, " 2d " " " "
Paul Micheau, " 3d " " " "

Representatives in Congress.

Daniel D. Tompkins, 9th Congress, 1805—'6.
Henry Crocheron, 14th " 1815—'17.
James Guyon, Jr., 16th " 1819—'21.
Jacob Crocheron, 21st " 1829—'31.
Samuel Barton, 24th " 1833—'37.
Joseph Egbert, 27th " 1841—'43.
Henry I. Seaman, 29th " 1843—'47.
Obadiah Bowne, 32d " 1851—'53.
Henry G. Stebbins, 38th " Resigned.
Dwight Townsend, 38th " 1863—'65.
Henry B. Metcalfe, 44th " 1875—'77.

State Senators from Richmond County.

Paul Micheau....................1789—'90—'91—'92.
Jacob Tysen....................1828.
Harman B. Cropsey........ .....1832—'33—'34—'35.
Minthorne Tompkins.... ....1840—'41.
James E. Cooley.................1852—'53.
Robert Christie, Jr ....1864—'65.
Nicholas La Bau ....1866—'67.
Samuel H. Frost................1870—'71.

Judges of the County Courts.

1691	Ellis Duxbury.	1786	Paul Michean.
1710	Daniel Lake.	1797	Gozen Ryerss.
1711	Joseph Billop.	1802	John J. Murray.
1712	Thomas Farmar.	1803	John Garretson.
1739	Richard Merrill.	1823	Jacob Tysen.
1739	John Le Conte.	1840	Henry B. Metcalfe.
1756	William Walton.	1841	William Emerson.
	(He was also a member of the Council from 1758 to 1766, when he died.)	1844	Albert Ward.
1761	Joseph Bedell.	1847	Henry B. Metcalfe.
1775	Benjamin Seaman.	1876	Tompkins Westervelt.

Presidential Electors from Richmond County.

1808	John Garretson.	1844	John C. Thompson.
1812	Joseph Perine.	1848	James M. Cross.
1836	Jacob Crocheron.	1856	Minthorne Tompkins.
1840	John T. Harrison.	1864	Obadiah Bowne.

Members of the Colonial Assembly from Richmond County.

John Dally	1691.
Lambert Dorland	1691.
Ellis Duxbury	1691—'95—'98.
Thomas Morgan	1692—'98, 1702.
J. T. Van Pelt	1692—'94—'98.
John Shadwell	1693—'95.
Thomas Stilwell	1693—'98.
John Tunison	1694—'95—'98.
John Woglom	1698—'99.
Garret Veghte	1699, 1702.
John Stilwell	1702—'25.
Abraham Lakerman	1702—'26.
Richard Merrill	1725—'37.
John Le Count	1726—'56.
Adam Mott	1737—'39.
Richard Stilwell	1739—'48.
Paul Michean	1748—'51. App. N. (36.)
Wm. T. Walton	1751—'61.
Benjamin Seaman	1756—'75.
Henry Holland	1761—'69.
Christopher Billop	1769—'75.

Members of Assembly for Richmond County.

1st	Session.—	Abraham Jones....1777—'78.	App. N. (37.)
	"	Joshua Mersereau.	"
2d	"	No name recorded.1778—'79.	
3d	"	Joshua Mersereau.1779—'80.	
4th	"	Joshua Mersereau.1780—'81.	
5th		Joshua Mersereau.1781—'82.	
6th	"	Joshua Mersereau.1782—'83.	
7th	"	Adrian Bancker...1784.	
	"	Johannes Van Wagenen, 1784.	
8th	"	Joshua Mersereau.1784—'85.	
		Cornelius Corsen...	"
9th		Joshua Mersereau.1786.	
		John Dongan......	
10th	"	John C. Dongan...1787	
		Thomas Frost.....	"
11th	"	John C. Dongan...1788.	
		Peter Winant......	"
12th		Abraham Bancker..1788—'89.	
	"	John C. Dongan...	"
13th	"	Abraham Bancker..1789—'90.	
	"	Peter Winant......	
14th		Gozen Ryerss..... 1791.	
		Peter Winant......	
15th	'	Gozen Ryerss......1792.	
16th	"	Gozen Byerss......1793.	
17th	"	Gozen Ryerss......1794.	
18th	'	Lewis Ryerss......1795.	
19th	'	Lewis Ryerss......1796.	
20th	"	Lewis Ryerss......1797.	
21st	'	Paul J. Micheau...1798.	
22d	'	Paul J. Micheau...1799.	
23d	'	John P. Ryerss. ...1800.	
24th	"	Paul J. Micheau....1800—'01.	
25th	"	Paul J. Micheau....1802.	
26th	'	Paul J. Micheau .. 1803.	
27th	"	John Housman.....1804.	
28th	'	John Dunn........1804—'05.	
29th	"	John Dunn....... 1806.	
30th	"	David Mersereau...1807.	
31st	"	David Mersereau...1808.	

32d Session—	David Mersereau...	1808—'09.
33d	"	Richard Conner....	1810.
34th	"	James Guyon......	1811.
35th	"	James Guyon......	1812.
36th	"	James Guyon, Junr.	1812—'13.
37th	"	James Guyon, Junr.	1814.
38th	"	Jesse Oakley.......	1814—'15.
39th	"	Richard Corsen	1816.
40th	"	Richard C. Corsen..	1816—'17.
41st	"	Richard C. Corsen..	1818.
42d	"	Harmanus Guyon...	1819.
43d	'	Harmanus Guyon...	1820.
44th	'	Samuel Barton.....	1820—'21.
45th	"	Samuel Barton.....	1822.
46th	"	Isaac R. Housman..	1823.
47th	'	Henry Perine......	1824.
48th	'	Harmanus Garrison.	1825.
49th	'	No Election.	1826.
50th	'	Abraham Cole.	1827.
51st		Abraham Cole	1828.
52d		John Vanderbilt...	1829.
53d	"	John T. Harrison ..	1830.
54th	"	John T. Harrison ..	1831.
55th	"	Jacob Mersereau...	1832.
56th	"	Jacob Mersereau...	1833.
57th	"	Paul Mersereau...	1834.
58th	'	Lawrence Hillyer ..	1835.
59th	"	John Garrison, Jun.	1836.
60th	'	Lawrence Hillyer...	1837.
61st	'	Israel Oakley.......	1838.
62d	'	Israel Oakley	1839.
63d	"	Bornt P. Winant...	1840.
64th	'	Israel Oakley.......	1841.
65th	"	Henry Cole........	1842.
66th	'	Henry Cole........	1843.
67th	'	William Nickles....	1844.
68th	'	Peter Mersereau....	1845.
69th	'	George H. Cole	1846.
70th	"	George H. Cole....	1847.
71st	"	Ephraim J. Totten..	1848.
72d		Gabriel P. Disosway	1849.
73d	"	Benjamin P. Prall..	1850.

144   ANNALS OF STATEN ISLAND.

74th Session.—William H. Anthon . 1851.
75th   "   L'wr'nce H. Cortelyou 1852.
76th   "   Henry De Hart.....1853.
77th   '   Nicholas Crocheron. 1854.
78th   "   John F. Raymond..1855.
79th   "   William J. Shea....1856.
80th   '   Joshua Mersereau..1857.
81st   "   Eben W. Hubbard..1858.
82d   Robert Christie, Jun.1859.
83d   "   Theo. C. Vermilye..1860.
84th   "   N. Dane Ellingwood 1861.
85th   '   Smith Ely.........1862.
86th   "   Theodore Frean....1863.
87th   "   William H. Rutan..1864.
88th   '   James Ridgway.. 1865.
89th   "   Thomas Child......1866.
90th   "   Nathaniel J. Wyeth.1867.
91st   "   John Decker.......1868.
92d   '   John Decker.......1869.
93d   "   John Decker.......1870.
94th   "   John Decker*......1871.
95th   "   David W. Judd....1872.
96th   "   John B. Hillyer .. 1873.
97th   "   Stephen D. Stephens, Jr.....1874.
98th   "   "   "   1875.
99th   "   Kneeland Townsend 1876.
100th   "   Samuel R. Brick   1877.

* The Certificate was given to John Decker, but the seat was subsequently awarded to Willet N. Hawkins.

Members of the State Constitutional Conventions from Richmond County.

Convention of 1788, Abraham Bancker, Gozen Ryerss.
    "   1801, Joseph Perine.
    "   1821, Daniel D. Tompkins.
    "   1845, John T. Harrison.
    "   1868, George Wm. Curtis.

School Superintendents, &c., of Richmond County.

Harman B. Cropsey, County Superintendent, appointed 1843.
David A. Edgar, County Commissioner, elected.
Henry M. Boehm, " " "
Isaac Lea, " " "
James Brownlee, "

Clerks of Richmond County.

1682	Francis Williamson,	1810	John V. D. Jacobsen,
1684	Samuel Winder,	1811	Joseph Perine,
1689	Jacob Corbet,	1815	Jonathan Lewis,
1691	Thomas Carhart,	1828	Walter Betts,
1698	Thomas Coen,	1843	Joshua Mersereau, Jr.,
1706	William Tillyer,	1852	Israel C. Denyse,
1708	Alexander Stuart,	1855	James Cubberly,
1728	Adam Mott,	1858	Israel C. Denyse,
1738	Daniel Stilwell,	1861	Abraham V. Conner,
1739	Daniel Corsen,	1864	Michael P. O'Brien—Ap.L(28.)
1761	Paul Micheau,		Joseph Egbert,
1781	Abraham Bancker,	1869	John H. Van Clief, Jr.,
1784	John Mersereau,	1873	David H. Cortelyou,
1798	Joseph Perine—App. N. (38.)	1876	Abraham V. Conner.

Surrogates of Richmond County.

Under Colonial Government.
1733 Walter Dongan,
1759 Benjamin Seaman.
Under Federal Government.
1787 Adrian Bancker,
1792 Abraham Bancker,
1809 John Housman,
1810 Cornelius Bedell,
1811 Jonathan Lewis,
1813 Cornelius Bedell,
1815 Tunis Egbert,
1820 Richard Conner,
1820 John Garrison,
1821 Tunis Egbert,
1830 Richard Crocheron,
1843 Lewis B. Marsh,
1847 Henry B. Metcalfe--Ap.N.(40)
1876 Tompkins Westervelt.

Sheriffs of Richmond County.

1683	John Palmer,	1810	Daniel Guyon,
1684	Thomas Lovelace,	1811	Jacob Crocheron,
1685	Thomas Stilwell,	1813	Jacob Hillyer,

1689	Eli Crossen,	1815	Henry Perine,
1691	Thomas Stilwell,	1819	John Hillyer,
1692	John Stilwell,	1821	Jacob Crocheron,
1698	John De Pue,	1825	Walter Betts,
1699	Jacob Coulsen,	1828	Harmon B. Cropsey,
1700	Christian Corsen,	1831	Lawrence Hillyer,
1701	John De Pue,	1834	Israel Oakley,
1702	Lambert Garrison,	1837	Andrew B. Decker,
1709	William Tillyer,	1840	Jacob Simonson,
1722	Benjamin Bill,	1843	Israel O. Dissosway,
1730	Charles Garrison,	1846	Jacob G. Guyon,
1736	Paul Micheau,	1849	Israel O. Dissosway,
1739	Nicholas Larzalere,	1852	Abraham Ellis,
1751	John Hillyer,	1855	Abraham Lockman,
1775	Thomas Frost,	1858	Isaac M. Marsh,
1784	Abraham Bancker,	1861	Moses Alston,
1788	Lewis Ryerss,	1864	Abraham Winant,
1792	Benjamin Parker,	1867	Jacob G. Winant,
1796	Isaac Cubberly,	1870	Moses Alston,
1799	John Hillyer,	1873	William C. Denyse,
1802	Jacob Crocheron,	1876	Benjamin Brown.
1806	Jonathan Lewis,		

District Attorneys of Richmond County.

(This was made a County office in 1818.)

1818	George Metcalfe,	1850	George White,
1826	Henry B. Metcalfe,	1853	Alfred DeGroot,
1838	Thorn S. Kingsland,	1850	Abraham W. Winant,
1839	George Catlin,	1865	John H. Hedley,
1840	Roderick N. Morrison,	1872	Sidney F. Rawson,
1841	Lot C. Clark,	1875	John Croak.
1849	George Catlin,		

Regents of the University from Richmond County.

Abraham Bancker, John C. Dongan, first board, 1784; Harmanus Garrison, second board, 1784; since which time the county was not represented in the board until April 12th, 1864, when George Wm. Curtis was appointed, and still continues in office (1876).

Supervisors of the several Towns in Richmond County since the beginning of the year 1766—alphabetically arranged.

Castleton.

Barnes, George 1792—'93.
Barrett, Nathan 1887—'88.
Burbanck, Abraham 1794—'98.
Cary, Richard S. 1804.
Christopher, Richard 1846, 1849, 1857,-'8-'9, 1868-'9, 1874-'5-'6.
Clute, John J. 1860.
Conner, Richard 1766 to-'84, 1786 to-'92.
Crabtree, James H. 1865.
Crocheron, Abraham 1832—'3.
Davis, George B. 1853.
De Groot, Jacob 1839.
Dongan, John C. 1785.
Ely, Smith 1861-'2.
Esterbrook, Joseph 1866.
Gardiner, David L. 1864.
Garrison, John 1803.
Garrison, John Jr. 1834—'5—'6.
Hazard, Robert M. 1847—'8.
Heal, Nathan M. 1867.
Herpeck, Charles A. 1877.
Housman, John 1799 to 1802, 1810.
Housman, Isaac R. 1822 to—'31.
Laforge, Peter D. 1841—'2.
Martling, Joseph B. H. 1850 to—'52.
Martino, Gabriel 1855.
Mersereau, Joshua 1854.
Minturn, Robert B. 1871.
Pell, D. Archie 1870.
Thompson, John C. 1840.
Tysen, Jacob 1811 to—'21.
Tysen, John Jr. 1805 to—'09.
Vermeule, John D. 1872—'3.
Vreeland, Eder. 1844—'5.
Ward, Albert 1843.

Northfield.

Bedell, Cornelius 1790, 1794.
Burger, James G. 1855.
Child, Thomas 1863.
Coreen, Cornelius 1779 to—'84.
Crocheron, Henry 1800 to-'04, 1808 to—'14.
Crocheron, Nicholas 1805 to-'7, 1825 to—'30, 1846—'7.
Crocheron, Richard 1816 to—'28.
Denyse, Israel C. 1866—'7.
Hillyer, John 1767.
Hillyer, John B. 1872.
Hillyer, John Jr. 1772-'3.
Hillyer, Lawrence 1851, 1856.
Laforge, Peter C. 1862.
Lake, Daniel 1795 to—'97.
Latourette, Henry 1767.
Latourette, Richard 1876—'77.
Martin, Oliver R. 1848.
Mersereau, David 1815.
Mersereau, Jacob 1792—'3, 1799.
Mersereau, John 1788.
Mersereau, Peter 1841 to—'44.
Moore, Richard C. 1854.
Perine, James 1831—'32.
Post, Garret G. 1850, 1857 to—'61.
Prall, William 1824.
Ryerss, Gozen 1785 to—'87.
Simonson, Bornt 1774 to—'78.
Simonson, Garret 1873 to—'76.
Simonson, Jacob 1833 to-'40, 1849.
Tysen, John 1789, 1791, 1798.
Wright, Garret P. 1852.
Van Clief, John H. 1868 to—'71.
Van Name, Charles 1853, 1864.
Van Name, Michael 1845.

Southfield.

Barnes, George 1789, 1800.
Barton, Edward P. 1869.
Barton, Samuel 1852, 1857.
Brady, Philip 1870.
Britton, Alexander H. 1844.
Clark, Ephraim 1866—'67.
Cocroft, James 1865.
Coddington, Samuel 1857, 1841 to —'43.
Cole, George H. 1845.
Corry, William 1876, 1877.
Cortelyou, Peter 1789—'98.
Egbert, Joseph 1855—'56.
Fountain, Anthony 1767, '69, '84.
Garrison, John C. 1849, 1858 to —'60.
Greenfield, George J. 1872 to ——
Guyon, Harmanus 1816 to—'20 1822 to—'38.
Guyon, James 1782—'3, 1785—'6.
Guyon, James 1838 to—'40, 1847— '8, 1850—'51.
Hall, Farnham 1846.
Jacobson, Christian 1772 to—'81.
Jacobson, John V. D. 1802 to—'15.
Johnson, Anthony 1834 to—'36.
Keeley, Dennis 1861 to—'64, 1871.
Ketteltas, J. S. 1868.
Mersereau, Jacob W. 1853—'4.
Perine, Henry 1821.
Poillon, John 1766, 1768.
Tysen, John 1795 to—'98.

Westfield.

Bancker, Adrian 1772—'78.
Cole, Cornelius 1788, 1794.
Cole, Gilbert A. 1857, 1862.
Cropsey, Jacob R. 1844—'45.
Depuy, Nicholas 1766 to—'69.
Eddy, Andrew 1846.
Ellis, George W. 1870—'71.
Frost, Samuel H. 1851 to—'56.
Guyon, Jacob M. 1876.
Jackson, Richard 1828.
Larzelere, Benjamin 1789, 1795 to 1801.
Latourette, David 1835—'36.
Mersereau, Daniel 1829—'33.
Micheau, Paul 1790-'98.
Oakley, Israel 1840.
Oakley, Jesse 1850.
Perine, Henry 1774—'83.
Rutan, William H. 1858—'61.
Seguine, Henry H. 1874, 1877.
Seguine, Joseph 1826, 1837—'39.
Totten, Ephraim J. 1847, 1849.
Totten, Gilbert 1802—'25, 1827.
Totten, John, 1784, 1809-'25, 1827.
Winant, Peter 1785—'87.
Winant, Bornt P. 1834,'41-'43,1848.
Wood, Abraham H. 1864—'65.
Wood, Abraham J. '66-'69, '72-'78.

Middletown.

Armstrong, John E. 1878.
Bechtel, John 1864.
Bradley, Alvin C. 1872.
Brick, Samuel R. 1868—'71.
Davis, George B. 1861.
Frean, Theodore 1866, 1877.
Frost, Henry 1876.
Hornby, Alexander 1862.
Lord, D. Porter 1865, 1867.
White, Frederick 1874.
Wood, Jacob B. 1860

N. B.—There is no record of Supervisors' names earlier than 1766, except in a few instances noticed below. The names of the Supervisors of 1770 and 1771 are not recorded. It is possible that the names of some of the earliest Supervisors are arranged under the wrong town, as in no case are the names of the towns and Supervisors connected.

Supervisors prior to 1766.

1699. William Tiljeu, North.
Anthony Tyson, West.
Abm. Lakeman, South.
1703. Richard Merrill, North.
Stoffel Garrison, South.
Anthony Tysen, West.
1704. ——— Merrill, North.
Tunis Egbert, West.

1705. Aaron Prall, North.
Tunis Egbert, West.
Stoffel Van Sant, South.
1706. Tunis Egbert, West.
Aaron Prall, North.
1709. Alex'r Stuart, South.
Jacob Corsen, North.
Tunis Egbert, West.

County Taxes from the year 1766.

Year	Amount	Year	Amount
1766	$485 06¼	1823	$3,615 84
1767	1,382 50	1824	3,518 16
1768	408 23	1825	2,928 81
1769	282 12½	1826	3,169 46
1770	203 74	1827	3,552 72
1771	187 51	1828	4,255 04
1772	242 05	1829	5,442 17
1773	357 07½	1830	4,505 53½
1774	142 92	1831	4,424 61
1775	261 59	1832	3,909 09
		1833	4,409 77

There are no taxes recorded except Excise during the war, or until after the organization of the Federal Government.

1834 Incomplete on the record.
1835 .... 3,867 51
1836 Incomplete.

Year	Amount	Year	Amount
1784	$1,037 50 a	1837	5,942 55
1785	637 50	1838	8,659 55
1786	625 00 b	1839	8,458 93
1787	562 50 c	1840	9,211 51
1788	375 00 d	1841	7,268 58

a By Act of Legislature, £5000 additional was levied this year.
b £1600 additional levied by law.
c £3250 State tax additional.
d $1134.25 State tax this and the following year.

Year	Amount	Year	Amount
1789	750 00	1842	9,251 00
1790	875 00	1843	8,890 13
1791	700 00	1844	12,727 21
1792	750 00	1845	10,879 81
1793	1,000 00	1846	13,453 77
1794	812 50	1847	13,536 84
1795	875 50 [a]	1848	15,174 85
1796	1,187 09 [b]	1849 Not recorded.	
1797	1,347 58	1850	17,202 65
1798	811 61	1851	20,244 16
1799	874 96	1852	22,224 54
1800 No tax recorded.		1853	25,439 87
1801	2,488 01	1854	32,275 26
1802	1,100 00	1855	38,925 54
1803	1,216 51	1856	37,656 47
1804	1,234 71	1857 Not recorded.	
1805	1,123 52	1858	47,001 84
1806	1,005 63	1859	55,920 58
1807	625 88	1860	53,789 94
1808	676 55	1861	64,374 61
1809	965 27	1862	107,126 51
1810	606 66	1863	129,275 03
1811	1,356 99	1864	218,388 86
1812	1,004 67	1865	190,251 70
1813	1,517 88	1866	295,548 98
1814	2,169 13	1867	272,778 79
1815	3,259 40	1868	248,982 68
1816	4,424 41	1869	290,624 74
1817	4,305 69	1870	
1818	3,883 90½	1871	332,666 06
1819	3,746 89	1872	224,787 38
1820	3,412 31	1873	304,295 17
1821	3,305 42	1874	274,807 89
1822	2,943 50½	1875	274,997 34

[a] $238.37½ additional for school tax.
[b] Including school tax.

N. B.—The books were kept until 179— in Colonial currency. There was great irregularity in making up the amount of tax some years. Sometimes the Dog tax was levied with the other taxes, sometimes by itself, sometimes it was paid out of the surplus Excise money when there was any. The State, school and poor tax were sometimes collected in the same way.

"B."

EXTRACTS
From Old Records, &c.

EXTRACTS FROM THE OLD COUNTY RECORDS, WITHOUT SPECIAL REGARD TO DATES, *verbatim et literatim.*

I under writen Poules Marlet out of my own free will have giuen to my brother Abraham Marlett the half of my Lott of Land that I Am to haue out of the paten (patent) with my father which I gaue out of my free will as a frend sheep (friendship) and I Ingeage to giue A Transport when my Brother Abraham Shall Requier it this A sined (assigned) out of good will on Staten Island on this 17th day of March, 1678 as wetnes our hands

Poules Richards   the mark P. M of
Peter ferche   Pouls Marlet
 This is a Trew Record out of the O Rigonell (original)
By order on this 9th day Jenewery 1682
order of Abraham Marlett   o BADIAH HULMES Clk

Upon the Ingagment of Capt. John Palmer for the fidelity of ffrances willjamson to a fisheat (officiate) the ofes of A Clarke for the Court the said Court By Joynt Consent have Mead choys of the A foorsaid ffrancis willjamson this 12 day of June 1682

By reference to our civil list, it will be seen that this individual was the first county clerk.

Thes Ar In his Maiests (Majesty's) Neam to will and Requiar you At sight hearof to giue nootes to the A Boue (above) meintioned parsons to Meet to gether In sum Conueient plas and then and ther to Act A Cording to ther Instruction and for soe Doeing this shall Be your soefishent warrant giuen under My hand on this 26 day of Jenewery 1681
       RICHARD STILLWELL Justes

Oct 10. 1698 To Tho Stillwell for a Wolve £0. 15. 0
To Cornelis Tysen for a wolves head £1. 00. 0

Richard Merrill Plf
Lambert dorlont Deft } in A Action of the Caues

The Plf not A pearing to Ancer to his Action the Court ordereth that the Plf shall pay the Cost of sewt (suit)

Thes Are to giue notes to whome It may concarn that Richard Fathfall (?) and Elisabeth Larans (Lawrence) hath bin Publeshed A Cording to Law

by DANILL STILLWELL
on this 15th day of Jenewery 1682   Oversear

The A Boue (above) Mentioned Parsons Ar Mared (married) By Me on the 25th day of Jenewery 1682

RICHARD STILLWELL Justes
By order   OBADIAH HULMES Clarck

Jacob Jeyoung (Guyon) Ptf) In A Action of the Caus
Isaac See (?) Deft   } At A Court held on Staten Island By the Constable and oversears of the seam on this present Munday Being the 7 day of febraery 1680 wharas the caus depending Between the Ptf and deft hath Bin heard the Court ordereth deft to Cleer his flax forthwith and his Corn out of the Barn within ten days from the deat hearof and to clear up his other A Counts at the next Court.

A A Court held on Staton Island By the Constabl and oversears of the Seam on this present Munday Being the 5 day of September 1680 Sarah whittman Ptf William Britton Deft. in A Action of the Case to the valew of ℔ ⁘ The Caus depending Betwixt the Ptf and Deft hath Bin heard and for want of farther proof the Caus is Referred till the next Court.

Sarah Whittman Ptf
William Briten Deft

At A Court held on Staton Island by the Constabll and

oversears of the seam on this presont Munday Being the 3 day of october 1680 the Court ordereth that the Deft shall seat (set) up and geett (get?) forty panell of soeiisiont (sufficient) fence for the yous (use) of Sarah whitman at or Be foor the first of november next in sewing (ensuing) with Cost of sewt.

Capt Thomas Young Ptf   Dec 5 1681
Edmond Arow Smith Deft   The deft Most humbly declareth —the Ptf hath detained four small peeses (pieces) ov hed Band —on duble Rigan (rigging) for wich I paid in Ingon Com—half a Scepll of pees as not paid for and wheras he hath Charged me—for six and twenty pound of Buter there was no more than 26 p pot and all the waight of the pot was 8 pound. By this and other Consideration doth Caus me to detain the debt.

☞ The "Buter" was charged at six pence per pound.

March 7th 1736-7 John Bodine and Hester his wife sold to Joseph Bedle a parcel of land on the North side of Fresh Kills—"Being on the Poynt of Karles Neck, being irregular pees of land—" Containing Eighty Acres as likewise his "proporshanable quantity of Meadow Ground." Consideration £300 ($750.)

        signed   JEAN BODIN
                        HESTER ✕ BIDEN
                              her mark

1769 Rojer Barnes Esquire and Joseph Ralph Esq. for the tryel of Joshua Marcheroe Esq. and Mr. Dromods Negroes £2.17.

Joshua Marchero Esq. and Joseph Ralph and Richard Conner Esquires for the tryel of Mr Roper Dossons wench £3.00.

Received of Mr. Thomas Billop fourteen hundred and forty five Bushels of Wheate In full for his Magistis Quit rent Due from the Manor of Bentley to the 25th of March Last.

    Witness my hand April 30th 1736
                      ARCH° KENNEDY Rec. General

January 6. 1770 then the Supervisars Examined into the account of the arms that was bought for the county and Benjamin Semans Esq Brought in the account of What quantity Was in his hands, thair Was in his hands £36—Delivered to Captain Wright 12 guns and 12 hangers and guns With Bagnits to Mr. Broons and one Gun With a bagnit to Cornoral Dongan.

John Bedeel Esq. to cost for to transport Hannah fich and to cash paid to Lewes Dubois for the gale, (jail)—to sundrey Workmanship and nales for the gale and to a false york Bill taken of the collecttors.

March 30th Annoq Domini 1774
Gilbert Tottons ear mark for his cattle & sheep &c is a slit in the end of both ears viz. from the tip end down towards the head & a half moon on the upper part of the right ear.
Entered the day and year above written by
PAUL MICHEAU Clk.

1775 To John Bedeel Esq for Extrodany troble	£1. 12. 0	
" John Hillyer Jun for a quoire of Paper	0. 1. 6	
" Jonathan Lewis Crowner for inquist	2. 8. 0	

March 1776 To Thomas Frost for four double spring Pad locks for the goil (jail) two Pounds.
1780 to three visits to Cornelius Slaght and Dressing his wounds   £1. 9. 0
1781 May 2 to a visit to Mr Van Pelt at Mr John Deckers.   0. 5. 0
Bleeding him £0. 2. 6, a vomit £0. 2. 6 an anod.
Bolus £0. 4. 0   Total   4. 3. 0
for which he received a voucher March 15th 1790.

In 1778 there was paid to
"Christian Jacobson for 3 years services as supervisor £4. 4. 0
Henry Perine   "   "   "   3. 19. 6

Barnt Simonson for 3 years services as supervisor   2. 2. 0
Richard Conner   "   "   "   4. 4. 0

The whole amounted to £14. 9. 6 or $36.18¼. We quote this for the benefit of the same officers of the present day.

"Sept. 28th 1779 Richmond County. Received of John Bedel Esq. the sum of Fifty one Pound six shill for the use of the Gun boat as appears by the following receipt
Richmond County Sept the 28. 1779
Received of Mess^r Richard Conner, Christian Jacobson Henry Perine, Cornelis Corson supervissors for said County the sum of Eighty four Pound being in full for my selfe & Eight men belonging to the gun boat commenceing the fourteent of august last and continued for one month
                     by me JAS. STEWART Capt"

There are allusions to the gun-boat in several places in the records; it was probably one of the means used by Col. Billop to enforce the order to prevent communication between New Jersey and Staten Island.

"October the 30: 1781 to Bedell & Micheau, for Powder delivered by Clonell Bilops order when the Island was inwaded."

The firm of Bedell & Micheau probably were the proprietors of the store kept at Fresh Kills during the war, and mentioned in another place.

Under date of Sep. 17th, 1785, we find the following:

"At a meeting of us the Supervisors we found that there had been a Leaf and part of a Leaf cut out of this book between the Dates of 1781 one and one thousand seven hundred and Eighty two, and we do hereby Certify the same, as Witness Our hands
                     GOZEN RYERSS
                     RICHARD CONNER
                     PETER WINANT
                     JAMES GUYON"

"Richmond Town Dec 16. 1786

At a Meeting this day of the Supervisors we did agree to advertise & Notify the Freeholders of the County of Richmond of a Law respecting the payment of arrearages and commutation of Quit rents passed by the Legislature y° 1st day of April 1786 and accordingly have wrote some Advertisements and put them up.

> GOZEN RYERS
> JAMES GUYON
> RICHARD CONNER."

In 1787, Benjamin Micheau, the county treasurer, announced to the Supervisors that he had been robbed, but the record does not inform us how the robbery had been effected, nor what amount had been abstracted; we infer, from reading the meagre statement of the facts, that the treasurer had applied to the Legislature for a special act for his relief, and that one had been passed authorizing the Supervisors to afford the relief sought, if upon investigation they should find just reason for so doing. Accordingly several meetings were held, and a large amount of testimony taken, the result of which was,—to copy the record,—"after having heard all The Proofs and alligations respecting the segested (suggested?) Robbery as aforesaid, and having duly and deliberately Considered the Evidince and alligations as the Law Directs, Do not Conceive That we the Supervisors are authoriz'd to raise the Money as Directed by said Law for the relief of Benjamin Micheau Late Treasurer of the County aforesaid. In Testimony Whereof we have hereunto set our hands This twenty Eighth Day June 1788

> JOSHUA MERSEREAU
> JOHN WANDEL
> RICHARD CONNER
> CORNELIUS COLE."

"1786 June 26 To Martinus Swaime
      for transporting Sam perkins   £ 1. 9. 0

To Abraham Barbanck for transporting
Mrs. Ogg & a mulatto fellow   £2. 18. 5"

Dec 20th 1787 John Vanderbilt sold to Benjamin Michean conditionally for £14. 11. 10 current money of New York (about $36.50)

One Negro wench named Ann
One pide (pied) cow
One red cow with white face
One feather bed.

The above is of the nature of a chattel mortgage.

"1778 Oct 14 Met agreeable to ajornment, Examined the Loan officers Books and accts and found the £200 paid in to the Loan officers be again Let out; and the Interest Paid as pr Receipt vz.

Rec⁴ Sept. 18. 1788 from Messʳ Garrison & Dubois Loan officers for Richmond County Twenty nine Pound Which together With one Hundred & seventy six pound they paid the 14th July last, and Twenty Pound their Sallery is in full for the Interest on £4500 put out on Loan in said County to the third Tuesday in June last.

GEORGE BANCKER Treasurer

RICHARD CONNER
CORNELIUS COLE
JOHN WANDEL
JOSHUA MERSEREAU
} Supervisors"

A record under date Dec. 1, 1789, contains the following accounts:

"To Richard Scarret for digging a Grave £0. 10. 0

To Lewis Dey for Boarding the Carpenters when repairing the County House & Building the Gallows & Furnished 100 shingles 1 Bushel of Lime a pair of hinges & For fetching Anthony Cornish from New York Goal fees &c &c £6. 0. 0

To Lewis Ryerss (then sheriff) for two locks for the Goal, for going to New York for to Report Anthony Cornishes

Escape from Goal, for Going to New York when he was apprehended, for Fetching him from New York, Making the Gallows & Executing of Anthony Cornish, for Expence of Apprehending of sd Cornish at New York, Goal costs £16. 16. 0"

We have been unable to find a more detailed account of this case. A very aged man, living when this was written (1875,) and nine years old at the time of the execution, and who remembered it well, said that the prisoner was known as "Black Antony," being a negro; he had committed a murder on board of a vessel in the Sound. The place of execution was near the site of the present school-house in Richmond Village.

"Oct. 19: 1790. The following is the amount of the Inhabitants of the county of Richmond as numbered by the Supervisors and Assessors of said county Agreeable to an Act of the Legislature passed the 18th day of February 1790.

	Males.	Females.	Slaves.
Town of Southfield	309	330	258
Town of Westfield	440	451	267
Town of Northfield	463	409	167
Town of Castleton	381	340	127
Souls in Richmond Co.	—	—	—
In all 3942	1593	1530	819"

"March 1790 Benjamin Larzalere, To drawing an Inquisition of a child found in a spring & duties therein required £1. 0. 0

Benjamin Parker for attending the Jurors as Surgeon On the above Inqnisition £0. 8. 0

Lewes Dey for suppœneaing of evediuces in the above Inquisition £0. 5. 0

Aug. 31 Dr. Benjamin Parker for Bord & Doctering of Peter Corkins in his last sicknis Untill his Death £26. 0. 0

The clothing which said Corkins had at the time of his death was allowed on said Parker's bill

To Joseph Taylor by order of Doctor Parker for sundries for the Burial of Peter Corkins £. 0. 8. 3.

Nov. 30. 1790 To Dr. William Young for Doctering of Peter Breestead in his last Illness £16. 0. 0"

"1790 To Richard Taylor Undersheriff for Transporting John Fannatle to John Simonson constable for the town of Westfield and Victualing a his house £ 0. 7. 0

To John Simonson Constable for Transporting John Fannatle from his house to Amboy and from Thence to Wood Bridge as there was no Constable in Amboy as by account Brt in £ 0. 19. 0

"July 7: 1792 At a meeting of the Supervisors Together with the Judges of the Court of Common Pleas for the County of Richmond the 26th of June 1792 Lawrence Hillyer, Joseph Barton Jun. were unanimously appointed Commissioners to Superintend the Building of a Court House in the Town of Richmond on a Lott of ground given by Doctor Thomas Frost, and Thomas Frost having since been appointed a Commissioner to be with the said Lawrence Hillyer and Joseph Barton to Superintend Said Court House and to Advertise for Undertakers & to receive proposals that may be Consistent with æconomy and the Interest of the County.
RICHARD CONNER Clk Supervisors"

In 1792 a tax of £315 ($787.50) was levied upon the county for building the court house, and the sum of £15 ($37.50) was paid to Dr. Thomas Frost in payment for the "Lott" which the previous entry says he had *given* for the purpose. The record does not give the name of the "undertaker" to whom the contract was awarded.

This building is still standing opposite the hotel known as the Richmond County Hall. When the present court house was built, the old court house property was sold to Walter Betts, who converted it into a dwelling. It is now (1875) owned and occupied by Isaac M. Marsh, Esq. While this building was used for a court house, the brick building on the opposite corner was the prison.

The same year, 1792, another tax of £84 ($210) was levied for finishing the court house. The completion of it was delayed for nearly two years, for under date of Oct., 1794, we are informed that the supervisors met in it for the first time.

The lot upon which the present court house stands was conveyed to the supervisors by Henry I. Seaman and wife by deed bearing date April 19. 1837, at a nominal price, for the purpose of erecting a court house thereon; according to the terms of the conveyance, when the property shall cease to be used for that purpose, it shall revert to the said Seaman or his heirs.

On the 22d December 1847 Farnham Hall and wife, in consideration of fifty dollars conveyed to the supervisors the lot in the rear of that upon which the court house now stands.

"Feb. 5. 1795 The Supervisors Met Agreeable to notice at the House of Daniel Turner in Richmond Town To Draw up Petitions to Send to the legislature of this State for a new mode of Election Laws."

1797 Dec. 14. Bernard Sprong for making a map of the towns of Southfield and Westfield & surveying Smoking Point Road £6. 6. 0.

Richard Conner for making a map of the towns of Castleton and Northfield & service of Clerk of Supervisors £. 7. 2. 0.

(Total $33.50)

1801 October 26. To Lawrence Hillyer Esq for Erecting a Public Stocks according to Law..................... $12 00

1801 July Peter Ogilvie attorney for the poor masters of Southfield against Britton and Kettletas was allowed $14.37½ for his services.

The following are from the Baptismal Records of St. Andrew's Church:

"1780 June 18, a Child Belongeing to a Corprel of the 22 Rigment."

"Armye Baptise a Child of yᵉ Army yᵉ 19 July 1776
Baptise a Child Charl by Name yᵉ 21 of yᵉ Scotch
Dunkin son of Daniel McDaniel & Catrine yᵉ Mother
Baptis'd yᵉ 28ᵗʰ of July 1776."

The baptism of parents and their child at the same time is an event of rare occurrence; the following is an instance:
"Larance Rolph Adult Was Born 10 of April 1742
Pacience Lake Adult yᵉ wife of Larance Rolph was Born Jaʸ 22 ——
William Roberson Son of yᵉ above adults was Born yᵉ 12 of february 1765."
They were all baptized on the 18th day of August, 1765.

Here is the age of four of James Howell Children & Elizabeths his wives

Richard Howell son of James Howell & Elizabeth his wife was Born April yᵉ 17, 1757 & thir Daughter Susana ware born yᵉ 20ᵗʰ of Decemb'r 1758 & thir son James ware born yᵉ 15ᵗʰ of february 1761 & Elisabeth thir Daughter ware born yᵉ 16 of february 1764

"William Sharp } son Samuel was Born July the 29 about sunset 1783 and was Baptised August th 17—1783."

"Reuben Son of Anthony & Mary Egberts Was born the 13th September 1770 on thursday about ten of the Clock in yᵉ Morning.

Martha Dauter of Antony & Mary Egborts born April yᵉ 25th about ten of yᵉ Clock in yᵉ Morning 1772 on Saterday.

Elener Daughter of Anthony & Mary Egberts Born yᵉ 7th of August about of one yᵉ clock in yᵉ morning 1774.

Burials 1763

The Order of Vestery for yᵉ Sactons fees
    for Digging a grave............. ....£0. 6. 0

for inviting................................	£0.	8.	0
for yᵉ pall	0.	8.	0
for tending.................................	0.	8.	0
for Sodding	0.	8.	0
for Ringing yᵉ Bell.......................	0.	8.	0
	£1.	6.	0

The Clarks ffees for publishing & Baptysing,

for writin the publishment	£0.	8.	0
for fetching yᵉ water to baptise a child.........	0.	0.	6
for Entering yᵉ Child on Record	0.	0.	6
for sweeping yᵉ Church for Every puew Pʳ year.	0.	1.	6

The following are copied from original receipts in the possession of a gentleman at Mariner's Harbor, who resides upon a part of the property alluded to therein:

"Received of Arent Van Amer Two Bushells & a half of Wheat in full for One years Quitt Rent of two Lotts of Land on Staten Island, one Granted to Philip Bendell & the other to John Taylor the 15th December 1680, being to the 25th March last, as Witness my hand this 12th August 1761

Richᵈ Nicholls Depᵗʸ Recʳ Genᵉ."

"Received of Arent Van Amer Five bushells of Wheat in full for two Years Quitt Rent of the two Lotts of Land above mentioned to the 25th March last. As Witness my hand the 10th June 1763.

Richd. Nicholls Depᵗʸ Recʳ Gen¹"

"Received of Aarnt Van Amer Five Bushells of Wheat in full for two years Quitt Rent of the two Lotts of Land above mentioned to the 25th of March last. As Witness my hand this 2'd May 1765.

Richd: Nicholls Depᵗʸ Recʳ Gen¹"

The above receipts are all written in a distinct, but very cramped hand on a scrap of paper 4 by 6 inches. The three following are written on the reverse side of the same paper.

"Received of Arent Van Amer two bushells and a half of

Wheat in full for one years Quit Rent of the before mentioned Lotts of land due 25 March last.

New York 14 May 1766   JOHN MOORE Dep. Rec^r. Genl."

"Received of Arent Van Amer Two Bushells & a half of Wheat in full for One Years Quit Rent of the before mentioned Lotts of land due 25 March last.

Witness my hand 13 May 1767

JOHN MOORE Dep. Rec^r. Genl."

Recd of Arent Van Amen Two Bushells & half of Wheat in full for one Years Quit Rent of the above mentioned Lotts due 25th March last.   Witness my hand the 6th July 1768.

There are three other receipts for wheat bringing the payment down to March 25th, 1775. Then on separate papers are the following:

"Patent granted to John Taylor for a Tract of Land on Staten Island dated 15th Decem^r 1680 at One & a half Bushel Wheat ⅌ Annum.

Aaron Van Naum { From 25 March 1775 to 25 May 1787 is 12 : 2
Deduct   . 8.—

4. 2 @ 9/   £1. 17. 6
14 years commutation —9/   6. 6. -
                                                £8. 3. 6

Recd New Yok June 21st 1787 from Aaron Van Naum ⅌ the hands of Joshua Mercereau Esq. Public Securities which with the Interest calculated thereon to the 25th May last amounts to Eight Pounds three shillings & Six Pence in full for Arrears of Commutation on the above Patent.

£8. 3. 6   PETER S. CARTENIUS State And^r'"

There is another drawn in similar terms for the patent

granted to Philip Bendell, amounting to £5. 9. 0. The individual mentioned in these documents by the names of Arent Van Amer,—Van Amen—Van Naum, was Aaron Van Name, the grandfather of Mr. Michael Van Name, and his brother Charles Van Name, both of Mariner's Harbor. It will be observed that during the royal government the quit rent was payable in wheat, according to the terms of the patent. Under the Federal Government it appears to have been commuted for money. Vide App. N. (41.)

The following is a copy of the Sheriff's bill for taking two convicts to state prison, in 1828:

"Nov. 24 Stage fare to Quarantine.................... $1 00
Steam boat passage to New York.......... 1 00
Drink on the road from New York to Yonkers. 81
Supper, horse feed & drink at Yonkers... 2 00
Toll gates....................... 50
Horse feed, lodging, drink & breakfast at Smith's in Tarrytown.................... 3 63
" 25 Horse feed & drink at Yonkers............ 50
Horse feed & drink at Manhattanville...... 50
Stage ferrage & 2 passages.................. 2 00
Stage hire......................... .... 10 00
2 days taking convicts to prison.......... .. 4 00
2 days do do for deputy.......... 2 00

N. B.—There were four persons on this journey — the sheriff, his deputy, and the two convicts.

"At a Court of Sessions held for the county of Richmond March 3, 1712.

Jos. Arrowsmith, Lambert Garrison, Nath' Britton, Abm. Coole (Cole), Peter Rezeau, Esq'.

March y⋅ 4th. Court opened and Grand Jury calld. The presentmts of the Grand Jury brought in; the Court orders prosess to be issued out against those presented—viz. Peter Bibout for beating Mr Mony (Manee) and his wiffe. Barnt

Marling, Andrew Bowman, William Foord & The Taylor peter peryne & Vn. Buttler, Peter Catherick and Nath¹ Brittin Junr. all for fighting. John Dove and John Bilew for carrying of Syder upon the Sabbath day. Abraham Van Tyle for allowing his negroe to Cary Irone to the Smiths on the Sabbath day, and Mark Disosway for being drunk on the Sabbath day."

As Richmond had not yet been made the County-seat, we infer, from the following entry, that the Courts convened in various places in the County, though Stony Brook was recognized as the County-seat: "March 2, 1713—— Court a journed till to morow at Ten of the Clock in the forenoon to the North Side To Coll Grahams Court opened, and ajourned Till y° fist Tuesday on 7ber (September) next.—God Save the Queen."

Col. Aug. Graham was one of the judges of the Common Pleas and Sessions.

At a Court of Sessions held March 5th, 1716, "it was ordered by the court that Nicholas Brittin pay Twelve shillings ffine for his misbehaviour to Nath¹ Brittin Esq. and also ordered that he beg Justice Brittins pardon and promise to doe so no more, and also to pay all the charges of this action."

Debtors were arrested, and obliged to give bail or be incarcerated. The return to the precept of arrest by the sheriff or constable was "Cepi Corpus."

"Att a Court held for the county of Richmond In the pro. of New York on the first day of March in the first yeare of His Majesties Reigne George by the Grace of God King of Great Brittain &c ann. Dom. 1714—Ordered That Garritt Weghtie (Veghte) may be admitted to preffer The Lysence that he and some others, In behalfe of the Rest of the Dutch protestant Congregation In this County Have obtained of His

Excelly. Coll. Robt. Hunter Esqr. &c. The Same being Read as also a peticŏn upon the Same, praying our approbacŏn for ther Erecting a Meeting House for the Exercise of ther protestant profession Contiguous to the Burial place on the North Syd of the Sd. Island They Esteeming it a place Most Convenient for that purpose, upon there pray' and Humble peticŏn—It is Ordered by The Court that having Considered thereof Have Granted the prayer of the Peticŏners accordingly, Ordered by the Court that this be Entered In our Book of Lysicns."

September 3d, 1717, all the retailers of strong liquors were summoned to appear before the court of General Sessions to show by what authority they retailed; thereupon appeared Mauris Williams, Jean Brown, Anthony Wright, Barnt Symerson, Daniel Lane, John Garrea, David Bissett, Cornelius Eyman, Lamb' Garrittson Jun. Benj' Bill, Jacob Johnson, Isaac Symerson, Joseph Bastido;—13 in the whole county.

In almost every instance where a prisoner was acquitted by the jury, he was discharged by the Court upon payment of costs.

September 6, 1720, "Ordered that a good suffic' publick pound be erected and made at or near the burying place by the Dutch Church in the North precinct; and Ordered Likewise that there be another pound erected in some convenient place at Smoaking point in the West precinct. Whoever will be at the charge of making sd. pounds shall have all profitt accruing by poundage."

At a Court of Sessions held in the Court House at Stony Brook, on the 5th day of March, in the ninth of his Majestys' reign (1723), "Benjamin Bill Eq' high Sheriffe of the County of Richmond Complains to the Court of the Insufficiency of his majesty Goal for the said County that it is all together soe Insufficiency that it is impossible to keep any prisoner safe as the Said Goal Divers prisoners having lately Escaped thereout and therefore the said sheriffe protest against the Inhabitants of the County of Richmond for Repairing the said Goal and against all waits Escapes that may Ensue for the Insufficiency of the said Goal and pray that his protest may be entered accordingly."

In 1725, Nicholas Larzelier, then High Sheriff, repeated the same complaint in the same terms. Two years after he repeats it again. The prison alluded to here was not at Stony Brook at that time, though the Court House was there until 1729. In 1710 the prison was built at "Cuckols towne" (Richmond) by order of the Court, as follows:

"Ordered that Mr. Lambart Garisone and Mr Wm. Tillyer (the late and then present sheriff) See the prison House built at Cuckols Towne—ye Dimensions Twelve foot in breadth, fourteen foot Long, Two Story high, six foot ye Loer Room from beam to plank, and the uper Story Six foot, all to be built with stone, and for building of the sd. prison the Said Undertakers have hereby power To take the Monys out of the Collectors hands for carying on the sd. work & the order of ye sd. Undertakers & Receipts shall be a Sufficient discharge to ye sd. Collectors."

The clerk, Alexander Stuart, evidently had an exalted idea of his abilities as a penman. His initial letters are of an extraordinary size, and ornamented in an extraordinary manner. He was withal something of a pedant, and makes a wonderful display of his knowledge of Latin. The title page of the record which he kept reads: "The book of Records of the Court of Sessions and Common Pleas Held in the County of Richmond in the province of New York. Comine^d ye 6th day of March an^o 1710-11 and kept by Alex^r Stuart Clk.

Quid faciunt Leges abi Sola pecunia regnit
Aut abi paupertas—Vincere Nulla potest."

Then anticipating apparently the inability of his successors properly to close the volume, on the last page he has again displayed his name, beneath which is another Latin line, "Vita hominis sine Literis Mors est. August y⋅ 12th 1712."

The Courts of General Sessions were frequently conducted by an overflowing bench, as for example, on the 22d Sept. 1761, there were present 1st, 2d and 3d Judges, and nine Justices—twelve in all. A bench of 8, 9, or 10 judges was not uncommon.

On the 26th day of September, 1775, there was a Court of Common Pleas and General Sessions held at the Court House, in Richmond town, after which there is no record of any Court having been held in the county until Monday the 3d day of May, 1784, "being the first Court held after the Declaration of Independence being published." This Court was held at the house of Thomas Frost, the court-house having been burned by the British, David Mersereau, Esq., being Judge.

The first case on the record is entitled—

"*The State* vs. *Thomas Frost*} The Grand Jury brought in a bill of Indictment against the Defendant for saying, 'Johnson that G—— d—— Reble, G—— d—— the Rebles, by G—— I will sacrifice every G—— d—— Sun of a b—— of them,' and the Deft. being in Court was called and the Indictment Read to him.—Whereupon he pleaded not guilty and entered into Recognizance himself in twenty pounds and Peter Mersereau his security in ten pounds to appear at the next Session to Try the Traverse." Unfortunately there is no record of the result of this indictment. The next court whose proceedings are recorded was held in September, 1794.

It may be a matter of interest to know the names of the officers of the first court held under the new government; they are as follows:

David Mersereau, Esq., Judge; Cornelius Mersereau, Hendrick Garrison, Peter Rezeau, Anthony Fountain, John Wandle, Gilbert Jackson, and Lambert Merrill, associate judges, Abraham Bancker, Esq., Sheriff; Jonathan Lewis, Coroner; Daniel Salter, James McDonald, John Baker and Abraham Burbanck, Constables. The first act was to read the Commissions of the several officers. The first civil suit on the calendar was Richard Housman against Henry Perine. Trespass, damages £50.

The following items relating to Staten Island, are taken from the "Journal of the New York Provincial Congress."

The deputies elected by the freeholders of Richmond County to the first Provincial Congress, were—

Paul Michau, John Journey, Aaron Cortelyou, Richard Conner, and Maj. Richard Lawrence; they were all in attendance at the first session in New York, May 22, 1775, except Lawrence, who did not present himself until June 1st.

When the second Provincial Congress convened, Richmond County was not represented, but the following communication from citizens of that county was read at the meeting of Congress:

RICHMOND COUNTY, Dec'r 15th, 1775.

Mr. President:

SIR:—Your favour of 2d Decem'r. we hereby acknowledge came safe to our hand, and with the majority of our committee considered the contents. We, agreeable to your request, have caused by advertisement the freeholders and inhabitants in our county to be convened on this day, in order that their sense might be taken whether they will choose Deputies to represent them in a Provincial Congress or not. Accordingly, a number of the said freeholders and inhabitants did appear; a regular poll was opened, and continued till 6 o'clock; at the conclusion of which it appeared that a majority was, for the present, for sending no Deputies. Our former conduct in sending of Deputies to represent us in Provincial Congress, was elevated with encouraging hopes of having, ere this, obtained the so much desired point in our view, namely, a reconciliation with Great Britain. But, with anxiety we express it, that the hopes of obtaining so desirable an event, is now almost vanished out of our sight; and, instead of which, we behold with horror, every appearance of destruction, that a war with Great Britain will bring upon us. Under these apprehensions, and in our particular situation, we hope you will view us, and when candidly considered, we trust will furnish you with sufficient reason, for the present, to forbear with us.

We wish and pray that if yet any hope of reconciliation is left, that measures might be adopted, if possible, to obtain that desirable end, in wishing of which we conclude ourselves,
Your most obt.
And most humble serv'ts,
JOHN TYSON,
CHRISTIAN JACOBSON.
DANIEL CORSEN,
PETER MERSEREAU,
JOSEPH CHRISTOPHER,
LAMBERT MERRILL,
JOHN POILLON.

To NATH'L WOODHULL,
Prest. of Provl. Congress, New York.

P. S.—Should the Congress think it necessary for further information of the state of our county, they will please to order two of our committee to appear before them for that purpose."

During the recess of the Congress, the Committee of Safety was in session. On the 12th of January, 1776, Richard Lawrence and Christian Jacobson appeared before the Committee, and represented that the majority of the people of Richmond County were not averse, but friendly to the measures of Congress; Lawrence was a member of the Committee for Richmond County.

Sept. 1, 1775, David Burger, of New York, sent a letter to the Congress complaining that sundry persons in Richmond County had supplied a transport with live stock, and the matter was referred to the members of that county to make inquiry on the subject.

On the 1st December, 1775, Paul Micheau, one of the Deputies from Richmond County, in the first Provincial Congress, addressed a letter to the Secretary of the Congress, in which he says that he had requested the county committee to convene the people to elect new deputies; that a meeting of the committee had been called, and that only a minority appeared, who for that reason declined to act, and requests Congress to write to them and learn their reasons for not convening the people, and concludes by hoping the Congress may be able to keep tranquility and good order in the Province, and make peace with the mother country. He then gave the names of the committee as follows:

Capt. John Kittletas, Capt. Christian Jacobson, Capt. Cornelius Dussosway, Henry Perine, David Latourette, Esq., Peter Mersereau, John Poillon, Moses Depuy, Lambert Merrill, John Tysen, Joseph Christopher, George Barrus and David Corsen.

To this communication Congress replied the next day in a letter addressed to "John Poillon, John Tysen and Lambert Merril, of the committee for Richmond County," urging them to elect Deputies to represent them without delay, and they added emphatically, "rest assured, gentlemen, that the neighboring Colonies will not remain inactive spectators if you show a disposition to depart from the Continental Union." They concluded their letter in these words: "We beg, gentlemen, you will consider this matter with that seriousness which the peace, good order and liberties of your county require."

The answer of the committee is given before under date of the 15th December, 1775.

On the 21st, Congress passed several resolutions, censuring Richmond county for its delinquency, and resolved that if within fifteen days a list of the names of those who oppose a representation in Congress be not sent to that body, the whole county shall be considered delinquent, and entirely put out of the protection of Congress, and that intercourse with them shall be interdicted, and that the names of delinquents shall be published in all the newspapers of the colony.

It was then that Lawrence and Jacobson had this interview with the Committee of Safety, on the 12th of January, 1776, as given before.

On the 23d of the same month the following letter was received by the Committee of Safety from the Richmond County committee.

"RICHMOND COUNTY, Jan'y 19, 1776.

Gentlemen—Whereas the committee for this county have caused by advertisement the freeholders to be convened on this day, in order to elect two members to represent this county in Provincial Congress; accordingly a poll was opened for that purpose, without any opposition, at the close of which it appeared by a majority, that Messrs Adrian Banker and Richard Lawrence was duly elected to represent this county in Provincial Congress until the second Tuesday in May next, which we hope will be agreeable to the rest of that body.

We are, gentlemen,
Your mo. obt. and most humble servts.

CHRISTIAN JACOBSON,
LAMBERT MERRILL,
JOHN TYSON,
PETER MERSEREAU,
GEORGE BARNES,
MOSES DUPUY,
DAVID LATOURETTE,
DANIEL CORSEN,
HENRY PERINE,
JOSEPH CHRISTOPHER.

To the Committee of Safety on recess of the Provincial Congress in New York."

In the interim, however, the delinquency of Richmond County had been represented to the Continental Congress, which body had passed the following resolve:

"IN CONGRESS, Feb'y 8th, 1776.

The inhabitants of Richmond county, in the Colony of New York, having refused to send Deputies to represent them in Provincial Convention, and otherwise manifested their enmity and opposition to the system and measures adopted for preserving the liberties of America; and as a just punishment for their inimical conduct, the inhabitants of that Colony having been prohibited by the Convention from all intercourse and dealings with the inhabitants of the said county; and this Congress being informed by the Committee of Safety of that Colony, that the freeholders of the said county did afterwards, without any opposition, elect Deputies to represent them in Provincial Convention; but as the proceedings against them had been submitted to the consideration of Congress, it was apprehended Deputies would not be received until the sense of Congress should be communicated.

Resolved, That it be referred to the said Provincial Convention to take such measures respecting the admission of the Deputies, and revoking the interdict on the inhabitants of the said county, as they shall judge most expedient, provided that the said Deputies and major part of the inhabitants of said county shall subscribe the association entered into by that Colony.

Extract from the minutes.
CHAS. THOMPSON, Sec'y."

It was then ordered by the Provincial Congress that the resolution of the Continental Congress be transmitted to the Deputies lately elected by the people of Richmond County.

The Congress being apprehensive that Gen. Clinton would attempt to land upon Staten Island for the purpose of making depredations and carrying off live stock, had requested the Provincial Congress of New Jersey to send Col. Herd, with his regiment, to the Island to prevent it, and lest he might not get there in time, a like request was made to the committee of Elizabethtown. This measure excited the apprehensions of the people of Staten Island, who were suspicious of the errand of Col. Herd and his regiment. Accordingly, on the 19th of February, the two deputies, Adrian Bancker and Richard Lawrence, hastened to inform the Congress that they had subscribed to the association entered into by the

Colony, and that seven-eighths of the people had done so likewise "long since," and that the coming of Col. Herd, "with a large body of men, to call the people to account for their inimical conduct," just then when many of the people were coming into the measures, and the cause gaining ground daily, would have an injurious effect, and they suggest that the stopping of the New Jersey forces would quiet the minds of the people.

On the same day Congress replied and assured the Deputies that Col. Herd's errand to the Island did not in any manner relate to the people of the county, except to protect their property, and that a counter request had been forwarded to New Jersey. The two deputies were requested to attend the Congress and to bring with them the proof that the majority of the people had subscribed to the association, to enable them to take their seats.

The committee of Elizabethtown had caused the apprehension and imprisonment at that place, of Isaac Decker, Abm. Harris and Minne Burger, and had held Richard Conner, Esq., under bonds to appear before them, upon charges not specified. The Congress of New York entered into a correspondence with the committee of that place, and requested them to send the delinquents to the county where they belonged, to be tried by the county committee. The committee of Richmond were also informed of the action of the Congress, and were instructed to try the delinquents and mete out to them impartial justice, and report to Congress.

On the 23d of February, Mr. Adrian Bancker's name appears among those of the members of the Congress.

On the 28th of February, Decker and Burger were returned to their own county, and the charges against them and Richard Conner were also transmitted to the committee of Richmond. Nothing is said of Harris.

The committee of Elizabethtown, at the time of surrendering them, disclaimed all knowledge of their offences, but intimated that they had been arrested by Col. Heard, at the instance of either the New York or the Continental Congress.

On the 8th of March, Hendric Garrison, of Richmond county, forwarded a complaint to the Congress, that while he was attending as a witness before the committee of said county, and while under examination, the said committee permitted the defendants, Cornelius Martino, Richard Conner and John Burbank, to insult and abuse him, and asks the protection of Congress, as he considers his person and property unsafe.

Lord Stirling, as commander of the Continental troops in New York, issued a warrant to apprehend John James Boyd, of Richmond county, and to have him brought before the Congress. Capt. John Warner, to whom the warrant was delivered for execution, laid it before that body on the 14th of March, when it was considered and decided that the said Boyd is so unimportant and insignificant a person as not to deserve the trouble and expense of apprehending him. Boyd resented this depreciation of his importance, and on the 21st sent a note to the Committee of Safety claiming to be "a steady and warm friend to his country," and pronounces any accusation against him unfounded.

On the 1st of April, 1776, Christian Jacobson, as the chairman of the County Committee, reported the organization of four companies of militia in the county, the officers of which were ordered to be duly commissioned. App. N. (42).

On the 3d of April Mr. Lawrence, a member from Richmond, reported that the county was already furnished with 14 good flats or scows, which were sufficient for the removal of the stock from the Island, and that the building of two more, as previously ordered, would be a useless expense. These scows, or flats, were held in readiness to remove the cattle to New Jersey, if the English ships of war on the coast should attempt to seize them, as they had done in several other places.

On the 12th of April, Lord Stirling informed the Committee of Safety that he had Gen. Putnam's orders to march with a brigade of troops for Staten Island, and that he would be under the necessity of quartering the soldiers in the farm-houses for the present; he requests the people to be notified of the fact, so that they might prepare quarters most convenient to themselves, and to be assured that he would make the residence of the troops as little burdensome as possible. The Committee of Richmond were requested to prepare empty farm-houses, barns, &c., for the reception of the soldiers, and to use their "influence with the inhabitants to consider the soldiers as their countrymen and fellow citizens employed in the defence of the liberties of their country in general, and of the inhabitants of Richmond County in particular, and to endeavour accommodate them accordingly."

On the 2d of May, Mr. Garrison, (Hendric), chairman of the County Committee, was present at the meeting of the Committee of Safety, and inquired whether the people would be paid for fire-wood furnished to the troops in Richmond County, and for their labor in preparing the guard-house, at the request of Lord Stirling, and was referred to Col. Mifflin. Hence, we infer that some of Lord Stirling's troops had taken up their quarters on the Island.

On the 6th of May, Gen. Washington wrote to the Committee of Safety, informing them that Peter Poillon, of Richmond county, had been arrested for supplying the king's ships with provisions. On the 8th, Poillon was brought before the Committee and examined. He did not deny the charge, but pleaded in extenuation that the regulations for preventing intercourse with the king's ships had not been published in Richmond County until the 2d or 3d of that month, and that therefore he was ignorant of them; he stated further, that he left home with a considerable sum of money to discharge a debt in Kings County, together with some articles of provision for New York market, of the value of about three pounds; that while passing the ship of war Asia, at as great a distance as he safely could, he was fired at, and could not escape; he proved further, by reputable witnesses, that he was a respectable man, and had always been esteemed a friend to the liberties of his country. He was discharged, with a caution hereafter to keep at a safe distance from the king's ship, and to warn his fellow citizens of Richmond county to do the same.

May 18 to 1776, a certificate signed by Christian Jacobson, chairman of the Richmond county committee, dated April 22d, 1776, was presented to the Provincial Congress, and attested by Israel D. Bedell, clerk, and directed to Paul Micheau, Richard Conner, Aaron Cortelyou and John Journey, was read and filed, whereby it appeared that these gentlemen had been elected to represent Richmond county in that body, with power to any two of them to meet to constitute a quorum, with the second Tuesday of May, 1777.

On the 5th of June, 1776, Congress issued an order for the arrest of a number of persons in several counties who were inimical to the cause of America; those from Richmond county were Isaac Decker, Abm. Harris, Ephm. Taylor and Minne Burger. They also ordered that several persons who held office under the king should be summoned to appear before the Congress, and among them are found the names of Benjamin Seaman and Christopher Billop, of Richmond.

There is nothing in the Journal of the Congress to show that these orders and resolutions were ever carried into effect.

On the 9th of July the Provincial Congress convened at the court-house in White Plains, Westchester county; the British then having taken possession of Staten Island, there were no deputies from Richmond county in attendance. At this meeting the Declaration of Independence was received and read; it was also reported that the British had taken possession of Staten Island without opposition, and detachments had advanced towards Bergen Point and Elizabethtown. The Declaration having been read, it was *unanimously* adopted, and the Congress passed a resolution to support the same, "at the risk of our lives and fortunes." It was thus ordered to be published. It was then "Resolved and Ordered, that the style or title of this house be changed from that of the 'Provincial Congress of the Colony of New York,' to that of 'The Convention of the Representatives of the State of New York.'"

The Convention recognized the impracticability of electing Senators and Members of Assembly in the southern district of the State, Westchester excepted, and as it was reasonable and right that the people of that district should be entitled to representation in legislation, they proceeded to appoint these officers; and for the county of Richmond, Joshua Mersereau and Abm. Jones were appointed; the latter, as has already been noticed, was subsequently denied his seat, on account of his sympathy for the enemy.

The proposed expedition of Col. Herd to Staten Island to protect the live stock there, originated with Gen. Lee. Having communicated his apprehensions to the Committee of Safety, that body, on the 10th of February, 1776, addressed a letter to the Provincial Congress of New Jersey, in which they say: "The entrance of Genl. Clinton into our port on pretence of *merely* paying a visit to Govr. Tryon, though he has been followed by a transport with troops, which we have good reason to believe are only a part of 600 that embarked with him at Boston, renders it highly probable that some lodgement of troops was intended to be made in or near this city;" and as no troops from New York could be spared from its defence, and as Col. Herd's regiment was so near Staten Island, Gen. Lee deemed it proper that he should be sent over for its protection. The next day the Committee addressed another letter to the same Convention, informing them that the Mercury, ship of war, with two transports under her convoy, had left the port, and anchored near Staten Island, and express their fears that the Col. will arrive too late. In reply, the New Jersey Congress inform the Committee on the 12th that Col. Herd, with 700 men, have been ordered to march immediately to Staten Island. On the 17th, Congress expressed their thanks to Col. Herd for his alacrity in their service, but as the danger had now passed (probably by the departure of the ships) his services would not be required.

After the British had taken possession of Staten Island, the County of Richmond does not appear to have been represented in the Legislature of the State for a long time. There were representatives who were entitled to their seats, but they were not permitted to leave the Island. Communication with the main land, or with New York, or Long Island, was prohibited, except by permission, and consequently in the succeeding sessions of the Legislature the name of a representative from Richmond does not appear.

In the Journals of the Convention, Committee of Safety, etc., the days of the week were all recorded in Latin thus:

"Die Veneris 10 Hora A. M. April 21st, 1775;" that is, Friday, 10 o'clock, before noon.

  Die Solis, day of the Sun, Sunday.
  Die Lunæ " Moon, Monday.
  Die Martis " Mars, Tuesday.
  Die Mercurie " Mercury, Wednesday.
  Die Jovis " Jupiter, Thursday.
  Die Veneris " Venus, Friday.
  Die Saturnia " Saturn, Saturday.

The last was sometimes written "Die Sabbati," in allusion to the Hebrew Sabbath.

The Convention sometimes met on Sunday, but usually adjourned, unless business of the utmost importance demanded attention.

The first Staten Island newspaper was published on the 17th day of October, 1827; it was called the *Richmond Republican*, and was edited by Charles N. Baldwin; it hailed from Tompkinsville, but was printed in Chambers Street, New York. Its publication day was Saturday, and in politics it was rabidly democratic. Its editor announced that he also sold lottery tickets, and solicited orders for sign and ornamental painting.

A few notices and advertisements from some of the early numbers of this hebdomadal will interest the readers of the present day:

"Boat Found. Taken up on the beach of the subscriber, on the 22d of October last, a yawl about twelve feet long, garbed streaks, oak, cedar top, painted black, turpentine bottom.

CORNELIUS VANDERBILT."

Under date of November 10th, 1827, is the following:

"STEAM BOAT BOLIVAR,
Capt. Vanderbilt (Oliver), will run regularly during the winter months, after Monday 12th, as follows:

Leave Staten Island at 8 A. M. and 1 P. M.
Leave New York at 10 A. M. and 3 P. M.
Fare 25 cents. All baggage at the risk of the owners."

In May following two steamboats ran on the ferry, viz.:
The Bolivar, Capt. Oliver Vanderbilt, and the Nautilus, Capt. Robert Hazard. They advertised to leave Staten Island at 7, 8, 10 A. M.; 12.30, 2.30, 4.30 and 6 P. M. New York at 8, 10 A. M.; 12.30, 2.30, 4.30, 5.30 and 7 P. M. Fare 12½ cents.

Frances B. Fitch—though probably not a votary of the muses—advertised that he had started a ferry "at the Blazing Star, with a first rate scow, and will put on a horse-boat when the travel will allow."

The ladies of Tompkinsville met at the school-house on Monday, March 5th, 1828, "to purchase and make up clothing for the suffering Greeks," and the next month the "New York Greek Committee" acknowledged the receipt of 173 garments from the inhabitants of Tompkinsville.

The people of Holland's Hook gave notice that thereafter their place would be called Jacksonville.

On the 29th day of March, 1828, a stage commenced running between Quarantine and Richmond, fare 37½ cents; but in June of the same year it was reduced to 12½ cents.

In July, 1828, Dr. Samuel R. Smith advertised that he had commenced the practice of his profession in Tompkinsville.

1836, September 14th, Aaron Burr died at Port Richmond, in the hotel now known as the Continental, in the second story northeast room.

"C."

ANECDOTES, &c.

AT THE TIME of the Revolution, and for more than half a century thereafter, there stood on the Shore Road, New Brighton, at the foot of the hill upon which St. Mark's Hotel now stands, a long, single-story, stone house, known as Van Buskirk's tavern; but, towards the latter part of the time, as Brower's tavern, so called from the names of the individuals who kept the house. On the evening of May 24th, 17—, there was a gay assembly at this house, composed of many young ladies from the vicinity, and a corresponding number of young men, many of whom were officers of the army encamped on the Island. They had met to celebrate the King's birthday. A few of the young ladies, who were the daughters of farmers living on the Shore Road, had been brought there by water, as the most convenient way of reaching the place, and now, as the hour of midnight was about to strike, were wending their way to the shore, where their boats were in waiting to convey them home. There were four of them, each one escorted by an officer, their oarsmen being negroes. The party was equally divided, occupying two boats. They were joyous and mirthful as they sailed on the calm surface of the Kills until they reached a point opposite the little cove, which is now filled up and occupied by the New Brighton wharf, at the foot of Jersey Street, when suddenly four boats, each containing five or six men, shot out of their concealment, and surrounded the homeward-bound party. The ladies manifested a good deal of alarm until they were told that no harm should befall them; but the officers remained silent and calm, whatever they might have apprehended. At length one of them arose and inquired, "Who are you? What do you want? Where did you come from?"

"Too many questions in a bunch," replied one of the intruders, who appeared to be regarded as a leader. "Ask your questions singly, and I will reply to them."

"Well, then," resumed the officer, "Who are you?"

"Citizens of the United States of America," was the reply.

"Where did you come from?"

"From New Jersey."

"What do you want?"

"You—so make no ado about it, but each one of you get into a separate boat without delay."

They saw at once that neither remonstrance nor resistance would be of any avail, and quietly obeyed the order they had received; "trapped," said they, as they did so.

The leader told the ladies that he was sorry to interrupt their enjoyment, but if they were afraid to return home without their red-coated protectors, he would furnish them with some who wore blue coats. This proffered civility they at once and unanimously declined, and were sent on their way under the care of their colored oarsmen.

The four officers were taken to a prison in New Jersey, where they were confined until duly exchanged.

Towards the close of the war, a scout or spy, who had visited New York and had returned to New Brunswick, where he resided, reported that the British had loaded two large barges or batteaux with powder and other munitions of war, and intended to have them towed into Great Kills, Staten Island, after dark that evening, to escape the observations of the Americans. Several whale boats were at once prepared and manned for the purpose of capturing or sinking these batteaux. They timed their enterprise so as to reach the mouth of the Raritan after dark. The night was rainy and exceedingly dark, but with muffled oars, they pushed on, guiding themselves by the lights upon the Island until they entered the Great Kills. Here they concealed themselves and their boats, awaiting the arrival of their prey. About midnight the measured strokes of the tow-boats were heard, and lights were seen to enter the Kills; voices were heard speaking in subdued tones, and presently the dropping of the anchors in the water was distinctly audible at no great distance; then the departure of the row-boats, and all became silent. The Jerseyman waited patiently an hour or two, and then went in quest of the batteaux. These were readily found and examined as well as the intense darkness permitted. A consultation was briefly held in whispers, and it was decided that as the boats were so large, they would scuttle one and take the other in tow. Each batteau had a sentry on board, who, to escape the drenching of the rain, had comfortably ensconced himself under the tarpaulin which had been drawn over the hatch of each boat; and the beating of the rain upon their shelter, if it had not soothed them to slumber, would have effectually prevented them from hearing the slight noise made by the augers used in boring a number of holes in the bow of one of the boats. This done, the cable of the other boat was severed, a rope attached, and it was quietly towed out into the bay.

They were well up the Raritan with their prize when day began to break, and then the bewildered sentry awoke and came out from his retreat; he was immediately secured and disarmed by two men, who had been placed on board for the purpose. He very soon comprehended the situation, and when it was offered to release him and put him ashore, he declined, saying that he would never go back to the army again, as he was sure of being shot for suffering himself to fall asleep on his post, when a shout or a shot would have been heard on the land and brought a rescue. The sentry on the other boat was probably drowned when the boat sunk, as in the deep darkness it was impossible to see which way to swim to reach the shore. The captured boat was brought to New Brunswick in safety, and was found to contain many articles which the Americans were in need of.

Sir William Howe, though a strict disciplinarian, holding every man sternly to the line of his duty, nevertheless appears to have been of an amiable disposition, not disposed to molest any one for the expression of an opinion hostile to the government represented by him, except under extraordinary circumstances. Though a century has passed since he dwelt upon the Island, tradition has transmitted to us a few anecdotes of his intercourse with the people. On some public occasion a number of the citizens had congregated at Richmond, and in the course of their conversation, one of them, whose name we shall probably be able to discover before we conclude the narrative, in speaking of military commissions, alluding to that of David Alston, signed a few days before, remarked, "I would rather have one commission with the name of the American George attached to it, than a dozen with that of the English George." Some of his friends and neighbors reproved him for uttering a sentiment which might be construed as treasonable, and intimated that he might yet be called upon to answer for it. The remark, it would appear by the sequel, had been reported at headquarters, but no official notice was ever taken of it.

Some time, probably several months after, during one of Sir William's official visits to the Island,—for after the capture of the city of New York, his headquarters for a time were there—he, with his staff, were riding along one of the dusty Island roads, and being very thirsty, they entered a large gate which stood invitingly open, and stopped at the door of a comfortable farm-house without dismounting. The farmer came out and inquired what he could do to serve Sir William Howe and his friends. "We are exceedingly thirsty," said the commander-in-chief, "and have called to obtain a drink of milk if you have any to spare." "Yes," replied the farmer, "I will bring you some, if you will not dismount." This they declined to do, so the milk was brought to them by the farmer in a huge earthen pitcher, while his wife accompanied him, carrying a number of glasses. After they had all partaken of as much as they desired, and the proffered payment being positively declined, Sir William remarked, "You are very kind, sir; may I know to whom I am obliged for this favor ?" The farmer gave him his name. "Indeed," exclaimed he, "I have heard of you before"— the farmer looked up inquiringly,—"you are the man who prefers one of George Washington's commissions to a dozen of King George's"—the farmer's countenance fell,—"though I differ with you widely," he continued, "you need be under no apprehension ; we are both entitled to our respective opinions, and the right to express them, so long as we do no harm thereby." Bidding the alarmed farmer and his wife adieu, the party rode on. Sir William having observed that the farmer would shortly have an increase in his family, called him aside and whispered something in his ear which created a smile upon the countenances of both, and a reply from the farmer; "if so, it shall be as you wish."

Now, it so happened that in the course of a few days after the brief visit of Sir William and his staff, the farmer's family was increased by the birth of a son. Though he and his family were attached to the Reformed Dutch Church, and all his other children had been baptized in that church, on the baptism of this son, he was taken to St. Andrew's, where the ceremony was performed; Sir William Howe was present, and the name given to the child was William Howe.

In the baptismal record of that church there is but a single instance of a child having been baptized by that name, and that reads as follows:

"William Howe, son of Daniel and Elizabeth Corsen, was born y* 24th of November, 1776, & was Baptised by mr Charlton 25th of Febreary, 1777."

Thus, we think, we have discovered the name of the man who preferred George Washington's commission to that of King George, and this discovery is corroborated by the fact that the Corsen family, so far as we have been able to learn, were all consistent whigs. For the subsequent fate of William Howe Corsen, see App. L, Corsen family.

A party of three or four officers on horseback being overtaken by a shower, took advantage of the first shelter which presented itself, which happened to be a long shed attached to a barn. The owner of the place came out and offered to take care of their horses, if they would enter the house and wait until the shower had passed. The invitation was accepted ; in going into the house, they were led through the kitchen, where the good housewife was engaged with her churn. They paused for a moment to observe the process of making butter, and then passed on. After they had seated themselves, they inquired whether they could be furnished with something to eat. The man of the house replied in the affirmative, and said that his wife would attend to their wants as soon as she had finished churning. "If," said one of the officers, "that only prevents her from attending to our wants immediately, I'll do the churning for her while she prepares something for us;" so going into the kitchen, he good-humoredly informed her of the arrangement which he proposed to make, to which she, also good-humoredly, assented, but stood for a few moments to see how he managed matters. At length she exclaimed, "Oh, sir, this will never do; if you can't use your sword any better than you do the churn-dasher, you ain't much of a soldier; why, you are splashing all the milk out of the churn, and you will be a pretty looking object by the time you have finished ; here, let me pin this apron before you, then I'll show you how to do it." So saying, she fastened an apron upon him, to which he laughingly submitted, then showed him how to use the dasher, and went to work preparing something for the party to eat. His companions occasionally would look at him and make some jocular remark, to which he would reply that he was creating an appetite. The good woman, too, would sometimes glance through the door at him, when she would exclaim, "Oh, oh, but he is an awkward man ; but if he keeps on long enough, he will fetch the butter." This remark of hers became a by-word among the officers of the army when anything requiring unremitted exertion was to be done, "keep on long enough, and you'll fetch the butter," and continued to be used long after the origin of it had been forgotten.

By the time they had finished their repast, the rain had ceased. As they were preparing to depart, the officer who had performed at the churn inquired of the woman how much they were to pay her. "Pay!" she exclaimed, "why, sir, we don't keep a tavern; we don't take pay for such trifles; you are, all of you, heartily welcome to what little I have done for you." No amount of urging could induce her to accept money from them, and they rode off, promising that she should hear from them before long. In less than a week thereafter, a package containing the materials for a black silk dress for the lady of the house, was received, together with a brief note from Sir William Howe, requesting her to accept it as a remuneration for learning him how to churn.

In one of the companies of infantry attached to the British army, was an Englishman who was very tall, standing a head above his fellows, and proportionately stout; he was of a quarrelsome disposition, and frequently in trouble, and thoroughly disliked by his comrades. For some breach of military discipline, he was confined in the guard-house for several days, and fed on bread and water. To the confinement he made no very strenuous objection, but he protested, though in vain, against the fare allowed to him. When he was discharged, and permitted again to mingle with his fellows, he repeatedly expressed his intention of revenging himself upon his captain, on whose complaint he had been punished. The captain was informed of the threats made by the soldier, and warned to be on his guard. A few mornings after the release of the prisoner, while the company were being drilled in firing blank cartridges, the captain became conscious that a bullet had passed his head within an inch or two, and buried itself in a tree just behind him, beneath which he stood. He suspected whence the bullet had come, but paying no attention to the matter, he maintained his calmness, and announced to the company that as the weather was very hot, there would be no further drill that morning, but on the following morning, at an early hour, it would be resumed; each man was directed to furnish himself with three blank cartridges. The next morning at an early hour they were on the ground again, and their exercise began. When preparing for firing at the word "make ready," the captain cried out, "that was awkwardly done; it must be repeated—shoulder arms—make ready;—a great deal better," said he, "take aim,"—very badly done, that must be repeated,—shoulder arms." This was as far as he meant to go in that direction; he had detected his enemy taking direct aim at him. He continued the drill in another direction, and caused every man to lay his musket down upon the grass in front of him, and take one step backward.

One of the minor officers of the company, having been previously instructed, took his stand, sword in hand, directly by the musket of the vindictive soldier. The captain then delegated two other officers to begin, one at each end of the company, and draw the charge out of each musket. The guilty soldier made an effort to seize his musket, but the sword of the officer standing in front of him was at his throat in a twinkling, and he was obliged to desist. The examination resulted in finding every musket loaded with blank cartridges except the one belonging to the suspected individual—that was loaded with ball. He was immediately seized, his cartridge-box examined, and two more ball cartridges found therein. A court-martial was convened the same day, the prisoner tried on the charge of attempting to kill his captain, found guilty, and sentenced to be shot the day following, which was done by a file of soldiers detailed for the purpose, to the great relief of the captain, and not at all to the regret of his comrades.

We have had occasion to allude to a gun-boat which was kept at the expense of the people of the county on the Sound, to prevent intercourse between the people of Staten Island and those of New Jersey. This boat, for a time at least, appears to have been under the direction of Col. Billop, and was an unpopular affair to the people on both sides of the water. It was an almost daily occurrence that those on board fired upon any person within their reach on the Jersey shores; with what effect, however, is not known. A company of half dozen Jerseymen once attempted to get possession of the boat, but failed. It was lying at anchor one bright moonlight night under the shore of the Island, and as no person was seen moving on board, they supposed their opportunity had come. Accordingly, one of their number was sent in a small boat to row up some distance above the gun-boat, and then to drift silently down with the ebb tide, and, as he passed, to observe whether there was any person on her deck. He succeeded in accomplishing his purpose, but discovered a man sitting flat upon the deck, apparently engaged in strapping a knife upon his boot. When he reached the shore he made his report, and the enterprise was abandoned for the time, nor do we know that it was ever after renewed.

Though there were, in the royal army, both among the English and Hessians, a great many idle, dissolute and very wicked men, officers as well as privates, there were also among them many exemplary and industrious men, some of whom were mechanics and some agriculturists. An army doing garrison duty, has generally a good deal of idle time, which was employed by these men to their own profit and advantage. Shoemakers, for instance, frequently made boots and shoes for the officers and their families, when they had any, and for the citizens of the county; and were permitted to take their surplus work to the city to sell to dealers, for all of which they were generally well paid. The government supplying all their personal wants, the money thus earned accumulated, until at the close of the war, many had large sums at their command. It was generally this class who contrived to stay behind, purchase land, or commence business on their own account, sometimes, it is said, under assumed names. Some of the agriculturists obtained permission from the neighboring farmers to clear and cultivate an acre or two of land which the owners, in many instances, had considered worthless, because it was overgrown with bushes and briars, and would cost more to clear, as they said, than it was worth. It was wonderful, indeed, to see the amount these industrious soldiers would raise on a single acre—"more," said our venerable informant, "than I could raise from five." They suffered no thorns, hedges or briars to grow along their enclosures, remarking that where a useless plant would grow, a useful one would grow as well. Thus not only in this, but in many other instances, teaching the farmer's lessons in economy and thrift, which they would have done well to imitate.

It is, after all, a doubtful matter whether there were many of the people of Staten Island who were really tories from principle. The Seaman and Billop families, and two or three others not quite so prominent, were all beneficiaries of the British government; they were the proprietors of large and valuable estates bestowed upon them for merely nominal consideration; they were also the incumbents of lucrative offices which gave them a power and an influence which otherwise they would not have possessed. The British officers, both of the army and navy, were lavish of their gold, and the people of the Island, so far as money was concerned, were never in better circumstances. The temptation then to infringe the resolutions of the Provincial Congress, prohibiting all intercourse with the vessels of the enemy, were irresistible, more especially as the Congress was powerless to enforce its own ordinances, or to punish the infraction of them. But the local committees of the Province of New Jersey were not idle, neither were they blind. At times, when the demand exceeded the supply, the dealers on the Island were under the necessity of obtaining their articles from New Jersey, either personally, if they choose to run the hazard, or through agents, who sometimes contrived to smuggle them successfully. There was, however, no lack of patriots on the Island who dared to strike a blow whenever it could be done with security. The following anecdote is an instance:—A man named Taylor—not of the Staten Island family of that name—came over from New York, and took up his abode here for the avowed purpose of trading with the English vessels. He carried on the business for several months openly, and in defiance of all the cautions he had received by means of anonymous letters, which he openly exhibited in public places, and held up to ridicule. He defied any power which the rebels possessed to prevent his doing as he pleased in the matter of trading with the ships. One very dark and stormy night, five men entered his dwelling unannounced; they were all disguised, and while a part of them seized and bound him, the remainder performed the same service for his wife. With pistols at their heads, they were cautioned to make no outcry. Having secured Taylor, they led him to his own barn, put a noose around his neck with a pair of his own horse reins, threw the rope over one of the beams, and hoisted him from the floor by his neck; then having fastened the rope to a post in the manger, left him and went their way.

His wife hearing the men depart, apprehended something serious had occurred, and made most desperate efforts to loose the thongs which bound her, and finally succeeded. Fortunately a lighted lantern stood in an adjoining room, which she seized and ran into the barn, where she found her worst apprehensions realized by seeing her husband struggling in the agonies of death. Finding she could not untie the knot around the manger post, she found a hatchet with which she cut the rope and let him down upon the floor. Having removed the noose around his neck, and finding him insensible, she ran to a neighboring house for assistance, and at length succeeded in restoring him to consciousness. Two or three days afterwards Taylor removed back again to New York, but he was accompanied by a guard of soldiers all the way to the city.

It was at some time between the cessation of actual hostilities and the evacuation of New York, Long and Staten Islands by the British, that the following incident is said to have occurred: There were many ships of war lying at anchor in various parts of the harbor, mostly in the vicinity of the city; there were some, however, which laid in, and even beyond the Narrows, and these were anchored near the shores of Long and Staten Islands, as could safely be done, for the convenience of easy access to the land in all conditions of the weather, in order that the officers might obtain supplies of butter, vegetables, &c., from the farms in the vicinity. One day, a boy, some seventeen or eighteen years of age, whose father was a relative of the narrator of the anecdote, was in search of some stray cattle in the woods near the water, and saw a ship's boat with two sailors approaching. Supposing he might as well keep out of their sight in that solitary place, he concealed himself behind a large tree; he saw them land, and while one of them remained in charge of the boat, the other, with a basket in his hand, entered the wood. After having proceeded a few rods, until he was out of sight of his companion, and of everybody else, as he supposed, he took off his coat, knelt down at the foot of a large, gnarled tree, and, with an instrument resembling a mason's trowel, dug a hole in the earth, partly under a huge root, and having deposited something therein, carefully filled the hole again with earth, and laid a large flat stone upon it. Having accomplished his purpose, whatever it might have been, he rose to his feet, and took a long and careful survey of the surroundings, then proceeded on his way. The youth kept in his place of concealment for two full hours, when he saw the sailor returning with his basket apparently filled with vegetables; he passed by the place where he had dug the hole, scrutinized it closely, and then proceeded to the boat, which was still in waiting for him, and returned to the ship. Assuring himself that the coast was clear, the young man went to the place, re-opened the hole, and found therein a heavy canvas bag, evidently containing, as he judged by its sound, a quantity of money. Securing his prize, and without waiting to re-fill the hole, he hastened away, and found some other place of deposit, known only to himself. A day or two thereafter posters were put up in every public place, offering a large reward for the recovery of three hundred guineas, which had been stolen from one of his majesty's ships, being the property of the government, and an additional reward for the detection of the thief, but the boy kept his own counsel. The theft occasioned a good deal of talk at the time, but it was soon forgotten in the excitement consequent upon the declaration of peace, and the preparations for the departure of the British from the country. For nearly four years the young man kept his own secret, at which time he had attained his majority; and then, when he purchased a farm for himself, and paid for it, did he first reveal, to his parents only, the manner in which he obtained his means.

Sometime between the close of the Revolution and that of the century in which it occurred, a remarkable character made his appearance on the Island; he was tall and lank, and had a complexion so dark that many believed him to be either half negro or half Indian. He appeared to be well educated, and was remarkably circumspect in his conduct and conversation. He professed to have once been in a trance, during which he had visited both heaven and hell, and had seen and heard things which he dared not repeat. While in heaven, he, with eleven others, all strangers to each other, were commissioned to return to the earth and preach the true and everlasting gospel to every creature, all over the world. The others, without doubt, were now fulfilling their mission, as he was his. He said he had traveled over the States of Virginia, Pennsylvania, New Jersey and New York, and was now closing his work on Staten Island, where he was predestined to die. It had been revealed to him that he was first to have a very narrow escape from death, and then in a very short time thereafter he should die suddenly. He professed to have a limited power to work miracles, but that power was confined to healing the diseases of those who had faith; and it was said, he actually did cure some who professed to have unlimited faith in him. His method of cure was to place his hand on the patient and say, "according to your faith be it done unto you." If he failed in effecting a cure, he ascribed it to no want of power in himself, but to a want of faith in the patient. He denounced churches, and said they were the inventions of men who desired to go to heaven in an easy carriage drawn by angels over a road made of blossoms and perfumed flowers. He admitted there had been good people among them, for he had seen some of them in heaven. God, he said, had his temples, but he had built them Himself in the shape of trees, bowers and shady retreats. He preached repeatedly wherever he could find an umbrageous tree and an audience. He was very severe in his denunciations of personal pride, however manifested, and made humility in all its phases the principal virtue of his system, because, he said, without humility there could possibly be no religion. He never accepted any gifts which were offered, except food when he was hungry, or clothing when he required it. He accepted a night's lodging when it was offered, but if not, any place which afforded shelter and protection was sufficient. People regarded him as a sort of harmless lunatic, and he was never molested. One day, as he was passing a place where some men were felling trees, he stopped to see a very large tree fall, but as he stood too near, he was cautioned to stand back further; he had moved but a step or two when the tree fell, apparently directly upon him, but to the surprise of all who saw it, he stood unhurt amid the branches, which in falling had passed on each side of him without touching him. "This," "said he, "is the great peril I had to encounter and escape; now I shall die soon, and suddenly." The next day he was overtaken by a shower, and sought shelter in a barn, which was struck by lightning and he was killed, thus verifying his own prophecy.

There are those still living who can remember the great panic which pervaded the Island somewhere about the year 1820. Somebody had predicted the positive sinking of the Island on a certain day. There were hundreds of people whose apprehensions were excited, and the prophecy became the subject of universal conversation. Some sold their property, others removed from the Island, and when the day dawned, even those who had derided the prophecy were conscious of a choking sensation. There were many people who spent that entire day on the shores of New Jersey and Long Island, with their eyes fixed upon Staten Island, expecting momentarily to see it go down. There was one man, it was said, conveyed a boat to the highest point of the Island, and spent the day in it, that he might be ready to slide off when the catastrophe came. He conveyed his boat back again at night. When the day had passed, and the absentees began to return, not a solitary individual could be found who had ever given the least credence to the prophecy.

Tradition says that thirty or thirty-five years before the war of the Revolution began—that is to say, if the Declaration of Independence is assumed to be the beginning of that war—between 1741 and 1746, the agricultural community of Staten Island, which then probably embraced nine-tenths of the population, became terribly excited by the frequent and mysterious killing of their cattle. They were found dead in their pastures with their throats cut, in every instance close to their heads. At first it was ascribed to some enemy of the owner, who adopted this method of gratifying his vindictive inclinations, but it was at length discovered that in every case the animal's tongue had been cut out and taken away. Slight as it was, this appeared to be the sole motive of the perpetrator or perpetrators of these outrages. Three or four nights after the offence had been committed in one locality, it was repeated in another, miles away, and again, after another interval, in another place in quite a different direction. Three, four or five cattle were killed each night the perpetrators were abroad. Some farmers had their pastures watched every night; others drove their cattle into inclosures during the night, near their dwellings; the roads were patrolled during the darkness, but all these precautions were of little avail; if an animal happened to be exposed, or a watchman, through weariness or any other cause, became temporarily remiss, the crime was repeated, and the criminal escaped. The people at length became desperate; public meetings were held in the several towns, and rewards offered for the capture of the offenders, but none were captured. The slaves were suspected and closely watched, but no discoveries were made.

At length a farmer residing near the locality known as the "Elm Tree," was aroused one night by the barking of his dogs in a distant part of his farm; arousing his two sons, and two or three of his slaves, and arming them with guns and clubs, they hastened away in the direction of the still barking dogs, but observing the utmost silence. When they had reached the place where the dogs were, they were seen to be barking at something in a large tree in the edge of a piece of woods. A consultation in a subdued tone was held; some thought the dogs had driven a wild cat into the tree—others that it might be a bear—but the old man said that a wild animal would have fought and torn the dogs, and perhaps killed one or both, and therefore he differed from them, but he said, "There may be a cat in that tree, but I think it is the cat that killed our cattle; we shall see in the morning." A close watch was kept around the foot of the tree during the remainder of the night, and when it became sufficiently light, a man was discovered sitting on one of the upper branches. Convinced that he had at length caught the slayer of the cattle on the Island, he hailed him and directed him to come down, but received no reply. The summons to descend was repeated several times without effect; he sat immovable, crouched into as small a compass as possible, leaning upon the main trunk of the tree. The farmer was at a loss what to do; he dared not fire, for he might kill him, while as yet he was only suspected; at length he sent his negroes to notify two or three of his neighbors, and requested them to meet him, while he and his sons continued their guard over the prisoner. In less than an hour a dozen of the neighboring farmers were assembled under the tree, who all shared the farmer's suspicions, until one of them, in endeavoring to obtain a better view of their prisoner, stumbled upon an object which at once verified their suspicions. This was an exceedingly dirty, blood-stained bag containing two or three fresh beef's tongues and a long sharp knife in a leather sheath. With such a formidable weapon in his possession, it was surprising that he had suffered the two dogs to drive him into the tree, unless in the suddenness of the attack he had dropped the bag, and either had not had time, or could not see, in the darkness, to recover it. There was now no diversity of opinion as to the character of the prisoner, though there was as to the best method of disposing of him. It was at length decided that if he persisted in his refusal to reply to their questions, or to descend from the tree, to shoot him. This decision was about to be carried into effect, when the prisoner, seeing the gun pointed at him, threw up his hands and exclaimed. "Don't shoot, massa, and I'll come down." It was then for the first time discovered that he was a negro. Slowly he descended, apparently looking about him for an opportunity of eluding his captors, but the moment he was within reach, a dozen hands seized and held him securely until his arms were pinioned. He was a stranger to all of those who surrounded him, and to all their questions as to his name and residence, he maintained a dogged silence. Growing impatient of the fellow's stubbornness, a noose was slipped over his head, and in a very brief space he was dangling to one of the limbs of the tree. It was never known who he was or where he resided, but there was an expression of satisfaction throughout the Island when the news of the capture and execution was heard.

During the whole time of their occupancy of the Island, the British kept a lookout on some convenient elevation, for the arrival of vessels. At one time a sentinel was stationed in the top of "a large chestnut tree, which grew upon the summit of the Island, about a mile from a small wooden church which stood near the King's highway." This description corresponds with some locality near the present residence of Mr. T. C. Bogart. There is a tradition confirmatory of this statement, which says that the British kept a number of soldiers on the top of Toad Hill to guard the road and to keep a look-out over the land and water. From the locality indicated, this might have been done very easily, for it commands a view of the outer bay and Sandy Hook in one direction, and of the Kills, and New Jersey beyond, in the other. The sentinel in the tree was provided with a platform upon which to stand, and signals to elevate upon a pole lashed to the highest limb of the tree. This position was a perilous one in a heavy wind, and peculiarly so during a thunder storm. It is said that upon one occasion a soldier on duty in that elevated place was overtaken by a sudden storm of rain, thunder and lightning; the ladder by which he had ascended was blown out of his reach, and he was unable to escape from the dangers which surrounded him. When the storm had passed away, his body was found upon the ground beneath the tree, with his neck broken, and certain livid marks upon his person, as well as the condition of the tree itself, indicated that he had been stricken with lightning, and had fallen to the ground. About a month thereafter, another storm passed over the same locality, and the look-out descended from his elevation as quickly as possible, but he had no sooner reached the ground than the tree was again struck, and he was killed at his foot. After that the place of lookout was changed, and brought down the hill nearer the church, probably in the vicinity of the light-house. The following season the doomed tree was again struck, and riven to splinters.

An aged man named Britton, residing in Southfield, with his wife and grand-daughter, a young lady about seventeen years of age, were seated before a bright fire on the hearth, one chilly autumn evening; on a table stood a mug of cider, and in the fire was one end of a long iron rod, placed there to become heated, with which the old man was in the habit of "mulling" his cider, a beverage of which he was very fond, and of which he partook every evening before retiring. While thus waiting for the iron to become red-hot, the outer door of the room suddenly opened, and a huge Hessian soldier entered. After regarding the family group for a moment, he walked to the corner in which the young lady was sitting, and seated himself beside her. "Hey, missy," said he, attempting to put his arm around her waist, "how you like a big Dutchman for a husband, hey?" "Go away, you Dutch brute," said she. "Oh, no," he answered, renewing his attempt at familiarity, "me not go away yet." "Go away," she repeated "or I shall hurt you." Laughing at this threat, as something extremely amusing, he persisted in annoying her by his insolence. Suddenly she stooped down, and seizing the iron rod, thrust the red-hot end of it into his face. He uttered a yell, and in the effort to spring up, fell over his chair; she continued her assault upon him by pushing the rod into any part of his person she could reach, and when he had regained his feet and made for the door, she continued to pursue him, even following him out of doors. He made repeated attempts to strike her, but her rod being longer than his arm, effectually prevented him from touching her. He also attempted to seize the rod, but it was too hot to hold, and every such effort only burned him the more. Foiled at every point, he turned and ran away.

"D."

GOVERNMENT.

The Government of New Netherland, under the original Dutch settlers, was committed to the Director and his Council, which at first consisted of five members. This Council had supreme executive and legislative authority in the whole colony. It had also the power to try all civil and criminal cases, and all prosecutions before it were conducted by a "Schout Fiscaal," whose duties were similar to those of a sheriff and district attorney of the present day. He had the power to arrest all persons, but not without a complaint previously made to him, unless he caught an offender *in flagrante delictu*. It was his duty to examine into the merits of every case, and lay them before the court, without favor to either party; he was also to report to the Directors in Holland, the nature of every case prosecuted by him, and the judgment therein. In addition to the duties above enumerated, it devolved upon him to examine the papers of all vessels arriving or departing; to superintend the lading and discharging of cargoes, and to prevent smuggling. He had a right to attend the meetings of the Council, and give his opinion when asked, but not to vote on any question.

Several of the patroons claimed in a great measure to be independent of the Director and his Council, and organized courts and appointed magistrates for their own territories, as did the Patroons of Rensselaerwyck and Staten Island, but they were at constant variance with the authorities at New Amsterdam.

It is true that all who felt themselves aggrieved by the judgment of the Director and his Council, had a chartered right to appeal to the XIX at home—that is, the West India Company—but the Directors of New Netherland generally played the despot during the brief terms of their authority, and if any suitor manifested an intention to appeal, he was at once charged with a contempt of the supreme power in the colony, and most severely punished, unless he contrived to keep out of the Directors reach, until his case had been heard and decided in Holland, as in the instance of Melyn, the patroon of Staten Island, who appears to have been a thorn in the sides of both Kieft and Stuyvesant.

The religion recognized by the government of the province was that of the Reformed Dutch Church, or the Church of Holland, and though other sects were regarded with a certain degree of suspicion, they were tolerated so long as they did not interfere with the privileges of others.

When Stuyvesant was compelled by the popular clamor to surrender the country to the English, he stipulated for the preservation and continuance of all the political and religious rights and privileges of the people as then enjoyed, allegiance alone excepted, which was conceded by Nicolls.

After the conquest, this stipulation was generally held inviolate, but the civil institutions of the country were modified to make them accord with English ideas of government.

There are instances on record of persecution for opinion's sake on religious subjects under the Dutch, but all such matters were at once rectified when brought to the notice of the home government. This continued to be the practice of the English government also.

From the date of the conquest to the arrival of Dongan as governor, the country had been governed by the "Duke's Laws," which prohibited the election of magistrates by the people, but in 1683 Dongan convened a general assembly, which modified some of these laws and abrogated others. Some of the important changes made by this assembly were the following:

The supreme authority was to reside in the governor, council and people represented in general assembly.

Assemblies were to be held at least triennially.

Freeholders or freemen were to vote for members.

The number of members were to be 21, or as many more as the Duke thought proper. Of these, Richmond was entitled to two.

Bills passed were to be approved by the governor, with the concurrence of the Duke.

No tax should be levied but by consent of the governor, council and representatives.

Trials by a jury of twelve, and a grand jury authorized.

All offences except treason and felony to be bailable.

No man's land to be liable to sale under execution without his consent, but the profits and issues thereof to be liable for debt.

Married women's rights in their husband's estate not to be sold without their consent.

Widows to be entitled to thirds, as dower.

Full religious liberty to all professing faith in God by Jesus Christ.

A law was also passed creating the office of a sheriff for each county, and permitting him to have a deputy.

The province was divided in 1683 into the following counties: 1, New York; 2, Westchester; 3, Ulster; 4, Albany, including Schenectady; 5, Duchess; 6, Orange; 7, Richmond; 8, Kings; 9, Queens; 10, Suffolk; 11, Duke's; 12, Cornwall; the two last named now form a part of Massachusetts.

In March, 1688, Richmond was divided into four towns—Castletown, Northfield, Southfield and Westfield. The town of Middletown was not organized until 1860.

Before the legal division of the county into towns, it was divided into three precincts, the North, South and West: Castleton was not included in any of the precincts, but was designated "The Manor." The limits of the precincts were about the same as those of the towns as established by law on the 7th March, 1688.

Castleton derived its name from the Palmer or Dongan patent, in which the manor conveyed was called Cassiltown, corrupted into the present name, and the corruption legalized by repeated Acts of the Legislature; the other towns were named from their position in the county.

When the county of Richmond was first organized, the

county seat was fixed at Stony Brook, on the Amboy road, a short distance south of the Black Horse corner, and near the former site of the old Waldensian church. Tradition says that the county building consisted of a log cabin, containing two rooms, one for the residence of the jailor, and one for a prison, in which prisoners remained as long as suited their convenience.

The County seat was subsequently removed* to Cocklestown, which was the original name of the village of Richmond, then a mere hamlet of half a dozen small houses, and the name changed to that of the county.

The courts organized under the English authority were as follows:

1st. The Court of Chancery, consisting of the Governor and Council, to which appeals might be brought from any other court.

2d. The Oyer and Terminer, held once each year in each county, and consisting of a Judge of the upper court, and three Justices of the Peace of the county.

3d. In New York and Albany, the mayor and Aldermen held a court every fortnight, and from which there was no appeal except in cases where an amount over £20 was involved.

4th. Courts of Sessions in every county twice each year, composed of the Justices of the Peace of the county.

5th. Three Commissioners in every town to determine matters of difference between parties not exceeding the value of £5.

* Vide App. N. (43.)

"E."

STATEN ISLAND
200 YEARS AGO.

The following is an extract from a manuscript found in the city of Amsterdam, a few years ago, by Hon. H. C. Murphy, of Brooklyn.

On the 8th of June, 1679, two Labadists, Jasper Dankers and Peter Sluyter, sailed from Amsterdam in a ship called the *Charles*, Capt. Thomas Singleton, and arrived at Sandy Hook on the 22d of September following. They say: "When we came between the Hoofden (the Highlands of Staten and Long Islands—that is, in the Narrows)—we saw some Indians on the beach with a canoe, and others coming down the hill. As we tacked about, we came close to the shore, and called out to them to come on board the ship. The Indians came on board, and we looked upon them with wonder. They are dull of comprehension, slow of speech, bashful, but otherwise bold of person and red of skin. They wear something in front over the thighs, and a piece of duffels, like a blanket, around the body, and that is all the clothing they have. Their hair hangs down from their head in strings, well smeared with fat, and sometimes with quantities of little beads twisted in it, out of pride. They have thick lips and thick noses, but not fallen in like the negroes, heavy eyebrows or eyelids, brown or black eyes, thick tongues, and all of them black hair. After they had obtained some biscuit, and had amused themselves a little climbing and looking here and there, they also received some brandy to taste, of which they drank excessively, and threw it up again. They then went ashore in their canoe, and we, having a better breeze, sailed ahead handsomely." After narrating how they landed in the city, and describing the bay and the immense quantities of fish therein, they proceed with their journal.

"*October 9th, Monday.*—We remained at home two days, except I went out to ascertain whether there was any way of going over to Staten Island.

10, *Tuesday.*—Finding no opportunity of going to Staten Island, we asked our old friend Symon, who had come over from Gouanes (Gowanus?), what was the best way for us to go there, when he offered us his services to take us over in his skiff, which we accepted, and at dusk accompanied him in his boat to Gouanes, where we arrived about 8 o'clock, and where he welcomed us and entertained us well.

11, *Wednesday.*—We embarked early this morning in his boat, and rowed over to Staten Island, where we arrived about 8 o'clock. He left us there, and we went on our way. This Island is about 32 miles long, and four broad. Its sides are very irregular, with projecting points and indenting bays and creeks running deep into the country. It lies for the most part east and west, and is somewhat triangular; the most prominent point is to the west. On the east side is the narrow passage which they call the channel, by which it is separated from the high point of Long Island. On the south is the great bay, which is enclosed by Nayag, t'Conijnen island, Rentselaer's Hook, Neversink, etc. On the west is the Raritans. On the north or north-west is New Jersey, from which it is separated by a large creek or arm of the river called Kil Van Kol. The eastern part is high and steep, and has few inhabitants. It is the usual place where ships ready for sea, stop to take in water.* The whole south side is a large plain, with much salt meadow or marsh, and several creeks.

The west point is flat, and on or around it is a large creek with much marsh, but to the north of this creek it is high and hilly, and beyond that it begins to be more level, but not so low as on the other side, and is well populated. On the northwest it is well provided with creeks and marshes, and the land is generally better than on the south side, although there is a good parcel of land in the middle of the latter. As it is the middle or most hilly part of the Island, it is uninhabited, although the soil is better than the land around it; but

---

* Vide App. N. (45.)

in consequence of its being away from the water, and lying so high, no one will live there, the creeks and rivers being so serviceable to them in enabling them to go to the city, and for fishing and catching oysters, and for being near the salt meadow. The woods are used for pasturing horses and cattle, for, being an island, none of them can get off. Each person has marks upon his own by which he can find them when he wants them. When the population shall increase, these places will be taken up. Game of all kinds is plenty, and twenty-five or thirty deer are sometimes seen in a herd. A boy who came in a house where we were, told us he had shot ten the last winter himself, and more than forty in his life, and in the same manner other game. We tasted here the best grapes. There are now about 100 families on the Island, of which the English constitute the least portion, and the Dutch and French divide between them about equally the greater portion. They have neither church nor minister, and live rather far from each other, and inconveniently to meet together. The English are less disposed to religion, and inquire little after it; but in case there was a minister, would contribute to his support. The French and Dutch are very desirous and eager for one, for they spoke of it wherever we went. The French are good Reformed church-men, and some of them are Walloons. The Dutch are also from different quarters. We reached the Island, as I have said, about 9 o'clock, directly opposite Gouanes, not far from the watering-place. We proceeded southwardly along the shore of the highland on the east end, where it was sometimes stony and rocky, and sometimes sandy, supplied with fine constantly flowing springs, with which at times we quenched our thirst.

We had now come nearly to the furthest point on the southeast, behind which I had observed several houses when we came in with the ship. We had also made inquiry as to the villages through which we would have to pass, and they told us the "Oude Dorp" * would be the first one we would come to; but my comrade finding the point very rocky and

* Vide App. N. (46.)

difficult, and believing the village was inland, and as we discovered no path to follow, we determined to clamber to the top of this steep bluff, through the bushes and thickets, which we accomplished with great difficulty and in a perspiration. We found as little of r ..d above as below, and nothing but woods, through which no one could see. There appeared to be a little foot-path along the edge, which I followed a short distance to the side of the point, but my companion calling me, and saying that he thought we had certainly passed by the road to the Oude Dorp, and observing myself that the little path led down to the point, I returned again, and we followed it the other way, which led us back to the place from where we started. We supposed we ought to go from the shore to find the road to the Oude Drop, and seeing here these slight tracks into the woods, we followed them as far as we could, till at last they ran to nothing else than dry leaves.

Having wandered an hour or more in the woods, now in a hollow and then over a hill, at one time through a swamp, at another across a brook, without finding any road or path, we entirely lost the way. We could see nothing but the sky through the thick branches of the trees over our heads, and we thought it best to break out of the woods entirely and regain the shore. I had taken an observation of the shore and point, having been able to look at the sun, which shone extraordinarily hot in the thick woods, without the least breath of air stirring. We made our way at last, as well as we could, out of the woods, and struck the shore a quarter of an hour's distance from where we began to climb up. We were rejoiced, as there was a house not far from the place where we came out. We went to it to see if we could find any one who would show us the way a little. There was no master in it, but an English woman with negroes and servants. We first asked her as to the road, and then for something to drink, and also for some one to show us the road, but she refused the last, although we were willing to pay for it; she was a cross woman. She said she had never been at the village, and her folks must work, and we would certainly have to go away as wise as we came. She said, however, we must follow the shore, as we did. We went now over the rocky point, which we were no sooner over than we saw a pretty little sand bay, and a small creek, and not far from there, cattle and houses. We also saw the point from which the little path led from the hill above, where I was when my comrade called me. We would not have had more than three hundred steps to go to have been where we now were. It was very hot, and we perspired a great deal. We went on to the little creek to sit down and rest ourselves there, and to cool our feet, and then proceeded to the houses which constituted the Oude Dorp. It was now about two o'clock. There were seven houses, but only three in which anybody lived. The others were abandoned, and their owners gone to live on better places on the Island, because the ground around this village was worn out and barren, and also too limited for their use. We went into the first house, which was inhabited by English, and there rested ourselves and eat, and inquired further after the road; the woman was cross, and her husband not much better. We had to pay here for what we eat, which we have not done before. We paid three guilders in seewan, although we only drank water. We proceeded by a tolerably good road to Nieuwe Dorp, but as the road ran continually in the woods we got astray again in them. It was dark, and we were compelled to break our way out through the woods and thickets, and we went a great distance before we succeeded, when it was almost entirely dark. We saw a house at a distance to which we directed ourselves across the bushes; it was the first house of the Nieuwe Dorp. We found there an Englishman who could speak Dutch, and who received us very cordially into his house, where we had as good as he and his wife had. She was a Dutch woman from the Manhatans, who was glad to have us in her house.

12th, Thursday.—Although we had not slept well, we had to resume our journey with the day. The man where we slept set us on the road. We had no more villages to go to, but went from one plantation to another, for the most part belonging to French, who showed us every kindness because we conversed with them in French.

About one-third of the distance from the south side to the west end is still all woods, and is very little visited. We had to go along the shore, finding sometimes fine creeks well provided with wild turkeys, geese, snipes and wood-hens. Lying rotting on the shore were thousands of fish called marsbaucken, which are about the size of a common carp. These fish swim close together in large schools, and are pursued by other fish so that they are forced upon the shore in order to avoid the mouths of their enemies, and when the water falls, they are left to die, food for the eagles and other birds of prey. Proceeding thus along, we came to the west point, where an Englishman lived alone, some distance from the road. We ate something here, and he gave us the consolation that we would have a very bad road for two or three hours ahead, which indeed we experienced, for there was neither path nor road. He showed us as well as he could. There was a large creek to cross which ran very far into the land, and when we got on the other side of it we must, he said, go outward along the shore. After we had gone a piece of the way through the woods, we came to a valley with a brook running through it, which we took to be the creek, or the end of it. We turned around it as short as we could, in order to go back again to the shore, which we reached after wandering a long time over hill and dale, when we saw the creek, which we supposed we had crossed, now just before us. We followed the side of it deep into the woods, and when we arrived at the end of it saw no path along the other side to get outwards again, but the road ran into the woods in order to cut off a point of the hills and land. We pursued this road for some time, but saw no mode of getting out, and that it led further and further from the creek. We therefore left the road, and went across through the bushes, so as to reach the shore by the nearest route according to our calculation. After continuing this course about an hour, we saw at a distance a miserably constructed tabernacle of pieces of wood covered with brush, all open in front, and where we thought there were Indians, but on coming up to it we found in it an Englishman sick, and his wife and child lying upon some bushes by a little fire. We asked him if he was sick? "I have been sick over two months," he replied. It made my heart sore, indeed, for I never, in all my life, saw such poverty, and that, too, in the middle of the woods and wilderness. After we had obtained some information as to the way, we went on, and had not gone far before we came to another house, and thus from one farm to another, French, Dutch, and a few English, so that we had not wandered very far out of the way. We inquired, at each house, the way to the next one. Shortly before evening we arrived at the plantation of a Frenchman, whom they called La Chaudronnier, who was formerly a soldier under the Prince of Orange, and had served in Brazil. He was so delighted, and held on to us so hard, that we remained and spent the night with him.

13*th, Friday.*—We pursued our journey this morning from plantation to plantation, the same as yesterday, until we came to that of Pierre Gardinier, who had been in the service of the Prince of Orange, and had known him well. He had a large family of children and grand-children. He was about seventy years of age, and was still as fresh and active as a young person. He was so glad to see strangers who conversed with him in the French language, that he leaped with joy. After we had breakfasted here, they told us that we had another large creek to pass called the Fresh Kill, and then we could perhaps be set across the Kill Van Koll to the point of Mill Creek, where we might wait for a boat to convey us to the Manhatans. The road was long and difficult, and we asked for a guide, but he had no one, in consequence of several of his children being sick. At last he determined to go himself, and accordingly carried us in his canoe over to the point of Mill Creek in New Jersey, behind Kol, (Achter Kol.) We learned immediately that there was a boat upon this creek loading with brick, and would leave that night for the city. After we had thanked and parted with Pierre le Gardinier, we determined to walk to Elizabethtown, a good half hour's distance inland, where the boat was. We slept there this night, and at 3 o'clock in the morning set sail."

"F."

VILLAGES.

VILLAGE OF NEW BRIGHTON.

This village was incorporated by act of the Legislature, April 26th, 1866, and embraced the northerly half of the town of Castleton. It was about two and a half miles long in a straight line, and about one mile in width. This territory was divided into four wards, and the trustees appointed by the same act to carry its provisions into effect, were Augustus Prentice, 1st ward; James W. Simonton, 2d ward; Francis G. Shaw, 3d ward; and Willliam H. J. Bodine, 4th ward. The portion of the town remaining unincorporated was very sparsely populated, but was obliged, nevertheless, to have a full corps of town officers, some of whom resided within the village, and exercised their offices without, as well as within, and the duties of some, such as the commissioners of highways, which office had been abolished within the village, could be performed only in the unincorporated remnant of the town. The bills rendered by these officers for their services at the end of each year were so enormous, that the taxes outside of the village were greater than those within. The only method the people could resort to for ridding themselves of this burden, was to seek admission into the corporation, which they did, and in 1872 the remainder of the town was added to the village, and divided into two wards, the 5th and 6th. The dimensions of the village now are, length about 4 miles, breadth about 2.

In 1871, a large and elegant village hall was erected on Lafayette Avenue, corner of Second Street, at a cost of about $36,000, including the land.

The village contains eleven churches, viz:

In the 1st ward the Reformed Church, corner of Tompkins Avenue and Fort Street.

St. Peter's Roman Catholic Church, between Carroll Place and St. Mark's Place.

In the 2d ward, Christ Church, Episcopal, on Franklin Avenue, corner of Second Street.

Church of the Redeemer, Unitarian, on Clinton Avenue, corner of Second Street.

The Snug Harbor Church.

In the 3d ward, St. Mary's Church, Episcopal, on Castleton Avenue, corner of Davis Avenue.

Calvary Church, Presbyterian, Bement Avenue, corner of Castleton Avenue.

In the 4th ward, Church of the Ascension, Episcopal, on Richmond Terrace, or Shore Road.

Trinity Church, Methodist, on Richmond Terrace, or Shore Road.

Church of St. Rose of Lima, Roman Catholic, on Castleton Avenue, corner of Roe Street.

In the 5th ward a Moravian Chapel on Richmond Turnpike, Four Corners.

In addition to the above, the Young Men's Christian Association building, known as Association Hall, on the Shore Road, 4th ward, is used for religious purposes every Sabbath day, and several times through the week.

There are four public schools in the village, viz:

One on Madison Avenue, 1st ward. One on Prospect Avenue, 2d ward. One on Elizabeth Street, 4th ward, and one on the Manor Road, near Four Corners, 6th ward; there are also two or three excellent private schools.

The charitable and benevolent institutions in the village are: The Sailors' Snug Harbor, and the Home for Destitute Children of Seamen, which are noticed elsewhere.

The Shore Rail Road—cars drawn by horses—begins at the steamboat landing, foot of Arietta Street, and runs through Arietta Street, Richmond Turnpike, Brook and Jersey Streets, to the Terrace, and thence along the Terrace to the Mill Road, near the line of the village of Port Richmond, a distance of nearly four miles. The road is admirably conducted, and is considered a great public accommodation.

There are three steam ferries connecting the village with

New York city—one from the foot of Arietta Street, on the east side of the Island, and two on the north side, each of which stop at the West New Brighton, Snug Harbor and New Brighton wharves, and make from eight to twelve trips per day to New York, according to the season.

Of the industrial establishments in the village, the New York Dyeing and Printing Establishment, on Broadway, in the 4th ward, and the Staten Island Fancy Dyeing Establishment, on Cherry Lane, in the 6th ward, are the principal, and are described more at length elsewhere. Beside these, there are manufactories of paper hangings, carriages, silk dyeing, &c.

There are two weekly newspapers printed in the village.

VILLAGE OF PORT RICHMOND.

This village was incorporated by act of the Legislature April 24th, 1866, and is situated in the town of Northfield. Its length on its southern boundary, which is nearly a straight line, is about a mile and a half; its greatest width is about three-fourths of a mile. It is not divided into wards, like the other incorporated villages in the county, but into East and West Port Richmond by the Morning Star Road; three of its five trustees must reside in the former, and two in the latter. Its first trustees were George W. Jewett, Nicholas Van Pelt, William A. Ross, Garret P. Wright and Henry Miller, all of whom were repeatedly re-elected by the people, and some of whom are still members of the board; trustee Van Pelt was the first president, and has continued to perform the duties of that office without intermission until the present time (1876.)

There are five churches in the village, viz:

The Reformed Church, on Richmond Street, or Church Road.

St. John's German Lutheran Church, on Division Avenue, corner of Catharine Street.

THE GRIFFITH BUILDING,
Corner of the Church and Shore Roads, Port Richmond

Grace Methodist Episcopal Church, on Heberton Street, corner of Bond.

Park Baptist Church, on Broadway, corner of Vreeland Street, and

Baptist Church, on Union Avenue, near the western extremity of the village.

Summerfield Methodist Episcopal Church, on the Harbor Road, is but a few feet outside of the boundaries of the village.

There is but one public school within the limits of the village, which is situated on Heberton Street, corner of Elizabeth.

There is another public school a few feet outside of the village limits, near the southwest corner.

St. John's Lutheran Church has a parochial school on Catharine Street.

There are two steam ferries connecting the village with New York—the North Shore and the Peoples' ferries—both of which touch at the Elm Park and Port Richmond Landings.

Of the industrial establishments, the White Lead Manufactory of John Jewett and Sons, and the Linseed oil factory of Jewett & Dean, are the principal, and are noticed elsewhere.

In addition to these, are several ship-yards, the principal of which is that of William Lissenden. A century ago this place was known as Ryer's Ferry; on a change of owners of the ferry, it was called Mersereau's Ferry; there was also another Ferry in the vicinity of the former, known as Hilleker's Ferry, the wharf of which was next east of Jewett's White Lead Factory, where the remains of it may still be seen. Subsequently the place was called Cityville, and then Bristol; the paternity of the present name is due to Rev. Dr. Brownlee, at whose suggestion it was adopted, and it has now become permanently fixed.

While this work was going through the press, it was suggested to the author, that his description of the Village of Port Richmond would hardly be complete without some reference to the Centennial Celebration of the nation's natal day, especially as it was the only celebration on the Island. The celebration took place under the shade of the beautiful trees which overarch that splendid thoroughfare known as Heberton Street. The services consisted of an opening address by Ex-District Attorney S. F. Rawson, who presided. The Rev. Dr. Brownlee offered the opening prayer. The Rev. J. T. Bush read the Declaration of Independence. The author of these "ANNALS" then read an historical address relating to the Village of Port Richmond and the Town of Northfield. He was succeeded by the Hon. George William Curtis, who delivered an eloquent, patriotic address, which was universally admired and applauded. The closing prayer and benediction was pronounced by the Rev. S. G. Smith, of the Park Baptist Church. The services were interspersed with vocal and instrumental music. It was, on the whole, the most creditable and patriotic celebration that ever took place on the Island.

VILLAGE OF EDGEWATER.

This village was originally incorporated in 1866, and by its charter divided into nine wards, but some legal defect having been detected in it, a new charter was enacted the following year. The names of the first trustees under the new charter are as follows:

1st Ward—William C. Denyse.
2d   "   David Burgher.
3d   "   George Bechtel.
4th   "   Theodore Frean.
5th   "   Dr. Thomas C. Moffat.
6th   "   James R. Robinson.
7th   "   Alfred Wandell.
8th   "   Dennis Keeley.
9th   "   J. Duignan.

Theodore Frean, President; Henry F. Standerwick, Clerk; Thomas Garrett, Police Justice.

For a number of years the government of the village was injudiciously conducted, causing much dissatisfaction among the people, and the idea of abandoning the charter and returning to the original town government as it existed before the passage of the first act of incorporation, began to be entertained by a large number of citizens.

In 1875 another attempt at local government was made by an amended charter containing several important changes and modifications. The village was divided into only two wards, with one trustee each, and a trustee at large, to be elected by the whole village, who was to be the president of the village. The board elected under the amended charter consisted of William Corry, trustee at large, and president; Benjamin Brown, trustee of the 1st ward, Fellowes, trustee of the 2d ward; Henry F. Standerwick, clerk.

The churches within the corporate limits of the village are—
Old St. Paul's, Episcopal, minister vacant.
St. Paul's, Memorial, Episcopal, minister Stanley.
St. John's, " " J. C. Eccleston, D. D.
St. Simon's, Mission, " " "
First Presbyterian, " J. E. Rockwell, D. D.
German Lutheran, "
Kingsby Methodist Ep. " H. M. Simpson.
African Zion, " " "
St. Mary's, Rom. Cath. " John Lewis.

"G."

NOTED LOCALITIES.

TOAD HILL.

Geographically, this eminence, or succession of eminences, commences at New Brighton, and runs southerly and southwesterly until it terminates somewhat abruptly on the northerly side of the Fresh Kills, beyond Richmond Village. The Clove divides the ridge into two nearly equal parts, and it is to that part which lies between the Clove and the Moravian Church that the name is usually applied. The whole elevation abounds in minerals of various kinds, the most abundant, as well as most valuable of which is iron ore, which exists in immense masses, and is generally of a superior quality. Several of these iron mines have been extensively worked, and that lying nearest the Moravian Church was known and worked by the early Dutch settlers of the colony. The hill affords numerous splendid sites for dwellings, unsurpassed for extent and variety of prospect, as well as salubrity, by any in the country; some of these have been improved by the erection of tasteful and ornate villas, but many more yet remain to be occupied. In the beginning of the present century, when availability for cultivation, and not beauty of prospect, was the principal consideration in the purchase of land, the whole hill, from the Clove to the Moravian Church, could have been bought for less than one thousand dollars, as the soil, except in the valleys between the ridges, was considered almost valueless for the purposes of agriculture; half a century later, after the beauties of the location had become well known and appreciated, a single acre could not have been purchased for that sum, in many places. The origin of the uncouth name of the hill has been a subject of some speculation. The earliest reference to it in any existing document, is in the patent from Dongan to Palmer, in which it is called "the iron hill," and in other ancient conveyances of later dates, it is referred to by the same name.* It has been said that the name is not "Toad," but "Todt," from a person by that name who owned land upon it, but unfortunately for this theory, there is no evidence that there was ever an individual of that name on the Island, and certainly none that such a man was ever a land-owner in any part of the county.

An old man recently deceased, at almost the age of a centenarian, who had resided all his life either upon the hill or in its immediate vicinity, informed the writer that it was called "Toad Hill" before his time, and that he always understood it received its name from the following somewhat ludicrous circumstance. Before the war of the Revolution, how long he knew not, there was a young lady residing upon the hill, who was so fortunate as to have two suitors at the same time. As was quite natural under such circumstances, she had her preference, and the unfortunate wight who did not meet her approbation received a significant hint that his absence would be agreeable to her, by having a couple of large toads dropped into his capacious pocket by her own fair hands without his knowledge. On the next Sunday evening, as he was dressing for the purpose of making her another visit, he discovered that his Sunday coat emitted a *perfume* not agreeable to his olfactories. A close examination revealed the cause; the hint was understood, and his visits ceased. By some means the story became known, and his young acquaintances frequently taunted him by inquiring when he intended to go to toad hill again, or how the people on toad hill were. Thus the name which originated in a jest, became fixed upon the locality.

Another hypothesis is that during one of the Indian massacres, probably that of 1655, some of the inhabitants who had fled to this locality for concealment, were discovered and killed, and the hill in consequence became known as "doodebergh," or hill of the dead, which in time was corrupted into its present name. But it is never referred to in any of the old records by any other name than "the iron hill."

* Vide App. N. (44.)

WATCHOGUE.

Between Old Place and Chelsea, bordering on Staten Island Sound, is a level, sandy territory, sparsely populated, and, where not cultivated, is covered with a stunted growth of pines and cedars, though the low wet lands in some places bear a growth of larger trees of other varieties. The name of this territory is of Indian origin, but the meaning of the word has been lost. Indian names of places were usually significant of something peculiarly applicable to the locality, and as everything about the place has been changed since their day except the musquitoes, the name probably had some reference to these insects. It cannot be denied that this place is more than ordinarily infested with them, but this is owing more to its proximity to the extensive and prolific nurseries of them on the Jersey shores, than to any local cause. Nevertheless, the people of Watchogue appear to be almost as indifferent to their presence as if they were absolutely musquito-proof. Almost every place has some drawback, and, except this, Watchogue is rather a pleasant place for one who loves to cultivate strawberries, melons and sweet potatoes; these articles are produced here in great perfection. A rather pedantic attempt has of late years been made to Anglicise the Indian name by calling the place "Watch-Oak," which, as it is meaningless and inapplicable, no known event in its local history warranting the innovation, the name will not adhere. Perhaps the more recent name of "Bloomfield" which it has received, may be more fortunate. Watchogue, being so near "the lines" during the war of the Revolution, and being much more sparsely populated then than at present, had, no doubt, its local histories and traditions, but as the people of that period have all passed away, the histories and traditions have passed away with them.

THE ROSE AND CROWN.

Lossing, in his very valuable contribution to American history, "The Field Book of the Revolution,"* says: "The main body of Howe's troops landed near the present (late) quarantine ground, and encamped upon the hills in the vicinity. The fleet had anchored off Vanderventer's (Vandeventer's) point, (the telegraph station at the Narrows), and three ships-of-war and some transports brought the English troops within the Narrows to the landing-place. Howe made his headquarters at the Rose and Crown Tavern, upon the road leading from Stapleton to Richmond, near New Dorp. The house is near the forks of the Richmond and Amboy roads, and overlooks the beautiful level country between it and the sea, two miles distant. It is now (1852) the property of Mr. Leonard Parkinson, of Old Town, Staten Island. The house was built by a Huguenot, one of the first settlers upon that part of the Island."

We regret to add that since the above was written, the house has been demolished. It stood on the westerly side of the road, almost directly opposite the entrance to New Dorp lane. It was built of stone, and was but one story in height, having several dormer windows in the roof. It had a hall through the middle, with rooms on either side of it; a low stone kitchen was attached to its southerly end, and the whole shaded by an immense tree in front. Howe himself, and a part of his staff, were quartered in this house, the remainder taking up their residence in the house, still standing, and known then, as now, as the "Black Horse" Tavern. After the battle of Long Island, and the capture of New York, Howe removed his headquarters to that city, and Dalrymple, who was left temporarily in charge of the Island, occupied the apartments vacated by his commander-in-chief. The venerable Mr. Isaac Housman, who for many years owned and occupied the Black Horse property, and where he

* Vol II, p. 800, note.

died, informed the writer, that on several occasions, aged British officers from Canada, who had served on the Island during the Revolution, accompanied by their sons, or some other young companions, revisited these scenes of their early life, and so little change had taken place in the vicinity of these two taverns, that they readily recognized the particular localities where the events which were still fresh in their memories, had taken place. On one of these occasions, an aged soldier, pointing to a rock by the side of the road, said to his companion, "This is the identical rock upon which Captain ———— was seated by his seconds, after his duel with Captain ————, in which he was mortally wounded, and upon which he expired while they were waiting for the conveyance which had been sent for." "Here Col. ————, while riding rapidly, was thrown violently to the ground by his horse stumbling, and broke his neck. They were, he said, both buried in a little cemetery in Richmond, and he thought he could place his feet upon their graves, for they were buried by the side of each other. He even pointed to a window in a neighboring house, which lighted the room he had occupied for a period of several months.

If the history of these two houses could be written, it would abound with narratives of intense interest.

They received their names from the emblems, or picture upon their respective signs; that of the Black Horse was still swinging thirty years ago, but the horse had ceased to be black; it much more resembled the ghost of an old gray nag, afflicted with the rheumatism.

THE BULL'S HEAD.

This is at the intersection of the Richmond Turnpike and the road leading from Port Richmond to New Springville. The sign which swung between two high posts in front of the small low tavern which stood on the northeast corner, gave name to the locality. Some rustic artist had evidently exhausted all his talents and resources in transmitting to posterity the picture of a very fierce looking bull's head, with very short horns and very round eyes, which looked very much like a pair of spectacles. Long before, and during the Revolution, the locality was known by the name of "London Bridge," but why, is not so clear, unless the bridge over the little stream in the vicinity had some connection with it. After the war, and the erection of the new sign, the tavern became somewhat noted as a place of rendezvous for such young men, and probably old ones, too, as had a propensity for gambling. Some fearful stories were sometimes told of the place and its frequenters; especially of one of them, who was a mysterious character, whom everybody desired to avoid, but who would not be avoided. Sometimes he appeared as a man of exceedingly dark complexion, but with fiery eyes; that he had a hoof and a tail, nobody doubted, though nobody had actually seen them. Sometimes he would present himself in the shape of a huge black dog, or other forms as his fancy dictated, but he always remained until the party broke up, and then accompanied some one of them on the way home, never speaking by the way, because no one dared to address him, and all attempts to escape from him by speed proved utterly ineffectual. At length, so great became the terror which his frequent visits inspired, that the house was entirely forsaken by those who had patronized it, and then the mysterious visitor forsook it, too. We allude to these stories because they were once inseparably connected with the place, and half a century ago implicitly credited by people generally. Within a few years the locality has been visited by conflagrations, which consumed the houses on three of the corners, the fourth corner being vacant, and now the people who reside there, or some of them, endeavor to call it Phœnixville, because these houses, perhaps, will some day arise from their ashes.

THE CLOVE.

The name of this locality is of Dutch origin; "het kloven," the cleft;—the hill being here cleft through. As the early settlements on the north and south sides of the Island increased, intercourse between them gradually became a necessity, especially as many on the south side worshipped in the Dutch church at Port Richmond, and there was no available place, but this, where a road could be laid. Long before the Clove road was surveyed and recorded, it was used as a public highway, and is one of the earliest roads in the county; nature appears to have made it for the purpose. The following accident occurred here in the latter part of the last century. A fool-hardy young man undertook, on a wager, to ride down the high, bald hill on the southerly side of the Clove, on a sled, the surface of the snow which covered the ground being a thick hard crust of ice. He descended the hill like lightning, but losing control of his vehicle, he was dashed against a tree near the base of the hill and instantly killed. During the war of the Revolution, it is said, the British kept guards constantly traversing this valley, by day and by night, and none were permitted to pass through without the countersign.

THE FINGER-BOARD ROAD.

The road which connects with the Richmond road next south of the Clove road, is known to this day by the above name, which it received from a guide-board and post, standing at its entrance, directing the stranger which road to take to Richmond. A robbery and murder was once committed on a small elevation over which the road passes, and which from that circumstance received the name of "Roguery Hill," and the road became known as the "Roguery Hill Road," until the guide-post, above mentioned, gave it the name it still bears.

HOLLAND'S HOOK.

This locality occupies the extreme northwest point of Staten Island. Its name is derived from the fact that the place was first settled by several families from Holland, and was, in consequence, originally called "Holland's Hook," the word Hook, or Hock, signifying a point or corner. The descendants of many of these families still reside there.

It has been said that the place was named from Hon. Henry Holland, for several years a member of the Colonial Legislature from this county, and an ardent friend of St. Andrew's Church; but Henry Holland never resided there, nor ever owned any real estate there, his property being entirely on the south side of the Island, in the vicinity of the Black Horse; in fact, as may be seen by some old conveyances, the place was so called long before Holland's name was in any way connected with the Island, and probably before he was born; on some of the recent maps of the county, this locality is known as "Howland's Hook," which is a corruption of the original name, and the result of ignorance of its origin. It is said that the use of the Dutch language continued here long after it had ceased to be used in other parts of the county.

THE MORNING STAR—THE BLAZING STARS.

These were taverns, from which ferries were run across to New Jersey. They were so called from the emblems or figures on their signs. The former had a star, but how it was represented to enable it to be distinguished from the evening star, we are unable to say; the road which led to it is still familiarly known by that name. Of the latter, there were two, the Old Blazing Star, and the New Blazing Star. These stars were comets. The Old Blazing Star ferry ran across the Sound near Rossville, and was a very important locality during the Revolution. After Governor Tompkins had laid out and opened the Richmond Turnpike, stages ran regularly over the whole length of the new road, in connection with steamboats from New York, and constituted part of the route of travel between New York and Philadelphia. At the western terminus of the Turnpike, stages were carried over the Sound by means of large scows, and this ferry received the name of "The New Blazing Star." But these stars have all set, probably never to rise again.

KILL VAN KULL—ARTHUR KULL.

The precise meaning of the Dutch word "Cull," we are unable to give, though it probably had some reference to the water, as Newark Bay was emphatically called "the Cull," and was universally known by that name. The Dutch word "Kill" meant a small stream or passage of water; therefore, the name Kill Van Kull means the stream or passage from the Cull, or Kull, as it is now spelled. Arthur Kull, or Kill, as it is now sometimes written, is a corruption of the Dutch word "achter," after, or behind; therefore, Achter Kull meant behind or beyond the Cull. An attempt has recently been made to change the orthography of the word Van, by substituting the letter o for a, thus, Von, which is neither Dutch nor English, and arises from ignorance of the fact that the Dutch a in this connection has the sound of the English o in the same connection; therefore, to spell the word correctly, it should be written Van, and pronounced Von. We give the above as the explanation of the origin of the Dutch names of these waters.

THE OLD PLACE.

In the first, and for many years, the only house built on the road known by this name, religious evening services were held for a long time, its situation being central for a widely scattered population. After a while, the house became so dilapidated as to be uncomfortable, and the place of holding these meetings was changed. This proved to be so inconvenient for many, that an apartment in the old house was repaired, and notice was given that the meetings would be resumed in the "Old Place," and thus the vicinity became known by that name. We do not know how reliable the above account of the origin of the name may be; it has, at least, the merit of being natural and probable. The people of the vicinity have of late caught the mania for changing old names for new ones, and have called the place "Summerville," a name appropriate enough during a part of the year at least; and the "Old Place Road" is now "Washington Avenue," which is not at all complimentary to the illustrious character whose name has been thus appropriated.

Made in the USA
Coppell, TX
16 October 2022